for better

HOW THE SURPRISING SCIENCE OF HAPPY COUPLES
CAN HELP YOUR MARRIAGE SUCCEED

Tara Parker-Pope

A PLUME BOOK

PLUME
Published by the Penguin Group
Penguin Group (USA) Inc., 375 Hudson Street, New York, New York 10014, U.S.A. ·
Penguin Group (Canada), 90 Eglinton Avenue East, Suite 700, Toronto, Ontario, Canada
M4P 2Y3 (a division of Pearson Penguin Canada Inc.) · Penguin Books Ltd., 80 Strand,
London WC2R 0RL, England · Penguin Ireland, 25 St. Stephen's Green, Dublin 2, Ireland
(a division of Penguin Books Ltd.) · Penguin Group (Australia), 250 Camberwell Road,
Camberwell, Victoria 3124, Australia (a division of Pearson Australia Group Pty. Ltd.) ·
Penguin Books India Pvt. Ltd., 11 Community Centre, Panchsheel Park, New Delhi –
110 017, India · Penguin Group (NZ), 67 Apollo Drive, Rosedale, North Shore 0632,
New Zealand (a division of Pearson New Zealand Ltd.) · Penguin Books (South Africa)
(Pty.) Ltd., 24 Sturdee Avenue, Rosebank, Johannesburg 2196, South Africa

Penguin Books Ltd., Registered Offices: 80 Strand, London WC2R 0RL, England

Published by Plume, a member of Penguin Group (USA) Inc. Previously published in a
Dutton edition.

First Plume Printing, May 2011
10 9 8 7 6 5 4 3 2 1

Ⓟ REGISTERED TRADEMARK—MARCA REGISTRADA

CIP data is available.

ISBN 978-0-525-95138-4 (hc.)
ISBN 978-0-452-29710-4 (pbk.)

Printed in the United States of America
Original hardcover design by Daniel Lagin

PUBLISHER'S NOTE
While the author has made every effort to provide accurate telephone numbers and Internet
addresses at the time of publication, neither the publisher nor the author assumes any responsibility for errors, or for changes that occur after publication. Further, the publisher does
not have any control over and does not assume any responsibility for author or third-party
Web sites or their content.

For Laney

CONTENTS

The Scientific Study of Marriage

What makes a good marriage?

The mystery of why some marriages succeed while others fail is something men and women have been trying to sort out for decades. What qualities make some people more successful at navigating the stormy waters of love while others lose their way? Why do some couples seem happy together while others are happiest apart? And is there any way to protect a marriage from the risks of stress, negativity, and divorce?

The answers to those questions come from a surprising place. Far from the therapy couch or self-help gurus, the best insights about love and relationships are coming from the scientific community. Top relationship researchers from dozens of universities around the world have devoted their careers to observing couples interact, collecting voluminous amounts of data about how men and women communicate, both in the words they use and in their body language and facial expressions. They have tracked pulse rates, blood pressure levels, and other physical responses that occur when couples talk, laugh, and argue. Scientists have even measured the effect marital conflict and stress can have on the immune system and the body's ability to fight off colds or heal a wound. Brain scan studies of the newly in love and the long married offer glimpses into the physiological underpinnings of both passionate and lasting romantic love.

It's now possible to deconstruct a marriage down to its most basic parts and predict, with surprising accuracy, the likelihood that a marriage will survive or end in divorce. Using computer-assisted coding programs and body sensors, scientists have analyzed thousands of hours of video recorded conversations between couples, tracking everything from facial movements and body language to pulse rate, sweat, and skin temperature. Computer-assisted word analysis programs have allowed researchers to pick apart conversations between couples and find meaning hidden in the rhythms and patterns of the words couples use when they communicate.

The insights these researchers have gained will give you an entirely new way of looking at your own relationship. The findings can be translated into surprisingly practical advice for couples. A gesture as seemingly minor as eye rolling or the manner in which a man retells the story of how he met his wife can be strong predictors of happy married life or a looming divorce. Scientists have even applied mathematical models to marriage, calculating, for instance, that strong marriages have at least a five-to-one daily ratio of positive to negative interactions. Simply translated, that means it's not enough to apologize for mistreating your spouse. For every mistake you make, you need to offer five more good moments, kind words, and loving gestures to keep your marriage in balance.

Scientists have also studied divorce and can now tell couples what risk factors make their marriages most vulnerable. How couples argue, who starts the fight, and even the pronouns they use in conversation can all signal the success or failure of a marriage. Age differences, children, how often a couple has sex, and numerous other factors have all been studied in a daunting scientific quest to apply the logic and rigors of science to one of the most complex emotional relationships of our lives.

The good news from the study of marriage is that today, far more people are succeeding at marriage than failing. While that may run counter to the conventional wisdom, in reading this book you'll learn the truth behind marriage and divorce statistics and why marriage today is stronger than it has been in decades.

You'll also discover that assessing the overall health of your marriage (or the marriage potential of a prospective partner) is easier than you think. The trick is learning to distinguish between the normal, everyday conflicts and frustrations of human relationships and to focus on the real issues that may be standing in the way of a better relationship.

Did you know that solving your money problems can help solve your marital problems? Or that when you fight with your partner, the first three minutes of the argument count the most? Or that the division of housework duties in a home can have a direct impact on a couple's sex life?

Whether you are embarking on a new marriage, hoping to rescue a troubled relationship, longing to get it right the second time around, or simply looking for ways to improve a good marriage, the scientific study of marriage has resulted in simple, practical advice for determining what matters most in a relationship and where to focus your energy to make it better.

My interest in the science of marriage stems from my own search for answers. As a longtime health writer who has spent hours reading medical and scientific journals, I often urge readers to take charge of their health and make decisions based on the available scientific evidence. But when my own seventeen-year marriage began to crumble, I found myself struggling to make sense of it. Bookstore shelves are filled with marriage advice books and self-help guides, but I couldn't relate to the "straight talk" and platitudes found in most of them. I knew where to look for answers about heart disease, diabetes, allergies, and numerous other health issues, and I wanted the same objective, evidence-based advice about my marriage.

Using the Internet and medical and social science databases, I began to search for research on marriage and relationships. I was stunned to find a vast world of marital science beyond the self-help aisle. For decades, numerous scientists, from universities around the world, have been churning out credible, quantitative research filled with practical advice about marital health.

As a result, I set out to explore what science has taught us about lasting relationships and the complexities of courtship, love, and marriage. Over the past few years I've interviewed dozens of the world's top marriage and relationship researchers and pored over hundreds of published research studies.

I've seen seemingly happy marriages, including my own, come to an end. Many had fallen victim to infidelity, while others seemed to crumble under the burdens of parenting and the demands of modern living. Could any of us have known that it would end this way? Should we have seen it coming? Was there a way to inoculate a relationship from the devastation of divorce?

The answer to all these questions is yes. Understanding the science of marriage gives us a crystal ball of sorts, to better predict which relationships will work and who will struggle to stay together. I realize now that had I known more about the basic scientific truths of love and marriage, I would have seen the limits of my own relationship from the beginning and noticed the telltale signs of trouble years sooner. Armed with the knowledge, I might have made better choices that could have helped save my marriage, or at least given me more confidence about the choice my husband and I made to end our relationship.

What's so important about this scientific study of marriage is that it views the most important relationship of our life as a significant health issue that affects us both physically and emotionally. The goal is to diagnose and treat marital problems just as a doctor would diagnose and treat cancer, diabetes, or any other important health concern.

And just as doctors know that certain lifestyle habits influence disease risk, the scientific quest to better understand marriage has helped us identify important risk factors for divorce. Researchers have found practical ways that couples can better insulate a marriage against failure. And there's even advice to help long-married couples reignite the passion and excitement that they experienced during the early romance of their courtship.

Each chapter of this book will explore the science behind various aspects of marriage, such as monogamy, love, sex, children, money, housework, and conflict. Most important, this book will translate the science of marriage into practical, actionable advice—a prescription for marital health—that you can use to improve your relationship. In some chapters, you'll even find the measurement scales and quizzes researchers use to gauge the quality of a relationship or the depth of passion and commitment couples feel.

My hope is that in reading this book, you will gain insights about yourself, your relationship, and possibly even the marriages of your parents, in-laws, and others closest to you. While the title of this book and much of the research it explores focuses on marriage, the lessons learned often are applicable to any couple hoping to pursue a committed, long-term relationship. Understanding the science of love and marriage can help single people make better choices in the pursuit of their ideal mate. For some readers, the science may empower them to extricate themselves from a doomed relationship. But hopefully, for most readers, the findings will arm them with the information they need to save a struggling relationship or strengthen a good one, giving them a specific prescription to boost the health of the most profound relationship of their lives.

Saving or improving your marriage is worth the effort. Research shows that couples in stable relationships have more sex, more money, and live longer, healthier lives. Whether you are content in a long, stable relationship, in the idealistic throes of early romantic love, or leaving a failed marriage in hopes of doing better next time around, the scientific study of marriage has put the secrets of long-term love and happiness within your grasp.

part i

For Better

CHAPTER 1

For Better or for Worse:
Sizing Up Modern Marriage

The real soul mate is the one you are actually married to.

—J. R. R. TOLKIEN

In the throes of early love, in the excitement of planning for a wedding, and in the bliss of the honeymoon, a lifetime of love and happiness certainly seem possible, even probable.

And there's a good reason to be optimistic. Today most married couples *are* staying together. Does that surprise you? For years we've all heard the grim statistic claiming that 50 percent of marriages will end in divorce, but that bleak prognosis doesn't apply to most couples getting married today or even most of those who married in the last few decades. The truth about marriage is that divorce is getting less common. Divorce rates have dropped sharply since peaking in the late 1970s, for a variety of reasons. In many ways, the marital bond is stronger and better than it ever has been.

Of course, that doesn't mean that marriage is easy or that couples don't struggle. A sizable minority of marriages will eventually fail.

Even among marriages that do last, not everyone is satisfied with their relationship, and many husbands and wives long for happier times. There are ways to improve every relationship, and the science of marriage teaches you how to do it.

But to fully understand the potential of your own relationship, it helps to learn about the broader trends influencing marriage today. A closer look at marriage and divorce statistics shows that far more than half of married couples today stay married, and in any given year only a fraction of couples end their unions. For couples just starting out or those who are questioning the future of their relationship, the new patterns of marriage and divorce give you reason to feel the same optimism about marriage that you did when you walked down the aisle. Of course there are challenges, conflicts, and hard times, but overall, the average marriage is more stable than it was four decades ago and most married couples today are expected to stay together "till death do us part."

Making Sense of Statistics

So why do so many people believe the odds of staying married are no better than a coin toss?

Let's start by talking about how marriage is changing. People born in the 1930s and who married in the 1950s have the highest marriage rates of any generation—as many as 96 percent married. But among more recent generations the number has dropped to about 90 percent.

Today, fewer people are getting married and more couples are delaying marriage. These changing patterns of marriage began in the late 1950s, as women began to delay marriage to pursue college degrees and careers before settling into married life. In the 1950s, most women married before twenty-one. Today, the average age at first marriage for women is about twenty-six, while women pursuing college or professional degrees may wait until thirty or older to get married.[1]

The shifting age of marriage has had a positive impact on marital stability. Risk for divorce drops significantly when couples wait to wed until after the age of twenty-five. Exactly why isn't clear, but it may be that by the age of twenty-five, men and women have a clearer sense of their goals and common interests, allowing them to choose a more compatible mate. And with the delay of marriage, many of the weakest relationships are ending before a couple ever heads to the altar, leaving only the strongest couples to take that walk down the aisle.

"Today we have more selection pressure for stronger relationships," says Betsey Stevenson, assistant professor of business and public policy at the Wharton School at the University of Pennsylvania and the country's leading expert on divorce and marriage trends. "Some of the weaker relationships are washing out before marriage."

And with more women in the labor force, the traditional male-breadwinner, female-homemaker marriage has become less common. Today women are contributing more financially to relationships than earlier generations, and men are contributing more of the domestic duties. (That said, economists are quick to note that there still remains a wide gap in the amount of housework and child care performed by women versus men.) Compared to earlier generations, marriage today is less about dividing up economic and domestic duties and more about shared interests and mutual happiness. Men and women are more likely to marry someone like themselves, with a similar educational background, and that, in turn, leads to more stable relationships.

"It might be that those types of matches, people who are more kindred spirits, are more able to weather a small storm," says Dr. Stevenson. "You just have so much in common, you have so much invested together. A blip is just that, a blip, and it becomes easier to get over."

The dramatic changes in marriage have also led to changes in divorce. In addition to marrying more than current generations, couples married in the 1970s also are divorcing more. Among these couples the thirty-year divorce rate is about 47 percent. Given the increasing life span, the generation of couples married in the 1970s does appear headed toward a 50 percent divorce rate.

But the divorce rate of couples married in the 1970s isn't particularly relevant to people who have gotten married more recently or are planning to marry in the future. Couples who married in the 1970s typically married in their late teens and early twenties. They were born in the 1950s to a generation of breadwinning fathers and stay-at-home mothers who would eventually struggle mightily with their designated roles. Just as many of these couples were marrying in the 1970s, powerful social forces and legal shifts were leading to dramatic changes in divorce law and a widespread rethinking of marriage.

The divorce trends showing up in later generations are more hopeful. People married in the 1980s and 1990s are getting divorced at lower rates than their counterparts married in the 1970s. In fact, marital stability appears to be improving each decade.[2]

Dr. Stevenson has analyzed the ten-year divorce rates of three generations of women—those married in the 1970s, the 1980s, and the 1990s. Among female college graduates, the ten-year divorce rate for those married in the 1990s is extraordinarily low—just 16 percent. By comparison, 23 percent of female college graduates married in the 1970s were divorced at ten years.

Divorce rates are slightly higher for those who aren't college graduates, but still far better among more recent generations. Among male high school graduates who married in the 1990s, only 19 percent were divorced after ten years. By comparison, among men married in the 1970s who didn't attend college, 26 percent had divorced by ten years.

"We have evidence that marriages are changing and divorce rates are falling," says Dr. Stevenson. "It might be because marriages are more resilient. It might be because people are happier in the types of relationships they have, and they are more attached and their spouse is harder to replace."

Ten-Year Divorce Rates for Three Generations of Women

	COLLEGE GRADS	HIGH SCHOOL
1970s:	23 percent	26 percent
1980s:	20 percent	25 percent
1990s:	16 percent	19 percent

Source: Adam Isen and Betsey Stevenson, Wharton School, University of Pennsylvania

Dr. Stevenson also performed an analysis of twenty-year divorce rates on couples married in the 1980s. She decided to look at how factors like age of marriage and educational attainment can be used to predict divorce risk. She found that when couples from the 1980s who were college graduates waited to marry until the age of twenty-five, their divorce rates were far lower than those of couples who married younger or before finishing college. She also found that dropping out of college is a significant predictor for having an unstable marriage. College dropouts actually are less likely to stay married than high school graduates who never enrolled in college. The reason isn't clear, but Dr. Stevenson speculates that dropping out of college may be a sign that commitment and follow-through aren't top priorities.

The difference in divorce risk when age and education are taken into account is stunning. Marrying before the age of twenty five and dropping out of college predicted a whopping 51 percent divorce rate. What happened to couples who delayed marriage until after completing college and after the age of twenty-five? After twenty years of marriage, only 19 percent of them had divorced.

Divorce Rate Among Couples Married in the 1980s, by Age and Education

Overall 20-year divorce rate:	39 percent
College graduates, married after 25:	19 percent
College graduates, married before 25:	35 percent
Some college, married before 25:	51 percent

Source: Betsey Stevenson, Wharton School,
University of Pennsylvania

As these numbers show, your divorce risk is strongly affected by the age at which you marry, your educational attainment, and the decade in which you married. I wish I had known about these numbers when my own marriage began faltering. My husband and I were both college graduates who married in 1988 at the ages of twenty-three and twenty-one. While we were certainly in a higher risk category because of our young age at the time we married, our chances were better than we thought. In our demographic, about two out of three couples just like us have managed to stay together and work it out. But at the time, I believed that marriage was essentially a coin toss, that half of all marriages failed, and that I was just among the unlucky 50 percent heading to divorce court.

Would knowing the truth—that most people in marriages like mine were succeeding—have made a difference? Of course there is no way to know, but that's why I think it's so important to get the word out about what's really happening in marriage today. Inflating divorce statistics has the potential to increase *everybody's* risk of getting divorced. Just as we become inured to violence when we see a lot of it on television or in the movies, I think the 50 percent divorce rate myth has trained a generation to be ambivalent about marriage and divorce. If half of all married couples are getting divorced, what's the big deal?

Why are divorce statistics so often inflated? One reason is that we have the most data on people married in the 1970s, so those tend to be the statistics that are quoted and repeated. Another problem is the overly simplistic formula many people use to calculate the divorce rate. Typically, when you see a report about an alarmingly high divorce rate, the statistic is derived by comparing the number of people who divorce in a given year to the number of people who marry in a given year. It seems logical until you think about all the different types of couples getting married or divorced in a given year. If marriage rates were constant, this method would give you a pretty good approximation of the overall divorce rate. But marriage rates haven't been constant, and the overall rate of marriage is dropping. And as we explored earlier, divorce rates aren't constant, either, and are actually different for every generation. Finally, life expectancy rates are increasing, so the pool of married couples who could potentially get divorced is higher today than it was thirty years ago. Because so many variables in the marriage-and-divorce equation are changing, a simple calculation comparing marriages and divorces in a given year ends up distorting the result and suggesting that the divorce rate is higher than it really is.

So what is there to be gained by consistently distorting divorce rates? Some researchers speculate that fretting about the demise of marriage—and perpetuating the myth that half of all marriages will end in divorce—feeds a national agenda about family values that benefits both ends of the political spectrum. The inflated number can be used as ammunition to win funding or undermine a public program, depending on the goal of the person or group involved.

But in the end, I think we are all hurt when misleading statistics about the state of marriage are bandied about. It leaves us assuming marriage is more fragile than it really is, and it makes us ambivalent and more vulnerable to giving up when problems occur in our own relationships.

"What I find so disturbing about this fifty-percent-divorce-rate idea is that people aren't forming the right expectations about marriage," says Dr. Stevenson. "The fifty percent number makes people think, 'Will my kids be raised in a divorced household? Will I end up as a single mom?' I think in terms of planning for the future, it's useful to understand what really happens in your peer group."

Second Marriages and Divorce

Adela Rogers St. Johns, a celebrated journalist during the 1920s and '30s, had a theory about second marriages. "There is so little difference between husbands, you might as well keep the first," she noted.

She wasn't alone in her belief that second marriages are no better than the first. In fact, an oft-cited statistic is that second marriages have higher divorce rates than first marriages. This is, ostensibly, an argument for just sticking it out in a first marriage, since your odds of getting divorced the second time around are higher than they were for the first.

But for those of us who are hoping to make a second marriage work, are we really more likely to get divorced if we venture back into the marriage market a second time? Not necessarily.

A closer look at the data on second marriages and divorces shows we have reason to be optimistic. The problem with much of the data on second marriages is that they are skewed by "risky prospects."

A risky prospect is a man or woman who isn't all that committed to marriage and who isn't all that bothered by divorce. Some of these people might even become "serial" brides and grooms. (Think Elizabeth Taylor.) Among first marriages, these risky prospects account for a small percentage of the total sample. But once you start studying second marriages, the risky prospects account for a larger percentage of couples, and it's likely that they drag down the average when you start calculating divorce risk.

Consider these five-year divorce rates for women married between 1995 and 1998:

First Marriages: 9 percent
Second Marriages: 12 percent

Now look at these fifteen-year divorce rates for women married between 1985 and 1988:

First Marriages: 36 percent
Second Marriages: 45 percent

Only 3 percentage points separate the five-year divorce rates for first and second marriages. And an additional 9 percent of second marriages fail after fifteen years compared to first marriages. Dr. Stevenson believes the percentage difference is so narrow that, if the data could be adjusted to extract people headed for "serial marriage," the success-and-failure rate of second marriages would look pretty much the same as that for first marriages.

It's even possible, she speculates, that second marriages might fare even *better* than first marriages. The reason? One of the most important risk factors for divorce—getting married younger than twenty-five—typically disappears in a second marriage. People who get married at thirty or older have very low rates of divorce.

"For people who first married at a young age, you might actually find that second marriages are quite stable," she says.

If Marriage Is Stronger Than Ever, Why Does It Seem So Hard?

While the numbers show that the odds of a lasting marriage are in your favor, that doesn't mean marriage today is easy. In fact, it may be tougher than ever. That's because as couples today, we are asking for far more from our marriages than any generation before us.

Of course, people have been getting married and staying married for thousands of years. But the expectation that marriages should be happy, loving, and fulfilling is a relatively new idea. For centuries, the reasons people married had nothing to do with their affection for each other or the emotional and intellectual needs of the two individuals involved. Marriage was an economic and social institution—men and women married to acquire land or wealth or to bolster social or political connections. Love rarely had anything to do with it.

That doesn't mean men and women haven't loved each other through the ages. Of course they have—and sometimes, perhaps often, they've even loved their own husbands and wives. But throughout history, love has not been the driving force behind marriage—although, as marriage historian Stephanie Coontz notes, it has sometimes been a "welcome side effect."[3]

According to Dr. Coontz, the love-based marriage didn't emerge until the eighteenth century, when the spread of the market economy and the humanitarian reforms of the Enlightenment led to a focus on individual rights. It was the first time in history that marriage had been viewed as a private relationship between two individuals rather than something good for building family wealth, or political alliances.[4]

Over the next hundred years, a number of social and economic forces continued to redefine gender roles and relationships around the world. As economies expanded, women were drawn into the workforce. The invention of birth control pills gave women sexual freedom and control of their reproductive lives, shifting traditional timelines for marriage and family. The U.S. civil rights movement, coupled with cries for women's "liberation," led to a wholesale rethinking of the roles and rights of men and women at work, at home, and in the community.

Even modern economic changes, such as the rise of the packaged-food industry, had an effect on marital stability. When marketers introduced convenience meals like frozen "TV dinners" and boxed macaroni and cheese, for instance, life as a single person got a whole lot easier. Men who hadn't been trained by their mothers to cook for themselves, for the first time could imagine life as bachelors.

By the middle of the twentieth century, marriage as an institution entered a period of dramatic instability, says Dr. Coontz. Divorce rates began to accelerate in 1957 as men and women continued to seek personal fulfillment in their relationships and often discovered they couldn't find it with their current husband or wife. Even the rise to prominence of Hugh Hefner and *Playboy* magazine appeared to influence gender relations and, ultimately, marriage. *Playboy* encouraged men to take back their bachelorhood and rethink the burden of being a family breadwinner. And women attempted to make gains in the workplace, delaying marriage to pursue college degrees and careers before embarking on married life.

The changes were unsettling and disruptive to a generation of couples who had married under different social circumstances. But today, a woman working outside the home is the norm, not something extraordinary. Couples today often meet in college or the workplace. Unlike earlier generations of couples, women are less

likely to marry primarily for economic support, and men aren't usually just looking for someone to iron the shirts. Instead, marriages
have become partnerships of shared interests and common goals.
The version of marriage that emerged from the tumult of the 1960s
and 1970s has far more potential to be a satisfying, mutually joyous
relationship for both husband and wife.

But that also means that couples today have far higher expectations of marriage than did earlier generations. Marriage has become
an exceptionally high-maintenance undertaking. When men and
women finally do get married, they expect a lot from each other and
expect a relationship based on fairness, partnership, and personal
and emotional fulfillment. Rutgers marriage researcher Barbara
Dafoe Whitehead calls it the "soul mate" marriage.

How often have you heard someone say they are seeking a "soul
mate?" It's certainly an idyllic notion, but a soul mate spouse, by
definition, will require far more emotional investment and attention than a spouse who takes a more pragmatic view of marriage
and family.

"It takes lavish investments of time, attention, and vigilance for
lone couples to sustain high levels of mutual happiness," writes Dr.
Whitehead in a recent review of the state of modern marriage. "The
high expectations for personal satisfaction in marriage, though a
good thing to pursue and even better to achieve, have also made
such marriages harder to sustain."[5]

Lessons from Modern Marriage Trends

The fact that men and women today expect so much more from a
marriage compared with earlier generations is, of course, a good
thing that gives couples a greater opportunity for a lasting and
meaningful relationship. But our idealized view of marriage also
places an enormous burden on the relationship and each other. A

fight with your husband or wife, while inevitable in any relationship, is far more painful and feels more worrisome when the harsh words and anger are coming from someone you love so deeply. Finding time for romance and sex can be a daunting challenge in a marriage of equals, when both partners are juggling work and domestic duties. And when busy schedules lead to neglect, and boredom sets in, the feelings of loss and sadness are that much greater because you feel you've lost your best friend as well as your spouse.

The good news for couples today is that the changing patterns of marriage and divorce have improved the odds of staying married. But these same social shifts have also raised the bar for what constitutes a good marriage. Divorce is getting less common and marriage is stronger than ever. But despite these positive changes, the stakes are particularly high in a marriage based on love, equality, and shared values. As a result, sustaining a modern marriage takes more time, energy, and emotional investment, which is why staying married often feels like such a struggle.

But as we will explore in the following chapters, the struggle is well worth it. We are hardwired for love and long-term partnership. And by every measure, ranging from better sleep to more sex, it's clear that a good marriage is good for you.

CHAPTER 2

Forsaking All Others:
The Science of Commitment

If I get married, I want to be very married.

—AUDREY HEPBURN

When two people find each other, fall in love, and decide to get married, the plan, for all intents and purposes, is to stay married. When people say, "till death do us part," they usually mean it.

Marriage is, after all, inherently about commitment, about choosing one person with whom you want to share a life, children, pets, tax returns, and a mortgage. Although the love-based marriage is a relatively new concept in the long history of human relationships, commitment is not. Around the world, and across both primitive and modern societies, human beings consistently prize commitment and monogamy, even if they don't always practice it.

But whether humans are capable of lifelong monogamy and fidelity remains a hot topic of debate among scientists and even among some couples. There is certainly a vocal contingent of skeptics who believes that human monogamy isn't natural, as demonstrated by the fact that fidelity has rarely been documented in nature. Only a tiny percentage of creatures appear to mate for life, and even among ostensibly monogamous animals, genetic testing has since proven that adultery is rampant. Given the evidence, it's reasonable for any couple beginning a marriage or struggling to keep one together to ask, "Are we really meant to spend our life with just one person?"

While humans stand out in the animal kingdom in their desire for lifelong relationships, there are some surprising and powerful examples of monogamy in nature. Monogamy among animals is definitely the exception, but what an extraordinary exception it is. In both the field and the laboratory, scientists have carefully tracked, monitored, and tested monogamous animal pairs and their offspring to confirm their loyalty. In doing so, they have developed various theories about why, among some species, evolution appears to favor lifelong mating. Studying the habits and behaviors of these animals may ultimately yield insights into the biological and social factors that influence human fidelity. More important, these examples of fidelity and lifelong commitment among the lesser creatures make the challenges of monogamy and fidelity seem less daunting (and more natural) for human couples.

Looking for Loyalty Among the Animals

Years ago on the popular sitcom *Friends,* a character named Phoebe talked about lobster mating habits. She was using lobsters to reassure Ross that he would someday unite with his true love, Rachel.

"She's your lobster," she told him. "It's a known fact that lobsters fall in love and mate for life. You can actually see old lobster couples walking around their tanks holding claws."

It was both funny and oddly believable. After the "She's Your

Lobster" episode, the monogamy of lobsters was often repeated as fact. I certainly came to believe it. In my view, any creature that was so evolved as to be monogamous didn't deserve to end up on my dinner plate, so I actually stopped eating lobster. I didn't want to think about all the lobster widows and widowers left behind after my meal. (A clever friend told me that instead of giving up lobster, the better solution was just to eat two of them.)

Lobster expert Trevor Corson, author of the book *The Secret Lives of Lobsters,* set me straight on my illusions about lobster love.

"Phoebe did so much to popularize the idea of monogamy among lobsters," he says. "What really goes on is a rather more mercenary operation by all the females in the neighborhood, who drug the one alpha male into submission so they can all have their way with him, one after another."

Really? So where did the notion come from that lobsters are monogamous?

"The male and female do shack up together, but only for about two weeks," says Mr. Corson, who has developed a comedy routine about lobster mating rituals. "The technical term scientists use for this is, in fact, a form of monogamy, but it's called serial monogamy— not exactly mating for life. And after it's over, it's simply sayonara."

I was disappointed. I liked the idea of our long-lived crustacean companions coupling for life on the ocean floor.

But when it comes to studying animal relationships, it's best to toss aside all your romantic notions. From birds to bees, dogs to ducks, monogamy in the animal kingdom is rare, practiced by fewer than 5 percent of mammals. And even among those animals that do form pair bonds to raise their young, infidelity is nearly universal.[6]

Biologists had long believed that most birds were monogamous, with male and females building nests, gathering food, and raising chicks together. In the 1960s, the well-known ornithologist

David Lack suggested that 92 percent of the 9,700 bird species were monogamous. To observers of bird behavior, it certainly looked that way.

But what is often overlooked is the fact that monogamy and fidelity are two different things. Monogamy means forming a long-term pair bond. Fidelity means sexual exclusivity. In both animals and people, you can have the first one without the second.

In the bird world, as equipment and observation techniques improved, a sharp-eyed ornithologist would occasionally spot a "sneaker," a bird flitting off for a dalliance with another bird. There were enough sightings of bird infidelity that scientists decided to conduct paternity studies. On average, about 30 percent of baby birds aren't the offspring of the male who cares for them.

In the movie *Heartburn* by Nora Ephron, the lead character complains to her father about her husband's cheating. "You want monogamy?" he asks. "Marry a swan!"

It's true that swans have long been viewed as a symbol of fidelity and devotion. But Australian researchers who study *Cygnus atratus*, a regal black swan with a bright red bill, have found that the birds only give the appearance of monogamy.[7]

University of Melbourne zoologist Dr. Raoul Mulder and colleagues compared the DNA of numerous cygnets to that of the nesting pair of black swans that was raising them. The study showed that one in six of the young birds wasn't related to the male that was tending the nest. Female swans, it appears, are routinely stepping out on their mates, sneaking away from the nest to copulate with another bird. And the word "sneaking" is an apt description. Scientists can't quite figure out when and how and where the birds manage their clandestine couplings. But don't blame the ladies. Since all the swans are partnered up, male and female swans are cheating on each other at an equal rate.

The swan data are just the latest findings to implode our notions about animal partnership. In the past few decades, the science of monogamy has been upended, as study after study has shown that animals previously thought to be monogamous and faithful regularly engage in what is known as "extra-pair coupling." The bottom line: Many animals cheat on their partners.

Studies of black-capped chickadees, among the most loyal of nesting birds, show that female birds may stray if they have a low-ranking male as a mate. They let him build the nest, but when he's not paying attention they will swoop away to mate with a more senior bird in the flock. The advantage to the female: The original mate will help raise the chicks, but the higher-ranking male will give her offspring the more desirable genes. Barn swallows also trade up. Females are more likely to cheat on short-tailed mates, opting for adulterous liaisons with birds that sport longer tails—a sign of disease resistance and potentially healthier offspring.[8]

It's not just birds that are promiscuous. Female rabbits and squirrels may copulate with several males in a day. Marmosets routinely step out on their mates. The lesson from nature is that while pair bonding is important to reproductive success, infidelity can act as a sort of insurance policy. Pair bonding guarantees a reliable partner to help raise offspring; infidelity ensures genetic diversity and potentially healthier offspring.

Among mammals, the idealized relationship of sexually faithful mates raising offspring together is rare. Fewer than 5 percent of mammal species practice "social monogamy," meaning they stay together for life. And even social monogamists may occasionally stray to copulate outside the relationship.[9]

Monogamy Among the Mice

At this point, the case for monogamy looks bleak. Perhaps you're thinking that this whole marriage-and-commitment thing is a mistake, an idealized notion that challenges the laws of nature. While it's true that nature typically doesn't favor fidelity, there are some notable exceptions. Consider the heartwarming story of the tiny *Peromyscus californicus,* also known as the California mouse.

Much of what we know about *P. californicus* starts with a budding biology student named David Ribble, now chairman of the Department of Biology at Trinity University in San Antonio. In the early 1980s, Dr. Ribble was completing his master's degree at Colorado State University. The university's Department of Fishery and Wildlife Biology had been commissioned for a field study on a particular tract of land that the military wanted to use for training. Other biologists were studying the coyotes, pronghorn antelope, and birds that called the site home, and someone needed to study the mice and other rodents upon which the larger creatures preyed.

As it happens, in the world of biology, anyone who specializes in the study of mice is in high demand, in part because it's a lot of work. Field mice not only scurry away and conduct most of their business underground or in nests hidden in tree roots, but they are nocturnal creatures, and studying them is a night job. "The number of people who do this are surprisingly few," notes Dr. Ribble.

After the military contract was completed, Mr. Ribble began doctorate work at the University of California at Berkeley. He wanted to begin studying lizards—they can be studied during daylight hours—but his colleagues encouraged him that he would be wise to continue to develop his expertise in the field study of mice. At the time, there was growing interest in an unusually large mouse that dwelled in the foothills of the Sierra Nevadas. Weighing in at about forty grams, the California mouse was twice the size of other field mice. And it was known for rearing just two offspring at a time—most mice have about four pups per litter. In ecology, a creature that is so noticeably different from its relatives gets a second look. Why did the California mouse evolve differently from other field mice?

Dr. Ribble began extensive fieldwork documenting the behavior of the nocturnal *P. californicus*. It's a docile, unassuming mouse, and relatively easy to catch around sunset with a box trap and bait of rolled oats. The mice were caught and tagged and fitted with radio transmitters around their necks so the scientists could track their movements. The females were marked with fluorescent powder that would leave colorful evidence on the mice with which they were consorting. All in all, about two hundred mice were captured and studied. The scientists also attempted to film the animals, inserting a cable with a red light into the nesting area, but that experiment failed. "It may have looked too much like a snake," says Dr. Ribble.

But even without film, the scientists were able to document some startling patterns. The scientists used black lights to track the color-coded powder that had been sprinkled on the female mice. As they continued to capture mice and monitor activity around the nest, they discovered that the powder rubbed off only on the female's pups and male mate. Unlike other field mice, there were no promiscuous paramours sneaking into the nest of *P. californicus*. The radio transmitters showed that the male and female partners rarely strayed far from each other.

"With telemetry you can get an estimate of their position, and you can plot all the points where you know they're spending time," explains Dr. Ribble. "When you do that, you see that where the male is spending his time and where the female is spending her time—it's the same. It maps right on top of each other."

And in monitoring the nests, the researchers documented that except for nursing the pups, the male California mouse contributes just as much time and effort to the direct care of his offspring as the female.

But the real proof was in the DNA. Through genetic testing the researchers were able to confirm what they suspected based on their powder tracking and radio telemetry studies. DNA tests showed that 100 percent of the pups raised by a given pair were fathered by the female's lifelong mate. In the wild, the California mouse never cheats.[10]

While the mice haven't been caught cheating in the wild, animal researchers decided to put mouse monogamy to the ultimate test. Dr. David Gubernick was a psychology researcher at the University of Wisconsin in Madison, who had studied learning in lizards and maternal bonding in goats. That research led to studies of monogamy and male parent care among animals, an intellectual inquiry he concedes was likely sparked by the absence of his own biological father in childhood.

Dr. Gubernick had inherited a colony of California mice from a lab researcher at the University of California–Los Angeles and decided to study whether the mice were as loyal in captivity as they were in the wild. He took committed pairs of male and female *P. californicus* and tried to tempt each partner with an opposite-sex stranger. In one of the more troubling aspects of this experiment, sometimes the male or female partner remained present in the cage to witness the attempted seduction of its mate. The mouse could see and smell its partner through a hole in the cage, but a small, Plexiglas bar was tethered to its neck, preventing it from scurrying through the hole to reach its mate.

Here's where it gets interesting. *P. californicus*, in the face of seemingly irresistible temptation, surprised everybody.

When the female spouse mouse was put in the cage with a new male, she rejected his advances almost every time. In about 15 percent of the cases, the female did allow the unfamiliar male to mount, even when her partner was present. Whether this is really a fair test of her fidelity isn't clear. Normally, an advance from another male would occur in the wild and no doubt the partner mouse would be present to defend her honor. In this case, the male mouse was restrained, so the female couldn't rely on him to help her reject the advances of the larger and stronger male. But even then, most of the female mice still resisted.

Even more interesting was the response of the committed male mouse, who was tempted with a ready-to-mate single female. To the surprise of researchers, the husband mouse stayed loyal, resistant to the allure of the female and refusing to copulate even when his partner mouse wasn't watching.

"These results indicate that monogamy in *P. californicus* is maintained by a strong attraction and preference of pair mates for each other and by self-restraint from mating with others," the researchers concluded. "Males exhibit apparently more sexual fidelity than females."[11]

Why would the selective pressures of evolution favor mouse fidelity? Dr. Gubernick believes the monogamy of the California mouse is related to the importance of male care in the survival of the young. In a series of experiments, he studied mouse pairs in three different lab environments. Some of the mice had it easy, living in warm cages with easy access to food. Other mice had food, but their cage temperature was cold, similar to the winter nights in California during mouse mating season. The last group had to work for its food, running in a wheel before being fed, to simulate the fact that in the wild, the mouse would have to leave the nest and exert itself to find nourishment.

After the breeding pairs had mated, half of the males were removed. The absence of the male had no effect in the cushy environment—the mouse offspring fared just the same with or without male care. But in the cages where the mice had to work for food or live in cooler temperatures, far fewer young survived. When the lab conditions simulated natural settings, the young mice, who can't regulate their body temperature, needed male care to survive. Dr. Gubernick conducted a similar experiment in the field, removing wild male mice and documenting the effect it had on offspring. As expected, the offspring of males that were removed prior to birth had lower survival rates than the offspring that were attended by both parents.

Fidelity in the Genes

Another superstar of animal fidelity is a furry little rodent called the prairie vole, native to the Midwest. Prairie voles mate for life, sharing a nest and the raising of offspring. Although the prairie voles don't have a perfect track record (occasionally a male vole will copulate outside the pair-bond) they always return to their mate. What's particularly notable about the prairie vole is how differently it behaves compared to its close cousins, the montane and meadow voles. These closely related vole cousins do not partner up. They mate and move on, and don't even stick around to help with the pups.

What's the difference between faithful and philandering voles? Studies show that a slight genetic variation has created different brain circuitry for regulating the hormones vasopressin and oxytocin. These are the "cuddle" hormones released during sex and orgasm and when mothers nurse their young. Monogamous voles have brains loaded with receptors of these hormones. Frisky voles do not.

Studies of prairie voles show that the act of mating leads to bonding between vole partners as their brains are coated in cuddle hormones. Immediately after the male mates with a female, he begins to show distinct preferences for his partner, cuddling her and attacking other voles who stray too close.

To determine whether it was the hormones or some other

mechanism influencing vole bonding, researchers conducted a series of studies in which they injected prairie voles with a drug to block the hormone vasopressin. Without the hormone, the prairie vole acted like his promiscuous cousin. He didn't cuddle after mating but stayed on the prowl, mating with another available female. He also wasn't protective of the female after sex, and didn't show signs of aggression toward other voles.

In the same study, the researchers wanted to know if they could artificially induce vole fidelity by altering vasopressin levels. They gave males who hadn't mated a dose of vasopressin. Suddenly, the virgin voles, high on vasopressin, began to bond with a female, as if they had already mated, showing a distinct preference for her and defending her against strangers.[12]

Dr. Ribble, the California mouse researcher, is now studying African elephant shrews, which also appear to be highly monogamous. In the California mouse, evolution may have selected for monogamy to ensure the participation of the male in the raising of the offspring. But in other monogamous animals, like the elephant shrew, the males don't care for the young. The evolutionary explanation for shrew monogamy may center around male guarding. By focusing his energy and attention on guarding his mate, the male elephant shrew increases his reproductive odds. The female and her young benefit from his constant attention in terms of food, warmth, and protection.

"I think these mice and other animals have some interesting things to tell us," says Dr. Ribble. "You can't help but come to the conclusion that there are some advantages to monogamy."

The Science of Human Commitment

Do humans, like the swan and the black-capped chickadee, simply give the appearance of monogamy, but opt to step out when our partners aren't looking? Or are we more like the loyal California mouse and the prairie vole, steeped in bonding hormones and genetically mapped for fidelity under even the most extreme circumstances?

There is some suggestion that genetic factors may influence whether a person is monogamous. Recently, Swedish scientist Hasse Walum studied 552 sets of male twins to learn more about a variation of a particular gene and its association with relationship satisfaction. The gene is associated with the body's regulation of vasopressin and is the same gene linked with monogamy in prairie voles.[13]

The scientists found that a variation in this gene appeared to influence a man's relationship patterns. Men who carried the variant were less likely to have married their partner. Those who did marry had wives who were less happy in the relationship compared to the wives of men who didn't have a copy of the gene variant. And married men with the gene variant were also more likely to have experienced serious marital problems.

Men with two copies of the gene variant were twice as likely to have had a serious marital crisis within a year of the study, compared to men who didn't have a copy of the variant gene.

While the research marks the first time a specific genetic trait has been associated with marital happiness and fidelity, simply having a copy of the cheating gene doesn't mean adultery is a foregone conclusion.

"There are, of course, many reasons why a person might have relationship problems, but this is the first time that a specific gene variant has been associated with how men bond to their partners," says Dr. Walum. He notes that the overall effect of the genetic variation is modest and it can't yet predict, with any real accuracy, how someone will behave in a relationship.[14]

There is evidence that fidelity may have something of a biological basis for women as well. In a series of well-publicized experiments, researchers from the University of Bern in Switzerland collected sweaty T-shirts that twentysomething men had slept in for two days. Then they asked various women to take a deep whiff of each shirt. All of the shirts carried the manly odor of a dirty shirt, but the women showed distinct preferences for certain shirts and were repulsed by others. When the researchers analyzed saliva samples taken from both the men and women, they discovered that the women had sniffed out a preference for shirts worn by men who were the most genetically different from themselves.[15]

The women were apparently sniffing out differences in a set of immune system genes called major histocompatibility complex, or MHC.

Psychologist Christine Garver-Apgar at the University of New Mexico in Albuquerque wanted to know whether MHC similarities and differences between couples could influence a couple's sex life or risk for infidelity. To find out, Dr. Garver-Apgar and colleagues studied forty-eight heterosexual couples who had been together at least two years. The couples filled out questionnaires quizzing them about their sexual responsiveness toward their partner and whether they had ever been unfaithful. The study couples also gave saliva samples so researchers could analyze their MHC.

Their findings suggested that MHC compatibility appeared to be linked with sexual satisfaction and fidelity. The more similar a woman's MHC was to that of her partner, the *less* she seemed to enjoy sex with him. She was also more likely to report having had affairs, and was more attracted to other men.

But in couples with dissimilar MHC, women reported having better sex and were more likely to report being faithful. The researchers even came up with a formula for determining cheating risk based on genetic compatibility. If the man and woman shared 50 percent of their MHC genes in common, the women had a 50 percent chance of having cheated on another man.[16] Notably, MHC attraction appears to influence a woman's choice for a mate. Men don't appear to have developed an ability to sniff out compatible MHC.

There also are physical signs that suggest a human propensity toward monogamy, explains behavioral scientist David P. Barash, coauthor of *The Myth of Monogamy*. One of them is testicle size. If the female of a species is likely to mate with more than one male, the males of that species typically will have larger testicles that release more ejaculate and improve the odds of impregnation. But when the female is more likely to be loyal to one male, then large testicles aren't essential.

Consider the male silverback gorilla. He has relatively small testicles compared to the size of his body. But the gorilla competes for a female based on the size of his body, not the tenacity of his sperm. Once he gains control over a female, he's free to copulate with her at will with no competition from other gorillas.

By contrast, a male chimpanzee has evolved big testicles to produce large quantities of sperm. This may be because chimps compete with their sperm, not their body size. In a given troop, different males copulate with the same adult female, so a male who has sex early and often is more likely to father offspring.

What about the human male? The testicles of a man are larger than those of a gorilla but smaller than those of a chimpanzee. This suggests that when it comes to sperm competition, human males fall somewhere in the middle of the spectrum. Unlike chimps, humans aren't custom-made for promiscuity, but they face more competition than the average gorilla. The size of human testicles seems to suggest that while multiple couplings remain an option, humans are nonetheless well suited for long-term partnerships.[17]

Statistics on Human Fidelity

While cheating among animals is well documented, less is known about how often humans are sexually unfaithful to their partners.

We can't sprinkle women with fluorescent powder, and we can't tag men with radio transmitters to keep track of their movements. The only real way to document infidelity among humans is to ask them. While it's certainly possible for people to lie about past indiscretions, a large body of evidence collected over numerous years tells the same story: Cheating among married couples appears to be the exception rather than the rule. Most married couples claim to stay loyal and never stray outside the marriage.

The most consistent data on infidelity come from the General Social Survey, sponsored by the National Science Foundation and based at the University of Chicago, which has used a national representative sample to track the opinions and social behaviors of Americans since 1972. The survey data show that in any given year, about 10 percent of married people—12 percent of men and 7 percent of women—say they have had sex outside their marriage. Think about what that number really means. In any given year, 90 percent of married couples say they are faithful to each other. Lifetime infidelity rates also remain relatively low. In 2006, 28 percent of men over sixty said they have ever cheated on a spouse. Among women over sixty, 15 percent admitted to ever cheating.[18]

Why is there a perception that cheating is rampant among married men and women? Data on infidelity are all over the place. Some studies suggest sky-high cheating rates of 60 percent or more, while other studies have produced far more conservative estimates. Surveys appearing in sources like women's magazines may overstate the adultery rate, because they suffer from what pollsters call selection bias: The very act of asking about infidelity tends to attract a respondent who has either cheated or been cheated on. And marriage counselors, who see disproportionately high rates of infidelity in their practices, often estimate a high prevalence of infidelity in the community, but the cross-section of the population they see is skewed toward people having trouble.

Another problem with the data that have been collected on infidelity is that they fail to take into account the timing of infidelity. A person who is having affairs during a marriage clearly meets the conventional definition of an adulterer. But some people begin having outside relationships at the point that they feel their marriage is irreparably damaged. In these cases, infidelity is a sign of a failing marriage, not the cause.

Although infidelity is not common, there are some interesting shifts in infidelity rates. A detailed analysis of the General Social Survey data from 1991 to 2006, compiled by David C. Atkins, research associate professor at the University of Washington Center for the Study of Health and Risk Behaviors, shows that women appear to be closing the adultery gap: Younger women appear to be cheating on their spouses nearly as often as men. And lifetime infidelity rates have also increased. Among men and women over sixty, 20 percent of men and 5 percent of women admitted to ever cheating in 1991. Those numbers jumped to 28 percent and 15 percent respectively in 1996. The researchers also see big changes in relatively new marriages. About 20 percent of men and 15 percent of women under thirty-five say they have been unfaithful, up from about 15 and 12 percent respectively.[19]

Theories vary about why more people appear to be cheating. It may simply be that more people are admitting to cheating rather than there being a real increase in the number of cheaters. Today there is less of a stigma associated with infidelity than in the past. And studies show that different research methods can influence whether someone admits to being unfaithful. For instance, researchers from the University of Colorado and Texas A & M University surveyed 4,884 married women, using face-to-face interviews and anonymous computer questionnaires. During the in-person interviews, only 1 percent of women said they had been unfaithful to their husbands in the past year. But when women took the survey behind the anonymity of a computer, more than 6 percent admitted to cheating.[20]

Social trends also have likely had an effect. It stands to reason that lifetime infidelity rates would change as people live longer and healthier lives. For older people, drugs like Viagra that help treat erectile dysfunction are making it easier for older men to be sexual and, in some cases, unfaithful. Estrogen and testosterone supplements are now commonly offered to women to help them maintain their sex drive and vaginal health as they enter menopause. And even advances like better hip replacements can give an older person the physical mobility to stay social, interact with members of the opposite sex, and cheat, if so desired.

It's not entirely clear why younger couples, even newlyweds, appear more vulnerable to adultery, but perhaps marriage trends are to blame. Today, more couples than ever are living together before marriage. According to the U.S. Census, 6.4 million heterosexual couples were cohabitating in 2007, compared to fewer than 1 million thirty years ago. Studies show that infidelity rates are highest among couples who cohabit before marriage. Once those couples marry, it may be that the cheating habits that were developed before the couple got married continue into the marriage.

Virtually every study of infidelity shows that men are far more likely to cheat on their wives than vice versa. While it does appear men are at higher risk for infidelity in general, the gap likely isn't as wide as is often reported. Many researchers believe that women aren't necessarily more likely to be faithful. It may just be that they are more likely to lie about it.

Rutgers anthropologist Helen Fisher, whose book *Anatomy of Love* focuses on infidelity, notes that infidelity appears to occur in every culture and that in hunting-and-gathering societies there is no evidence that women are any less adulterous than men. The fidelity gap in developed countries like the United States may be explained more by cultural pressures than any real difference in sex drives between men and women. Men with multiple partners typically are viewed as virile, while women who take many partners are considered promiscuous. And historically, cheating simply has been logistically more difficult for women. Women have been isolated on farms or at home with children, giving them fewer opportunities to be unfaithful.

But today, married women are more likely to spend late hours at the office and travel on business. And even for women who stay home, cell phones, e-mail, and instant messaging have allowed women to form more intimate relationships without leaving the house, marriage therapists say. Dr. Frank Pittman, an Atlanta psychiatrist who specializes in family crisis and couples therapy, says he has noticed more women talking about affairs centered on "electronic" contact. Often these women become embroiled in emotional infidelity—sharing personal stories and intimate details of their lives—long before the relationship heads into physical infidelity.

But while infidelity rates do appear to be rising, it's important to remember that it's still relatively uncommon for men and women to stray outside of a marriage. "It's more fascinating and titillating to talk about the notion of playing around and evolutionary reasons for doing it," says the mouse researcher Dr. Gubernick. "But there are a lot of males in the world who are monogamous and remain monogamous and faithful to their partner. There tends to be a downplaying of that fact."

Just like inflated divorce statistics, the tendency to inflate cheating rates puts couples at risk. If we believe that most people get divorced or that most people cheat, we tend to become ambivalent about fidelity and marriage and our own behavior. The fact is that the vast majority of people still say adultery is wrong, and most men and women do not report being unfaithful.

Lessons from Commitment Research

Why are some people more committed than others? That was one
of the questions that interested experimental psychologist John
Lydon of McGill University in Montreal. He recalls his time as
an undergraduate at Notre Dame, when a spring senior formal in
Chicago seemed to make or break relationships. "It was always a
question of how many got engaged and how many broke up," he
says. "It was decision time."

Those memories were the basis for a series of commitment studies Dr. Lydon and his students began conducting at McGill. He
tracked students who left high school sweethearts behind as they
left for college, and he began studying how different people reacted
to temptation or perceived threats to a relationship. He found that
people in committed relationships respond differently to temptation depending on how big a threat it really is. In one study, heterosexual men and women in committed relationships were shown
a series of pictures of attractive people. On another occasion, they
were shown photos and told that the attractive person was personally interested in them. In the first condition, the men and women
were comfortable acknowledging the attractiveness of the people
in the photos. But in the second situation, when they were told
the person was interested in them, they were less likely to rate the
person as attractive. In essence, when the attractive person became
a threat and potential temptation, the reaction was to "devalue"
them and make them less attractive.[21] "The more committed you
are, the less attractive you find other people," says Dr. Lydon. "The
logic is this helps you maintain your relationships. A man would
defend his relationship from a potential threat by saying, 'She's not
so great.'"

But the McGill studies also found a reason why men may be at greater risk for cheating than women. Several studies showed that women are more likely than men to instinctively protect relationships in the presence of potential threat. When a woman is attracted to a man who isn't her spouse, the female brain appears to react differently from when a man is attracted to someone other than his wife.[22]

In one study of 300 heterosexual men and women, the researchers asked half the participants to imagine a sexy conversation with an attractive member of the opposite sex. The other half were asked to imagine a more routine encounter with people of the same sex. After visualizing a titillating or boring encounter, the participants were asked to play a fill-in-the-blank word game. Before you read about the results, try taking a quiz similar to the one the study participants took.

The *For Better* Quiz #1: What's Your Flirting Response?

Try to imagine the following scenario as vividly as you can, as if the events described are really happening to you. After the visualization exercise, you will be asked to complete some word puzzles. This is designed to distract your attention from the scene you just visualized. After you complete the word puzzles, you will be asked how vividly you recall the scenario, which is why it's important to imagine it as best as possible.

Imagine that you're in a coffee shop and you run into a friend or a co-worker whom you find attractive. Spend some time visualizing the scene and making it as real as possible. The man or woman you run into is really happy to see you, and you are also happy to see this person. The two of you strike up a warm, engaging conversation, and you lose track of time. You realize you need to get home. As you are leaving, the person gives you his/her phone number so you can get together again for coffee sometime.

Now, take a break from the visualization exercise and try to solve the following word puzzles.

    L O _ A L
    D E _ _ T E D
    C _ _ M I _ _ E _
    I N V E _ T E D
    B E _ A _ E
    T H R _ _ T

The goal of the study was to identify whether thinking about an attractive encounter with a member of the opposite sex might have triggered subconscious thoughts about cheating, as evidenced by how the word puzzles were completed. As it turns out, the word fragment puzzles consisted of words that have been identified as signaling commitment or a perceived threat.

After the participants had taken the quiz, striking differences emerged among the men and women who had flirting on the brain compared to those who had been imagining more mundane encounters. Women who had been flirting in their minds were most likely to identify the commitment and threat words.

Women were more likely to complete the quiz this way:

    L O Y A L
    D E V O T E D
    C O M M I T T E D
    I N V E S T E D
    B E W A R E
    T H R E A T

The men who had imagined flirting with an attractive woman were most likely to identify these words:

LOCAL
DELETED
COMMITTEE
INVENTED
BECAME
THROAT

Dr. Lydon said the differences between men and women were so striking, it suggests that for women, the mere thought of an outside temptation triggers "alarm bells" in their brains, but temptation doesn't seem to have the same effect on men.[23]

In another set of experiments, researchers studied real world encounters rather than imaginary experiences. They looked at how men and women treated spouses after encountering an attractive person in real life. The researchers mixed the study couples with good-looking actors who were trained to send subtle flirtation signals. The actors pretended to be other participants who had signed up for the research. A comparison group was mixed with aloof actors who made no conversation.

After spending time with the attractive, flirtatious stranger, the couples were then asked to imagine that their spouse had done something to upset them, such as being late for a date or lying about where they had been. After letting the person stew about the transgression, the researcher then asked the men and women to explain whether they could forgive their spouse.

Among the men, those who had been spending time with a flirtatious actress were less likely to forgive their wives' hypothetical bad behavior compared to the men who hadn't been flirting. But women had the opposite reaction. A woman who had been flirting was more likely to forgive her man's transgression, and even make excuses for him, than a woman who had been behaving herself with the aloof actor.

The finding suggests that when a man is tempted by an attractive person who seems interested in him, he begins to feel less committed because he sees the new woman as a good alternative. But women view a man who tempts them as a threat, so they reinforce their feelings about their partner by excusing flawed behavior.

The goal of the McGill research is to better understand how men and women react to flirtatious encounters in hopes of coming up with ways couples can protect themselves from the temptations of infidelity. By studying some of the differences between how men and women react to attractive people, the researchers can now offer some suggestions for reprogramming your brain to resist temptation.

One strategy is to plan ahead. Maybe it seems obvious, but men and women can avoid temptation by planning in advance how they might cope with it. This is not dissimilar to the reason building inhabitants are told to take part in fire drills. The act of simply walking down the stairs gives you the mental and muscle memory to react appropriately during a crisis, when you may not be thinking all that clearly. Using the same theory, people who come up with a strategy for dealing with a co-worker's advances or encountering an attractive stranger on a business trip may be more likely to resist during the moment of marital crisis when the temptation occurs in real life.

In one study, men were told to imagine meeting an attractive woman at a bar on a weekend that their girlfriend was out of town. Then some of the men were instructed to "train" themselves for the situation by completing the following sentence:

When the girl approaches, I will _____ to protect my relationship.

To study whether the training method could influence a man's reactions to women, the men were asked to play a virtual reality game that involved spending time in various rooms. In some of the rooms, pictures of attractive women flickered for a few thousandths of a second—so fast that they were imperceptible to the conscious mind but still noticeable to the subconscious, say researchers. The men who had just completed the training sentence tended to avoid the areas where the female images were flickering. But men who hadn't completed the training exercise ended up being drawn into the rooms with women.[24]

Studies also show that it's possible to dampen illicit thoughts when you're tempted to stray. Often a man might try this method, but he goes about it the wrong way, telling himself to "resist, resist, resist," when an attractive woman comes on to him.

But relationship experts say it's a mistake, when faced with temptation, to focus on how much you want to resist. Think about a person who goes on a diet, deciding they will stop eating their favorite foods, such as ice cream. What's their first reaction? They crave ice cream. Similarly, telling yourself that even thinking about another person is off-limits puts you at risk of doing just the opposite.

Instead, the better solution is to fill your head with thoughts of the person you love or look at his or her picture, which will in turn push the tempting thoughts out of your brain. Focus on warm and loving thoughts, not sexual desire, which would just fuel the sexual drive that is tempting you in the first place.[25]

The research shows that men and women can train themselves to resist temptation. And almost without exception, men and women say they value fidelity in a marriage and plan to stay faithful to their husband or wife. The science and the statistics clearly show that while monogamy may not be the norm in the animal kingdom, it is certainly possible for both animals and humans to remain socially and sexually faithful to a partner. Sure, the desire for fidelity among humans appears to be the exception rather than the rule in the animal kingdom, but in every other way, humans are exceptional creatures. Why shouldn't they also be exceptional when it comes to monogamy? The very essence of human nature is the ability to control our impulses—it's one of the many traits that distinguish us from the lower creatures. The reason we marry is to find a lifetime partner, and the science clearly shows that we are mapped for marriage and commitment.

But what is it that draws us to another person, fuels our desire for commitment, and motivates us to recite the marriage vow? The answer, of course, is love. It's perhaps the most essential factor in the biological equation of coupling, yet it's among the most complicated areas of study in the science of human relationships.

CHAPTER 3

To Love and to Cherish:
Flirting, Attraction, and Chemical Passion

Love is only a dirty trick played on us to achieve
continuation of the species.

—W. SOMERSET MAUGHAM

In the late 1960s, graduate student Elaine Hatfield was studying psychology at Stanford University, where her fellow students
were intently focused on issues of mathematical modeling and rat
behavior in hopes of gaining insights into the human mind. But
what really interested Ms. Hatfield were the after-hours conversations she often had with her fellow students. Almost without
exception, they were all struggling to make sense of dating, love,
and marriage and discovering how little each of them knew about
how to navigate human relationships. The budding psychologist
and researcher began to wonder if the scientific skills she was developing could be better put to use in the study of couples. Was love,
she wondered, a worthwhile subject of scientific research?

Dr. Hatfield soon embarked on an academic career focused on

the study of physical attraction, crushes, passionate love, and sexual desire. In 1975, she and a few colleagues applied for and received an $84,000 grant from the National Science Foundation to pursue their research.

But Dr. Hatfield's unorthodox love studies caught the attention of Wisconsin senator William Proxmire, who was making a name for himself by identifying wasteful government spending. He issued a press release blasting the research, arguing that love, one of the great mysteries of life, should remain safely beyond the grasp of science.

"I object to this because no one, not even the National Science Foundation, can argue that falling in love is a science," railed Senator Proxmire. "I'm also against it because I don't want to know the answer." Most people, the senator argued, "want to leave some things in life a mystery, and right on top of the things we don't want to know is why a man falls in love with a woman and vice versa."[26]

The controversy cast Dr. Hatfield and love research into the national spotlight. The *Chicago Daily News* even held a contest asking whether love and sex were reasonable subjects for scientific research. The result? Science lost, garnering just 12.5 percent of the vote.[27]

But fortunately, skepticism didn't win the day. The influential *New York Times* columnist James Reston defended the research, arguing that the study of relationships was an important scientific pursuit.

"If the sociologists and psychologists can get even a suggestion of the answer to our pattern of romantic love, marriage, disillusions, divorce—and the children left behind—it would be the best investment of federal money since Jefferson made the Louisiana Purchase," wrote Mr. Reston.

Eventually, the controversy faded, and more scientists began to quietly focus on love research as a legitimate academic discipline. Dr. Hatfield later gained national prominence for developing a widely used scale by which researchers could measure passionate love. (You can find Dr. Hatfield's quiz about passionate love later in this chapter.)

Today the scientific study of love has flourished. Scholars from a variety of disciplines—historians, social psychologists, evolutionary anthropologists, demographers, economists, microbiologists, and neuroscientists—have analyzed, dissected, and deconstructed this amorphous emotion and developed a deep and practical understanding of the science of love, passion, and romance.

The Biology of Flirting and Attraction

One of the most surprising revelations of love research is how much of our own romantic behaviors appear to be preprogrammed, mapped into our DNA by the selective pressures that guaranteed the survival of our ancestral gene pool.

In the animal kingdom, countless species offer various displays of courtship, prancing and thumping and preening to attract attention. If you've ever watched a wildlife film, you've seen lizards sway to their own internal mating song and watched birds strut and prance. Wolves nuzzle, nibble each other's coats, and walk pressed close together. Eventually the male may bow to the female and tilt his head in invitation. The goal is to draw the attention of a potential mate with an irresistible and showy display that suggests a high level of fitness and good genes.

If this all sounds quite familiar, that's probably because you've been there. Humans, too, have a strikingly similar repertoire of courtship rituals and gestures. We call it flirting.

The earliest studies of flirting were conducted in the 1960s by German ethologist Irenäus Eibl-Eibesfeldt. An ethologist is a scientist who studies the behavior of animals in their natural habitats. But Dr. Eibl-Eibesfeldt turned his camera on the human animal,

filming men and women interacting in the South Sea Islands, large
cities like Paris, New York, and Sydney, and smaller villages in
the Far East, Africa, and South America. His genius was in using
a special camera that took pictures from the side so that couples
wouldn't know they were being filmed.

Through his lens he discovered a silent language of courtship
that is strikingly similar around the globe. Women, whether they
were from primitive cultures or modern cities, engaged in virtually identical body language, gestures, and movements while in the
company of men. The language of flirting includes the smile, arched
eyebrows to widen eyes, a quick lowering of the eyelids, tucking the
chin down, and a coy glance to the side. After an averted gaze,
women consistently bring their hands near the mouth and giggle.

And just as animals exhibit submissive behaviors as they are trying to attract a mate, couples, too, show each other signs of submission and helplessness—palms turn up, shoulders shrug, and heads
tilt to expose the neck as a signal of vulnerability.

"Our closest animal relatives, the chimpanzees, greet each other
with compliant, upturned palms to show 'I am friendly,'" writes
psychologist and courtship researcher David B. Givens. "For human
beings everywhere, gesturing with an upraised, opened palm is a
convincing and time-tested way to say, 'Trust me; I mean no harm.'
Throughout the world, palm-up cues captivate, charm, and psychologically disarm partners who may be unsure of each other's
intentions."[28]

Dr. Givens, along with several other noted social psychologists, has studied human courtship rituals in modern societies by
immersing himself in the singles scene, camping out in dimly lit
bars, restaurants, and cocktail lounges to decode the verbal and
nonverbal signals men and women send to each other.

The scientific community has deconstructed all your best moves.
Michael Cunningham, a psychology professor at the University of

Louisville, and Anchorage psychology professor Chris Kleinke
have collected reams of data on pickup lines. Others have studied
the role of physical attractiveness and even the different types of
gazes and glances that men and women use to woo each other.

Even the seemingly endless trips women make to the restroom
are part of the ritual, and represent nothing less than a promenade
during which a woman demonstrates her interest in a man while
putting her own sexual availability and reproductive fitness on display. Remember those swaying lizards and strutting cranes? During the walk to the bathroom a woman may swing her hips, cast a
coy glance, lick her lips, twirl a strand of hair, and toss her head.

In turn, the man to whom this behavior is directed may then
lean back in his chair so that his chest puffs out and chin points
upward. (Think pigeon.) He'll make wide, sweeping gestures or
respond to a friend's joke with exaggerated laughter as a way to
continue to draw the woman's attention. (Think peacock.)

Dr. Monica Moore, an associate professor in the Department of
Behavioral and Social Sciences at Webster University in St. Louis,
has cataloged fifty-two flirtatious behaviors employed by women in
order to attract and keep the attention of a potential mate. Among
the moves: gazing, hair tossing, primping, caressing, leaning, and
dancing.[29]

Notably, Dr. Moore has found that physical attractiveness is
not the best predictor for finding a mate. Far more important is a
woman's ability to flirt—how well she sends the appropriate nonverbal signals that will reassure a man that it's okay to approach
her. A high-signaling but less attractive woman will win more male
attention than a more attractive woman who isn't sending out the
signals, Dr. Moore says.[30]

Once we've gotten somebody's attention, the silent language of
courtship eventually results in eye contact and then a face-to-face
encounter. In this early stage of contact, couples find excuses to

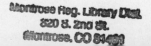

touch—brushing a hair out of place or picking a crumb off a lapel. And then, as the attraction intensifies and the couple begins to feel more confident in each other, they literally fall into sync.

Several studies have documented the concept of interactional synchrony, a phenomenon that occurs when two people, after spending time together, develop a unique rhythm to their gestures, either mirroring or complementing the other's movement. The pattern of common body movements has been widely seen in animals, and several studies have documented the phenomenon between mothers and children.[31] Anthropologist Edward Hall recounted the story of one of his students at Northwestern University filming a group of schoolchildren playing. In watching the children twirl, skip, and hop, he came to realize the patterns of movement translated into a rhythmic beat that he could even set to music. The children seemed to be unconsciously keeping each other's time.

"The rhythm of a people may yet prove to be the most binding of all the forces that hold human beings together," wrote Dr. Hall in *The Dance of Life: The Other Dimension of Time.* "I have come to the conclusion that the human species lives in a sea of rhythm, ineffable to some, but quite tangible to others."[32]

Several studies suggest that, just as children playing and mothers with their babies fall into a rhythmic groove, potential lovers also fall into a rhythm of movement as their interest in each other intensifies.

In one study, Austrian researchers studied ten-minute encounters between high school students of the opposite sex who didn't know each other. The students were told they were taking part in a simple experiment, which was interrupted when the researcher left for an urgent phone call. Video cameras rolled as the two teens sat alone in the room. Every head tilt, lean, and posture change was recorded and coded. Questionnaires revealed which of the students had developed attractions to each other during the waiting time.

The movement patterns that emerged were complex but still suggested that even in the earliest stages of attraction, couples develop their own unique rhythm of movement. One couple, for instance, repeated the same cycle of movements—the male leaned back, the woman touched her hair and then she touched her face—three separate times.[33]

Other studies suggest couples echo or mirror each other's movements when they become romantically attracted to each other. They pivot in their seats and lean in toward each other, raising their glasses to drink at about the same pace. "As we become attracted to each other, we begin to keep a common beat," writes Rutgers anthropologist Helen Fisher."[34]

Philadelphia social psychologist Timothy Perper, another researcher who spent hundreds of hours observing men and women in singles bars, restaurants, parties, and train stations, notes that the consistency of the human mating dance serves as a stark reminder of the powerful biological forces that compel us to seek companionship. The patterns he detected in his research, he notes, were not just about picking up a prospective date in a bar. The hair flips and movements and rituals, he said, are among the most visible signs that two people are falling in love.[35]

The Science of Sniffing Out Your Genetic Match

As noted earlier, a series of sweaty T-shirt studies have given scientists insights into the biological basis of our mate choice. Swiss researchers asked various women to take a deep whiff of dirty T-shirts belonging to a group of twentysomething men who had slept in the shirts for a few days. The women showed strong preferences for certain soiled shirts, and the scientists discovered the women actually were sniffing out a partner with whom they were the most genetically compatible.[36]

In the studies, the women were unknowingly sniffing out a set of immune system genes called major histocompatibility complex or MHC. A woman's body appears to be programmed to find a mate with very different MHC than her own. Studies show that laboratory mice won't mate with mice with too-similar MHC, and the T-shirt studies also suggest that women have a smell preference for men with different MHC. The ability to sniff out genetically different mates may have evolved to discourage inbreeding, leading to healthier children. Some researchers think kissing may even have evolved as a sort of MHC taste test to check out compatibility with a potential lover's immune system. The lesson for women may be that the more satisfying the kiss, the more pleasant you find his smell, the more likely you've found a genetically compatible mate. Notably, MHC attraction appears to influence a woman's choice for a mate, but men don't appear to have developed an ability to sniff out compatible MHC.

Some commercial firms have attempted to capitalize on the findings by offering genetic tests to help men and women determine their MHC compatibility with a partner. The MHC marketers promise a better sex life, more orgasms, lower cheating risk, higher fertility, and healthier children if you choose a genetically compatible mate.[37] Such a test is intriguing, but the marketing claims are well ahead of the science. Couples shouldn't make decisions about the future of a relationship based on the results of an unproven saliva test.

While there's not a lot men and women can do to make sure they are hooking up with genetically dissimilar partners, scientists do have one piece of advice for women: Get off the pill and use a different form of birth control if you are seriously considering a particular partner as a lifelong mate. Hormonal contraceptives have been shown to blunt our natural instincts about MHC differences, and research suggests a woman should be wary about choosing a husband if she's on the pill.

How does the pill interfere with the selection process? In more smelly T-shirt studies, women on birth control pills seem to choose badly, showing a preference for men whose MHC genes are too similar to their own. The theory is that the pill tricks the body into thinking it's pregnant, and the biological smell test for finding a mate is no longer needed. As a result, women on the pill may risk choosing a mate who is not genetically suitable.[38]

While men don't seem to be equipped to sniff out genetic differences, the scent of romance also appears to influence the choices a man makes. A man's olfactory senses appear to guide him toward a woman who is primed to conceive. Consider a recent study that looked at how much attention a woman received during various phases of her menstrual cycle—measured by tallying the tips men paid to various strippers. The study, published in the journal *Evolution and Human Behavior*, showed that women who work in strip clubs earn more money on their most fertile days. After comparing tips to the women's menstrual cycles, the researchers found that women who were ovulating earned about $335 in tips per five-hour shift. On nonovulating days in the cycle, the women earned just $260 per shift. And if a stripper was menstruating, the time of the month when a woman is least likely to become pregnant, her tips dropped to just $185 per shift. That's a 45 percent drop in a stripper's earning power between ovulation and menstruation.[39]

Martie Haselton, an associate professor of psychology at UCLA, documented other ways ovulation appears to affect female relationships. She found a link between fashion and fertility, finding that women pay more attention to their appearance as ovulation approaches.[40] During times of high fertility, a woman's voice becomes higher pitched and more feminine.[41] And women report that men appear to be more loving, attentive, and, significantly, more jealous of other men when their partners are ovulating.[42] That research suggests that men have a sixth sense that they need to more closely guard their mate to protect their reproductive territory.

The Chemistry of Love

Anyone who has ever fallen in love has felt helpless against the sheer force of the emotion. When love is new, it can be all consuming. Love fills our hearts, our bodies, and our brains, distracting us from our work, our friends, and pretty much everything other than the object of our affection. There is room for nothing else. Poets and philosophers often describe love as madness and misery.

As French philosopher and mathematician Blaise Pascal observed: "The heart has its reasons, which reason knows nothing of."

But while the whims of the heart remain a mystery, numerous love studies show that love is not just a wild, untamed emotion. Love is a physical state, a biological and chemical reaction that triggers numerous changes throughout the body.

It's been clear for some time that a variety of neurochemicals and hormones are linked with passionate love and sexual desire. Donatella Marazziti, a psychiatrist at the University of Pisa, Italy, has subjected the newly in love to regular blood tests, examining how the romantic state influences the body's levels of various brain chemicals and hormones.

In one study, Dr. Marazziti and her colleagues examined the link between love and the brain chemical serotonin, which is associated with mood, sleep, and memory. The researchers studied the blood serotonin levels of people recently in love compared to an average group of individuals who were not in the throes of a new romance. A third group also was observed—patients with obsessive-compulsive disorder, an anxiety disorder characterized by persistent thoughts and repetitive, ritualized behaviors. Among the three groups, the researchers found that the love-struck participants showed a striking similarity to those with obsessive-compulsive problems. The love-struck study subjects and the people with OCD showed similar declines in serotonin levels compared to the individuals who were not mentally ill or lovesick.[43] The finding helps explain the obsessive nature of early romantic love—when you can't stop thinking about the person you've just met, to the point that it becomes difficult to concentrate on daily tasks. Dr. Fisher, the Rutgers anthropologist, has observed that people who are newly infatuated spend as much as 85 percent of the day thinking about the one they love.

In other studies, Dr. Marazitti and fellow researcher Domenico Canale looked at how romance appears to affect other hormones, and again found dramatic chemical fluctuations related to love. Consider testosterone, the sex hormone that serves many functions in both men and women. When women fall in love, testosterone levels rise. When men are smitten, testosterone declines. The scientists also observed changes in cortisol, the hormone related to physical and psychological stress, as well as follicle stimulating hormone, a pituitary hormone linked to ovulation in women and sperm production in men. While these changes show that falling in love leads to physical changes in the body, it's notable that these chemical fluctuations don't last. When the Italian researchers retested the same volunteers twelve to twenty-four months later, hormone levels had returned to normal.

Several researchers have studied the role of the so-called bonding hormones oxytocin and vasopressin in relationships. Oxytocin induces labor during childbirth and is released when a woman nurses her child. It's also present in high levels during female orgasm. Vasopressin has a variety of effects on blood pressure and the brain, and scientists believe both chemicals play a role in bonding and commitment. These are the same hormones detected among the monogamous and sexually faithful prairie voles we learned about in Chapter 2.

Human studies have also suggested a role for oxytocin in passionate love. Dr. Marazitti and his colleagues measured oxytocin levels in forty-four volunteers, some of whom were newly in love while others were in long-term relationships or not involved with anybody. People who had high levels of anxiety about their loved one, a common characteristic of romantic love, also had higher levels of oxytocin.[44]

Measuring Your Passion

Because passionate love tends to mark the early part of every relationship, it is also the reference point couples often use in assessing the quality of their relationship. Couples in long-term happy marriages often recall with nostalgia the electric chemistry of their early days together. Psychology professor Elaine Hatfield suggests that there are two basic types of love that cover most married relationships.

- Passionate Love: When we are in the throes of passionate love, we experience a near constant state of intense longing for the other person, marked by profound physiological arousal. When the feeling is returned, we experience fulfillment and ecstasy. Unrequited love leaves us feeling distraught and empty.
- Companionate Love: This love is a far less intense emotion, but no less powerful. It combines feelings of attachment, commitment, and intimacy. It represents the affection we feel for those with whom our lives are deeply entwined.[45]

For most couples, passion and romance eventually fade over time, and a calmer, more contented love takes over as the years go by. Given that passionate love can be exhausting and emotionally draining, the shift to an easier, more committed love is often welcomed by couples.

Where is your relationship in the spectrum of love? The Passionate Love Scale, developed by Dr. Hatfield and Susan Sprecher, psychology and sociology professor at Illinois State University, was designed to assess the cognitive, emotional, and behavioral aspects of passionate love. While the Passionate Love Scale is widely used by relationship researchers, Dr. Hatfield notes that couples should take the test only for fun. Don't make major decisions based on how you score on the fifteen-item scale. "Love and life are very complex, and a person's emotions are always nuanced," says Dr. Hatfield.

The *For Better* Quiz #2: Passionate Love

Answer the following questions to test your level of passionate love. Think of the person you love most passionately now, and respond by circling the appropriate response. Answers range from (1) not at all true to (9) definitely true. Then, add up your scores and check the scale below to see how hot your love fires burn.

	UNTRUE . . . TRUE
I would feel deep despair if my partner left me.	1 2 3 4 5 6 7 8 9
Sometimes I feel I can't control my thoughts; they are obsessively on my partner.	1 2 3 4 5 6 7 8 9
I feel happy when I'm doing something to make my partner happy.	1 2 3 4 5 6 7 8 9
I would rather be with my partner than with anyone else.	1 2 3 4 5 6 7 8 9
I'd get jealous if I thought my partner was falling in love with someone else.	1 2 3 4 5 6 7 8 9
I yearn to know all about my partner.	1 2 3 4 5 6 7 8 9
I want my partner physically, emotionally, and mentally.	1 2 3 4 5 6 7 8 9

I have an endless appetite for affection from my partner.	1 2 3 4 5 6 7 8 9
For me, my partner is the perfect romantic partner.	1 2 3 4 5 6 7 8 9
I sense my body responding when my partner touches me.	1 2 3 4 5 6 7 8 9
My partner always seems to be on my mind.	1 2 3 4 5 6 7 8 9
I want my partner to know me—my thoughts, my fears, and my hopes.	1 2 3 4 5 6 7 8 9
I eagerly look for signs indicating my partner's desire for me.	1 2 3 4 5 6 7 8 9
I possess a powerful attraction for my partner.	1 2 3 4 5 6 7 8 9
I get extremely depressed when things don't go right in my relationship with my partner.	1 2 3 4 5 6 7 8 9

PASSIONATE LOVE SCALE SCORES

106–135 points—Extremely passionate. Your love is wild and reckless.

86–105 points—Passionate. The fires of passion still burn, but not as intensely.

66–85 points—Average. Contentment, with occasional sparks

45–65 points—Cool. Tepid, infrequent passion

15–44 points—Extremely cool. The fire is out.

Love on the Brain

Clearly, love creates chemical chaos inside our bodies, a finding that's not all that surprising given the jittery, exciting feelings we associate with a new relationship. But scientists studying the wide variations in brain chemicals and hormones during times of romantic love decided they wanted to know more. What does love look like in the brain?

It was a question that, until relatively recently, couldn't be answered. The ability of scientists to study brains in love was the result of a technological breakthrough developed in the 1990s called functional magnetic resonance imaging, or fMRI. Conventional MRI machines use a strong magnet and radio waves to produce detailed images of the brain and other body structures. MRI scanners can be used to diagnose brain tumors, stroke, and other brain problems.

But functional MRI goes a step further, tracking blood oxygen levels in the brain. Whenever any part of the brain becomes active, the small blood vessels in that region dilate, causing more blood to rush in. As a result, fMRI scans can be used to observe the brain's response to almost any kind of emotional stimulation, including sounds or visual images.

In 1993, a group of German neuroscientists are believed to have been among the first to scan the brain to see what it looked like in various emotional states, including passionate love. In the brain scanner, the scientists concluded, the patterns of romantic love look like "mental chaos."[46] It wasn't until seven years later that University College London scientists Andreas Bartels and Semir Zeki decided to tap the new technology in an effort to home in on the neural basis of romantic love. They wanted to understand what parts of the brain react when people experience the intense feelings of passionate love. They recruited eleven women and six men who scored high on the Passionate Love Scale. These volunteers professed to be "truly, deeply, and madly in love."

But studying love on the brain is tricky business. People in love care deeply about their lovers, of course, but they also experience strong emotions for close friends and loved ones. The question is whether the brain reacts differently to a lover, for whom we feel passionate love, compared to other people whom we love deeply, such as our children, parents, and close friends. To find out, the researchers showed the volunteers four similar photographs. Women in love saw photos of their boyfriends and three similarly aged male friends for whom they had affection. Men in love saw photos of their girlfriends and three similar female friends. And finally, to account for differences in affection among old friends and new friends, the researchers made sure that the volunteers had known their friends at least as long as they had known their lovers.

And as a final guarantee to make sure they were really studying people in the throes of passionate love, the volunteers were subjected to two additional measures. First, they were asked to rate their feelings of love and sexual arousal while viewing pictures of their lovers and their friends. Galvanic skin response, a component of polygraph testing that is used to study emotional arousal, was also measured as the volunteers looked at the photographs.

The results did not disappoint. The brain scan images showed that unique parts of the brain become active when humans view the face of someone about whom they feel passionate love. "We have shown that underlying one of the richest experiences of mankind is a functionally specialized system of the brain," the authors wrote.[47]

Passion produced increased activity in the brain areas associated with euphoria and reward, and decreased levels of activity in the areas associated with distress and depression. The findings showed that love is not just a powerful emotion; it's a dramatic physical state that produces real and visible changes in our brain patterns.

Does Love Cloud Your Judgment?

One of the more interesting findings of the brain scan studies showed that passionate love appears to deactivate parts of the brain associated with critical thought. In other words, being in love can impair your judgment.

The findings may help explain why people in love often seem to make bad decisions. How often have you seen a friend so smitten by a new lover, they ignore obvious signs of trouble ahead, like a bad temper, forgetting to call, or possibly even signs that the person might be married. A person in love may make trade-offs they wouldn't normally make—like showing up late to work or ignoring an important looming deadline—in order to accommodate their beloved. A person in love tends to idealize a partner and ignore a lover's seemingly obvious faults—after all, the parts of the brain that control critical social assessment and negative emotions have been shut down.

And the images shown in the brain scans also help explain the deep bonding we feel with a lover. The scans show that passionate love activates the same part of the brain as that involved with reward and addiction. When we're in love, we simply can't get enough of a person. The brain images, said the study authors, explain "the power of love to motivate and exhilarate."[48] Additional studies by Dr. Fisher, psychologist Arthur Aron at Stonybrook University in Stonybrook, New York, and researcher Lucy Brown from the Albert Einstein College of Medicine have shed further light on the unique brain system that fuels romantic love. Romantic attraction activates the parts of the brain with a high concentration of receptors for dopamine, the chemical messenger related to drug addiction, cravings, and euphoria.[49] Dr. Fisher notes that young lovers show signs of a dopamine effect—they have boundless energy, they can't sleep, they lose their appetites, and they crave attention from their beloved. Indeed, the person in love is an addict of sorts. Just like someone going through chemical withdrawal, a lover becomes anxious and unable to concentrate in the absence of his or her partner. But even a small dose of affection—a phone call or a text message—gives them their "fix" and calms them, at least for a while.

In many ways, the brain scan studies show that the maddening feelings of love are essentially a major mental-health crisis. The chemical storm of brain changes it causes are strikingly similar to drug addiction and obsessive-compulsive disorder. Love really does make us crazy.

"The brain system involved in romantic love is powerful," says Dr. Fisher. "Everything that is going on in the brain, everything that happens with romantic love, has a chemical basis."[50]

In one recent brain-scan study, Dr. Fisher and colleagues looked at fifteen subjects who were deeply in love but were nursing broken hearts. While in the scanner, they viewed "neutral" pictures of someone they knew but for whom they didn't have intense romantic feelings. Then they were shown a picture of their beloved.

The brain images of those scorned in love also give us clues as to why the breakdown of a relationship can cause such distress. The subjects dealing with failed relationships showed activity in the dopamine system—suggesting they maintained intense feelings for their loved one. But they also showed activity in brain regions associated with risk taking, anger control, and obsessive-compulsive problems. Notably, the scans showed activity in one part of the brain linked with physical pain.

The use of brain scans to study emotional changes is still a new science. But the images signal the potential toll of relationship problems, and why a fight with a spouse or a romantic breakup can be truly painful. A man or woman in love who has been scorned by a lover is "not a good combination," notes Dr. Fisher. "You're feeling intense romantic love, you're willing to take big risks, you're in physical pain, obsessively thinking about a person, and you're struggling to control your rage," she says. "You're not operating with your full range of cognitive abilities. It's possible that part of the rational mind shuts down."[51] Breaking up is hard to do.

In many ways, it's reassuring to learn that our most primitive instincts likely drew us toward our mate, and it's that ancient instinct that also helps keep us together with the best chance for healthy children, a robust sex life, and a greater likelihood of a faithful relationship. What's happening as love sets in seems so real, so powerful, at the time, yet so much of it is caused by stirring the chemical pot of our hormonal system. While biological drive and genetically based behavior patterns can fan the flames of attraction, that's not the end of the story. Once we find a partner, it's up to each of us to carefully tend to the fires of love and work to rekindle the passion that brought us together in the first place.

Lessons from Love Science to Improve Your Marriage

Love is such a complex emotion that the Arabic language uses more than a half-dozen words to adequately describe it, a phenomenon described in *The Map of Love* by novelist Ahdaf Soueif.

> "Hubb" is love, "ishq" is love that entwines two people together, "shaghaf" is love that nests in the chambers of the heart, "hayam" is love that wanders the earth, "teeh" is love in which you lose yourself, "walah" is love that carries sorrow within it, "sababah" is love that exudes from your pores, "hawa" is love that shares its name with "air" and with "falling," "gharm" is love that is willing to pay the price.[52]

Anyone who has ever loved doesn't need an Arabic lesson to understand that all love is not the same. The love we feel for our children is different from what we share with our friends, lovers, or spouses. And even within a romantic relationship, we experience varying degrees of love, and even the type of love we feel can change over time. There's the jittery passion of early romance, the settled contentment of marriage, and the deep devotion of lifelong relationships.

Dr. Fisher notes that the ability of humans to feel different types of love is a by-product of evolution. Feelings of lust, attraction, and attachment are associated with different neurotransmitters and hormones, and these "emotion motivation" systems evolved to influence three distinct aspects of reproduction. The sex drive motivates people to seek a partner. The neural circuits associated with attraction motivate men and women to choose a genetically compatible partner. And the brain system related to attachment sustains a relationship long enough to allow for the raising and protection of children.

But this scientific explanation belies the emotional complexity of the various types of love. If we are lucky, and thankfully most of us are, at some point in our lives we find love, although it can take many forms. Romantic love is dizzying, companionate love is comforting, and consummate love is lasting. Understanding the different forms of love and how love can change and evolve over time can help couples make sense of their emotions and their relationship.

Let's start with the most basic expression of love, the three-word phrase "I love you."

What do those words mean to you? Most of us think we know the answer, but the reality is that people often mean different things when they say, "I love you." California State University sociologist Terry Hatkoff has identified six basic styles of love. They are:

- Romantic—marked by passion and sexual attraction
- Best Friends—feelings of deep affection and caring
- Logical—when practical issues like money, religion, and values influence feelings
- Playful—the excitement of flirtatious and challenging interactions
- Possessive—marked by feelings of jealousy and obsession
- Unselfish—marked by nurturing, kindness, and sacrifice

Dr. Hatkoff has developed a love scale to measure the way different individuals personally define love. The scale has been tested on thousands of men and women and is now commonly used as both a research and diagnostic tool by family therapists.

Dr. Hatkoff says that when she administers the love quiz, most people discover they have two or three dominant forms of love. But often, husbands and wives answer the quiz differently. While it's helpful to understand your own meaning of love, it's even more important to know how your partner feels.

Consider this scenario:

A husband and wife go out to dinner. When the waiter flirts with the wife, the man doesn't seem to notice. Instead he mentions that he changed the oil in her car. The wife becomes upset by her husband's lack of jealousy, and the husband is bothered that she doesn't appreciate his efforts at car maintenance.

"She's thinking, 'If he loved me he'd be jealous when other men hit on me, and he's never jealous,'" explains Dr. Hatkoff. "But he doesn't define that as an important component of love. She defines it as important. She's judging him by her own meaning."

The love quiz would likely show that the woman scores high in the area of possessive love—in her mind, jealousy is one way to measure the level of someone's affection. But the husband scores low in the category of possessive love. Instead, he scores high in the area of logical love. If the woman realized this about her husband, she would understand that his having taken the time to change the oil in her car was a powerful sign of his love. And knowing that his wife scored high in possessive love, the husband could gently tease her about the waiter's flirtatious ways.

Taking Dr. Hatkoff's love quiz will help you identify what love qualities you value the most. You may be surprised by what you learn about yourself. Compare your results with those of your partner.

The *For Better* Quiz #3: Defining Your Love Style

Answer True or False to each question. Even if you feel a question doesn't quite describe your feelings, you must pick an answer.

  ⓉⒻ   1. I believe that "love at first sight" is possible.

  ⓉⒻ   2. The first time we kissed or rubbed cheeks, I felt a definite genital response (lubrication, erection).

  ⓉⒻ   3. We kissed each other soon after we met because we both wanted to.

  ⓉⒻ   4. Usually the first thing that attracts my attention to a person is his/her pleasing physical appearance.

  ⓉⒻ   5. At the first touch of his/her hand I knew that love was a real possibility.

  ⓉⒻ   6. Before I ever fell in love I had a pretty clear physical picture of what my true love would be like.

  ⓉⒻ   7. I like the idea of having the same kinds of clothes, hats, plants, bicycles, cars, et cetera, as my lover does.

  ⓉⒻ   8. I did not realize that I was in love until I actually had been for some time.

  ⓉⒻ   9. You cannot have love unless you have first had caring for a while.

  ⓉⒻ 10. I still have good friendships with almost everyone with whom I have ever been involved in a love relationship.

  ⓉⒻ 11. The best kind of love grows out of a long friendship.

  ⓉⒻ 12. The best part of love is living together, building a home together, and rearing children together.

  ⓉⒻ 13. Kissing, cuddling, and sex shouldn't be rushed. They will happen naturally when one's intimacy has grown enough.

  ⓉⒻ 14. It is hard to say exactly when we fell in love.

(T) (F) 15. The best love relationships are the ones that last the longest.

(T) (F) 16. When things aren't going right for us, my stomach gets upset.

(T) (F) 17. When my love affairs break up I get so depressed that I have even thought of suicide.

(T) (F) 18. Sometimes I get so excited about being in love that I can't sleep.

(T) (F) 19. When my lover doesn't pay attention to me I feel sick all over.

(T) (F) 20. When I am in love I have trouble concentrating on anything else.

(T) (F) 21. I cannot relax if I suspect that my lover is with someone else.

(T) (F) 22. Even though I don't want to be jealous I can't help it when my lover pays attention to someone else.

(T) (F) 23. At least once when I thought a love affair was all over, I saw him/her again and the old feelings came surging back.

(T) (F) 24. If my lover ignores me for a while I sometimes do really stupid things to try to get his/her attention back.

(T) (F) 25. From a practical point of view, I must consider what a person is going to become in life before I commit myself to loving him/her.

(T) (F) 26. It makes good sense to plan your life carefully before you choose a lover.

(T) (F) 27. It is best to love someone with a similar background to yours.

(T) (F) 28. A main consideration in choosing a lover is how he/she reflects on my family.

Ⓣ Ⓕ 29. A main consideration in choosing a partner is whether or not he/she will be a good parent.

Ⓣ Ⓕ 30. I couldn't truly love anyone I would not be willing to marry.

Ⓣ Ⓕ 31. I wouldn't date anyone that I wouldn't want to fall in love with.

Ⓣ Ⓕ 32. A main consideration in choosing a partner is how he/she will reflect on one's career.

Ⓣ Ⓕ 33. Before getting very involved with anyone, I try to figure out how compatible his/her hereditary background is with mine in case we ever have children.

Ⓣ Ⓕ 34. It's always a good idea to keep your lover a little uncertain about how committed you are to him/her.

Ⓣ Ⓕ 35. Part of the fun of being in love is testing one's skill at keeping it going and getting what one wants from it at the same time.

Ⓣ Ⓕ 36. As far as my lover goes, what he/she doesn't know about me won't hurt him/her.

Ⓣ Ⓕ 37. I have at least once had to plan carefully to keep two of my lovers from finding out about each other.

Ⓣ Ⓕ 38. I can get over love affairs pretty easily and quickly.

Ⓣ Ⓕ 39. I enjoy flirting with attractive people.

Ⓣ Ⓕ 40. My lover would get upset if he/she knew some of the things I've done with other people.

Ⓣ Ⓕ 41. It would be fun to see whether I could get someone to go out with me, even if I didn't want to get involved with that person.

Ⓣ Ⓕ 42. I try to use my own strength to help my lover through difficult times, even when he/she is behaving foolishly.

Ⓣ Ⓕ 43. I would rather suffer myself than let my lover suffer.

Ⓣ Ⓕ 44. I cannot be happy unless I place my lover's happiness before my own.

Ⓣ Ⓕ 45. When I break up with someone, I go out of my way to see that he/she is okay.

Ⓣ Ⓕ 46. I am usually willing to sacrifice my own wishes to let my lover achieve his/hers.

Ⓣ Ⓕ 47. If my lover had a baby by someone else I would want to raise it, love it, and care for it as if it were my own.

Ⓣ Ⓕ 48. I would rather break up with my lover than stand in his/her way.

Ⓣ Ⓕ 49. Whatever I own is my lover's to use as he/she chooses.

Ⓣ Ⓕ 50. When my lover doesn't see me or call for a while, I assume he/she has a good reason.

Now score your quiz by looking at where your True answers are grouped.

LOVE STYLE	QUESTIONS	NUMBER OF TRUE RESPONSES
Romantic	1–7	
Best Friends	8–15	
Possessive	16–24	
Logical	25–33	
Playful	34–41	
Unselfish	42–50	

You likely answered True at least once in most of the categories. But look at the two or three categories where you have the highest number of True answers to get a sense of how you define love. More important, learn what values your partner uses to define love.

"I've given this to thousands upon thousands of people and nobody ever scores a hundred in one area and zero in the other five. Everyone is usually a combination of all six," she says. "You don't have to share the same definition. You just have to understand your partner's definition so you don't make the mistake of miscommunication."

CHAPTER 4

The Science of Sex:
What Really Happens in the Marriage Bed

What a happy and holy fashion it is that those who love one
another should rest on the same pillow.

—NATHANIEL HAWTHORNE

Zsa Zsa Gabor, who has taken more trips to the altar than most of us ever will, once said she knew nothing about sex. "Because I was always married," she explained.

It is a common belief that the surest way to end your sex life is to get married. But the reality is far more complicated. While it's true that for many couples, sexual excitement fades in marriage, on average, statistics tracking the sex lives of men and women show that married couples are having more sex than anybody else.

Now, if you're like most married people, you find this statistic hard to believe. But for years, study after study has shown that frequency of sex is actually highest among married couples compared to the never married, divorced, or widowed or even compared to unmarried couples who are living together. This doesn't necessarily mean married people are having lots and lots of sex. But it does show that the grass isn't necessarily greener outside of marriage. Sure, the single life may result in occasional bouts of new, exciting, and regular sex with one or multiple partners, but being single also means frequent dry spells in your sex life. While husbands and wives may not be swinging from the chandeliers every night, the fact is, marriage is the surest way to guarantee consistent access to sex.

Even so, sex is a common source of marital conflict for heterosexual couples. (Gay and lesbian couples are less likely to argue about sex.) Many husbands are frustrated that they want to have sex more often than their wives. Wives are frustrated that their husbands seem oblivious to the many factors in a woman's day (job, housework, and children) that make her feel anything but sexy. In many marriages, sex is the ultimate catch-22. Women say they would be willing to have sex more often if their husbands would help more with the kids, shoulder more of the housework burdens, and offer up regular servings of love and affection that make them want to have sex. Husbands, meanwhile, say that without regular sex, they get frustrated and cranky, and more regular sex would make them more affectionate, helpful, and loving on a daily basis.

A number of factors—biological differences, health issues, stress, and relationship problems—can influence the quality and quantity of a couple's sex life. Understanding how these issues can influence a person's sex drive can help couples resolve conflicts surrounding intimacy. Some couples are resigned to having very little or no sex, and they have found a way to accept and care for their partner despite having a sexless marriage.

But for most couples, the more sex they have, the happier the marriage. Passion and sex are the distinguishing qualities of a romantic relationship. Chances are that physical attraction and sexual chemistry are a big part of what brought you together as a couple, and intimacy and sex remain essential ingredients in a good marriage. Of course, most of us know that already. The challenge for couples is how to maintain an active sex life throughout the course of a marriage or reignite a sex life that has begun to flicker out. Fortunately, numerous studies of marital sex offer insight and answers.

The Honeymoon Effect

Several researchers have tried to discern how the sex lives of married couples change over time. New York University sociologist Guillermina Jasso found that after the giddy first year of marriage, couples experience a precipitous drop in sex. By the thirteen-month wedding anniversary, couples are having sex about once a week less often (that's fifty-two fewer times a year) than they were having at their one-month anniversary. (Other studies have shown a drop of about 50 percent after the first year of marriage.) The decline continues into the second year but much more slowly. A month after the two-year anniversary, couples were having sex twelve fewer times than a year earlier. By the tenth year of marriage, sexual activity had declined to about once a month less than at the five-year anniversary.[53]

To compare the sex lives of couples around the world, University of Georgia researchers Alexandra Brewis and Mary Meyer studied a data set of more than 90,000 women in nineteen countries in Asia, Africa, and the Americas.[54] While there were subtle differences, overall the pattern was clear: The longer a couple is married, the less often they have sex.

Has your sex life followed a pattern similar to that predicted by the research? Take the following quiz to see how your sex life might change after ten years of marriage. Of course, these findings are averages based on a national sample.[55] Some people sustain robust sex lives over the course of a marriage, while others experience a dramatic decline. If you're having more sex than predicted, good for you! It's a sign that sex remains an important priority in your marriage. If you're having less sex than predicted, you may want to focus on your sex life and work on restoring physical intimacy to your marriage.

The *For Better* Quiz #4: Has Time Changed Your Sex Life?

Based on the findings of the national survey, estimate the effect the passing years are likely to have on your sex life. Start by indicating how many times a week you had sex during your first year of marriage.

  a) Once a week: 52 times a year
  b) Twice a week: 104 times a year
  c) Three times a week: 156 times a year
  d) Four or more times a week: 208 times or more a year

What will your sex life be by your third year of marriage? Pick the letter that corresponds to your first answer to estimate how often you'll be having sex with your spouse after three years.

  a) Once or twice a month
  b) About once a week
  c) Twice a week
  d) Three times a week

What will your sex life be by your tenth year of marriage? Pick the letter that corresponds to your first answer to estimate frequency of sex after ten years of marriage.

a) Occasionally
b) About three times a month
c) Nearly twice a week
d) Two to three times a week

Why does sex decline in marriage? Part of it may be that sex declines as people age. The exception to this rule is for younger women—some studies suggest that frequency of sex for women actually increases until the age of thirty. But overall, as people age, frequency of sex declines by about 20 percent each decade after the age of thirty, with greater drops after the age of sixty-five.

And most people who have been married for any length of time notice that the hot fires of romance that burned in the early courtship often begin to flicker out the longer a couple is together. Much of this has to do with the brain chemistry of romantic love, which fires up the dopamine system in the early days of courtship, but calms to a state of contented companionship and attachment the longer a couple stays together.

Cornell University professor Cindy Hazan set out to document exactly how long the fiery, sexually charged early phase of a relationship really lasts. She interviewed 5,000 men and women across thirty-seven cultures about their sex lives during courtship and marriage. She found that for most couples, the fires of passionate love burn out after about eighteen to thirty months. Other studies show that sex rates drop by about 50 percent in the first year of marriage, a finding that has been dubbed "the honeymoon effect."[56] Some research suggests that the drop in sexual activity after the early years of a relationship stems from the loss of novelty. When sex is new and exciting, you crave more and have a lot of it. But just like with a new car, a favorite vacation spot, or a favorite food, once the novelty fades, you just don't get as excited about it as you used to.

A more optimistic theory for the decline in sexual frequency after marriage is that married couples are more practiced at sex, and although the frequency declines, the quality improves. Data from the National Health and Social Life Survey, analyzed by relationship researchers Linda Waite and Kara Joyner, support the notion that married couples have more fulfilling sex than single people or couples who live together without being married. One great session of lovemaking in midlife, when both partners know how to hit all the right spots, may be far more satisfying than several less-skilled sessions typical of a couple's early years.[57]

Some studies have suggested that the very act of entering into a committed relationship can diminish a woman's interest in sex, a finding that may not be all that surprising to many men. Researchers from Hamburg-Eppendorf University in Germany interviewed 530 men and women about their relationships and interest in sex. They found that 60 percent of the thirty-year-old women studied wanted sex "often" at the start of a relationship. But within four years this figure dropped to fewer than half, and by twenty years, only one in five women wanted regular sex. The sharp decline in sexual interest wasn't seen among men in the study. The proportion of men who wanted regular sex remained between 60 and 80 percent.

The study identified another striking difference between men and women. About 90 percent of women said "tenderness" was important, regardless of how long they had been in their relationship. However, tenderness was a low priority for the long-married men in the study. Only one in four men who had been with their partners for ten years or more said they desired "tenderness" from the relationship.[58]

Sex by the Numbers

Researchers have spent a lot of time trying to understand the sex lives of humans. Scientists have created phalluses equipped with cameras and mixed up artificial semen laced with glowing tracers to study what goes on inside a woman's body during orgasm. The research team of William Masters and Virginia E. Johnson watched hundreds of couples having sex to document the phases of the human sexual response cycle. (For the record, they are excitement, plateau, orgasm, and resolution.) The noted sex researcher Alfred Kinsey recruited 300 men to take part in a study of the distance traveled by ejaculated semen. The research was designed to study whether the force at which semen is ejaculated was a potential factor in fertility. It wasn't.[59]

But while all of this is amusing and fascinating in a prurient sort of way, it isn't particularly useful for those of us trying to navigate human relationships outside the laboratory.

In the United States the best information we have about the sex lives of Americans comes from the General Social Survey, a major survey of attitudes and behavior conducted by the National Opinion Research Centers, headquartered on the University of Chicago campus. The survey focuses on Americans, but a sister study called the ISSP collects data from forty-one countries. Since 1988, the GSS has collected data asking individuals about their number of sex partners, frequency of intercourse, and extramarital relationships. Although the GSS detected ups and downs in sexual activity in the 1970s and 1980s, the numbers have stayed fairly constant since 1998.

The survey shows that the average adult has sex fifty-eight times a year or about once a week with a few days of extra bliss mixed in. The average sexual encounter lasts about thirty minutes.[60]

Of course, these numbers are averages. Some people are having a lot more sex; and some are having a lot less. About 5 percent of people in the survey reported having sex at least three times a week. About 20 percent of people, most of them widows, have been celibate for at least a year. Everyone else falls somewhere in between.

And married people, on average, are having more sex than everybody else. Remember, the average frequency of sex includes people who are recently divorced, widowed, older, or new to the dating scene. At some point, those people might get quite lucky and find themselves with frequent opportunities for sex. But as any never-married or recently divorced person knows, sometimes even the most sexually charged bachelor or bachelorette can go through a dating drought, leaving him or her without a sex partner for extended stretches. Married couples, on the other hand, may not be having the kind of sex they had when they were dating, but at least they are having sex.

The typical married person has sex an average of 66 times a year, although couples who are "very happy" have sex, on average, 74 times a year. Married people under thirty have sex about 112 times a year. By comparison, the average frequency of sex for single people between the ages of eighteen and twenty-nine is 69 times a year. Sex, on average, drops to 69 times a year for married couples in their forties, compared to 50 times for singles in their forties. For those over seventy, sex happens, on average, only 3 times per year, but for over-seventies who are married, sex occurs 16 times a year.[61]

Average Annual Frequency of Sex by Single and Married Adults

AGE	UNMARRIED	MARRIED
18-29	69	112
30-39	66	86
40-49	50	69
50-59	31	54
60-69	16	33
70+	3	16

Source: National Opinion Research Center

In parsing the data, the researchers noted the following trends:[62]

Sex declines with age. After about the age of thirty, frequency of sex drops by about 20 percent each decade until the age of sixty-four. The average plummets another 60 percent after the age of sixty-five, and drops again by 50 percent after the age of fifty. Much of the steep drop near the end of life is due to health problems and widowhood. Widows account for most of the 20 percent of people who report celibacy in the past year.

Sex, like wealth, is distributed unevenly. Studies show that most wealth is accumulated by a tiny percentage of the population. The same is true for sex. About 15 percent of adults are having half of all sexual encounters.

Hard workers are better lovers. Surprisingly, people who work the longest hours are the most likely to be having sex. People who report working a sixty-hour week or more have about 10 percent more sex, on average, than people who have lots of spare time.

Kids don't ruin everything. Parents often complain that they have no time for sex once kids arrive. But parents are still having more sex than single people.

If music be the food of love, play jazz. Jazz lovers are 30 percent more sexually active than other people.

Religious beliefs influence your sex life. People who are Jewish or agnostic have 20 percent more sex than their Christian counterparts.

Political passion ignites sexual passion. Being passionate about your politics in either direction is associated with more frequent sex. Extreme liberals have more sex than extreme conservatives. But people who are far on either side of the political spectrum have more sex than those who consider themselves moderates or just slightly conservative.

The rich and poor are having more sex than the middle class. The very low-income and the very high-income have sex more frequently than

everybody else. Men earning $75,000 per year average twelve fewer
days of sex a year than men who earn about $25,000 annually.

Active people have more sex. People who are involved in life are more
involved in sex, whether it's sports or social activities.

Sinners have more sex. People who smoke and drink have more sex.
Smokers report 10 percent more sex than nonsmokers. People
who drink alcohol have 20 percent more sex than teetotalers.
And people who both smoke and drink have twice as much sex
as those who don't do either.

College graduates have less sex. On average, extra education is associated with about a week's worth of less sex each year. People with
high school diplomas or those who didn't finish college have
more sex than those who graduated.

Marriage doesn't guarantee sex. In the survey 16 percent of married
people hadn't had sex for a month. And 7 percent hadn't had sex
for a year.

Some people are dying for sex. There are an estimated 11,250 deaths
related to sex in the U.S. each year.

When Sex Leaves the Marriage

While every couple will probably experience a lull in their sex life at
some point during marriage, some couples simply stop having sex.
About 15 percent of married couples have not had sex with their
spouse in the last six months to one year.

Denise A. Donnelly, associate professor of sociology at Georgia
State University, who has studied sexless marriages, says that failure to have sex at least once a month is a strong predictor of marital
unhappiness and divorce.

Low-sex and no-sex marriages aren't always destined to fail.
Sometimes, both spouses are content with little or no sex in their
marriage, and so the lack of sex doesn't create further problems.

A man who had been married more than thirty years wrote to me to explain why a low-sex marriage works for him and his wife.

"In the first two decades my wife and I could not get enough of each other," he explained. "Then in our forties health issues changed our love life forever. My wife had to have a full hysterectomy, I developed type II diabetes. Those two things alone significantly changed our individual drive for sex, but it didn't end the intimacy between us—actually it enforced and increased it."

He said that he and his wife still have sex occasionally, far less than in the past. But their thirty-year history, a life of mutual respect and love, seems to trump the loss of sex in their marriage. He says his relationship isn't defined by their "changing bodies," but is based on lifelong friendship and commitment.

But more often, one partner is unhappy with the lack of physical contact and intimacy with his or her spouse. A 1993 study by Dr. Donnelly showed that people in sexless marriages were more likely to have considered divorce than those in sexually active marriages.

"There is a feedback relationship in most couples between happiness and having sex," says Dr. Donnelly. "Happy couples have more sex, and the more sex a couple has, the happier they report being. But keep in mind that sex is only one form of intimacy, and that some couples are fairly happy (and intimate) even without sex. There is no ideal level of sexual activity—the ideal level is what both partners are happy with—and when one (or both) are unhappy, then you can have marital problems."

Michele Weiner Davis, a Woodstock, Illinois, therapist and author of *The Sex-Starved Marriage,* says as many as one in three couples struggles because one partner has a low sex drive.

After writing a story about sexless marriages, I heard from more than a thousand men and women who had experienced sexless relationships. A small number were from men and women who claimed to be content in marriages with little or no sex. But the overwhelming majority of people I heard from were devastated when sex ended and many had divorced and moved on to more satisfying relationships. Others noted that because of children or financial issues, they weren't free to divorce. A few readers even told stories about striking up affairs with another married man or woman who was also stuck in a sexless marriage. The arrangement allowed them to stay married to a partner whom they loved and to enjoy physical intimacy with a "safe" partner—someone who was in a similar situation and didn't represent a threat to their marriage.

For couples struggling with low-sex and no-sex marriages, the most important first step is to seek medical advice. For both men and women, a low sex drive can be associated with a medical condition such as low testosterone, erectile dysfunction, menopause, or depression and it can also be a side effect of certain medications or cancer treatment. A large number of readers who wrote to me explained that sex had been a casualty of illness, menopause, prostate surgery, or depression. A woman named Mary told me that health problems had ended sex in her marriage, but she and her husband have stayed together.

"Being in a relationship that once included sex, but no longer does or can, is challenging, to say the least," she told me. "The bottom line, I think, is for both people to ask, 'Do I want to continue sharing all the other parts of my life with this person? Can we be intimate in other ways? Is our shared history, respect, and continuing love worth more to me than sex?' For some, the answer continues to be yes."

Another reader, Tanya, told me that after her health problems improved, her sex life didn't.

"After I recovered from an illness that sapped much of my strength and life, my drive plummeted to the point that my husband and I have not had sex in months," she told me. "It's very depressing to both of us, and it's a real problem. I just don't have 'it' anymore. My brain tells me I should want it, but my body just doesn't care anymore."

The good news is that many of these problems can be treated if men and women are willing to seek help and discuss the issue with a doctor. For instance, Tanya notes that during her illness, she felt abandoned by her husband, and those hurt feelings remain and likely explain at least some of the reason she no longer wants sex with him. In some ways, Tanya is lucky, because she understands at least some of the psychological reasons behind her loss of interest. Couples therapy and medical counseling likely could bring her and her husband together if both were willing to seek help.

While women typically are blamed for losing interest in sex, research shows that men often are the ones who lose interest in sex. In a study of seventy-five married people in sexually inactive marriages, Dr. Donnelly found that in nearly two out of three sexless marriages, it was the man who had stopped wanting sex.

In writing about marriage and relationships, I have heard from many of these women. Often they say that their husbands simply refuse to discuss the problem, making it extraordinarily difficult to work on it as a couple.

"I've been in a sexless marriage for almost three years and my husband refuses to talk about it," wrote a woman named Jessica. "This total lack of intimacy with my husband is a dark shadow on the whole of my life. It makes me very lonely."

There are several explanations for a why a marriage becomes sexless. In studies of sexless relationships, some of the people never had much sex in the first place. Others identified a particular time or event like childbirth or an extramarital affair that doused the fires of their sex life.

Familiarity and boredom can take a toll on a couple's sex life. Sometimes it's stress—the daily demands of raising a family and work responsibilities—that gets in the way of an active sex life. Surprisingly, it was former U.S. labor secretary Robert Reich who brought national attention to this problem while speaking at a 2003 conference on work and life balance. You've heard of Yuppies (young urban professionals) and DINKS (dual-income, no-kids.) Mr. Reich talked about DINS—dual-income, no-sex couples. The assertion by the U.S. labor secretary that American couples were so fatigued by the work-life juggling act that they no longer had energy for sex made the pages of *The Wall Street Journal*.[63] Couples who find themselves in sexless marriages should consider whether the problem stems more from their frantic work life than from problems in their married life.

And some people may have naturally low sex drives or even be asexual. They may have some sex with their partners to begin with, but it becomes unimportant to them and sex fades. A small number of couples showed a mixed "feast-and-famine" pattern, meaning they have periods of a lot of sex, followed by a lengthy dry spell.

A woman named Sharon tells me that she has never been interested in sex. "For me, it's easier and more enjoyable to get my 'endorphin' rush from running forty to fifty miles per week," she says. "Sex is totally overrated!"

A man named Brennan agrees with her. "Sex is a heckuva lot of work for so little reward," he explains. "I'd rather spend the time cooking really great food."

Fatigue is a common reason women refuse to have sex, and isn't just a problem among women who work outside the home. Janet Hyde, a professor at the University of Wisconsin–Madison, studied more than 500 women and their husbands. Stay-at-home wives were just as likely to report fatigue-related loss of desire as employed women.[64]

It's not clear if the sexless marriage is becoming more common or we're just hearing more about it. Some scientists speculate that growing use of antidepressants like Prozac and Paxil, which can depress the sex drive, may be contributing to an increase in sexless marriages.

Dr. Donnelly says other factors may be influencing growing awareness of sexless relationships. "Back in the days before reliable birth control, having a sexless marriage was one way of limiting family size," she says. "Those were also the days when women were not supposed to enjoy sex and often used it as a bargaining tool in their marriages (because they were socialized to do so). Plus, unhappy couples (who are less likely to have sex) were more likely to stay together because of social expectations, or because they had children they were raising."

Once a marriage has been sexless for a long time, it's very difficult to rekindle a sex life. "One or both may be extremely afraid of hurt or rejection, or just entirely apathetic to their partner," says Dr. Donnelly. "They may not have been communicating about sex for a very long time (if ever) and have trouble talking about it. Couples who talk over their sex lives (as well as other aspects of their marriages) tend to have healthier marriages, but it's hard to get a couple talking once they've established a pattern of noncommunication."

There are mixed opinions about what to do to rekindle marital sex. For recently sexless couples, it may be as simple as a weekend away from the kids, taking a vacation or cruise, or just having some time off, alone. Others may need professional assistance. Dr. Donnelly advises couples to find a counselor who is willing to talk about a couple's sex life, rather than focusing on broader issues. "Talking explicitly about sex is essential," she says.

Many therapists will tell men and women to force the issue, to have sex even if they don't want to. What couples typically find is that within seconds, they begin to remember what they are missing. The body responds with a flood of brain chemicals, and within minutes, sex feels natural again. But forcing yourself back into bed can be tough. One man told me that his wife's attempts to reignite their sex life made his stomach knot up. A woman told me she recoiled from her husband's advances after years of not having sex. For these couples, the first step is not hopping into bed, but just talking about the problem and seeking professional help.

"To those people who are in sexless marriages and are unhappy, tell your spouses and get counseling," one woman told me. "After three children and two chronic illnesses, I thought I had lost interest in sex, and I thought my husband had also, until I looked on his laptop and discovered he had been spending thousands of dollars on Internet porn. After marriage counseling and some hormone therapy, we are no longer in a sexless marriage, and we are both happier."

Couples also need to consider the possibility that the lack of sex in the marriage may be a signal that all intimacy in the relationship is over. "Some of our former respondents have kept in touch with me, and the happiest ones are actually those that have moved on to other partners," notes Dr. Donnelly. "It may be a better solution than staying in a marriage that is hurtful and unfulfilling."

Lessons to Improve Your Sex Life and Your Marriage

While sex is a difficult issue in many marriages, it is also a highly effective way to solve problems and repair the daily missteps and grievances that occur in a relationship. It might seem like the opposite of what we're told—to always talk things out and clear the air—but the intimacy of sex can bridge a lot of gaps that talking simply can't. It sets off a physical and emotional chain reaction that short-circuits the discursive process. Keeping that physical connection—and even having sex when you might not want to—is crucial to the health of a marriage.

Couples often complain that they don't have time for sex, but experienced therapists say that's no excuse. Sheldon Isenberg, a Naperville, Illinois, psychotherapist and consultant, says that when clients complain they lack time for sex, "I tell them, 'You know, if you were having an affair, you'd find a lot of ways to do it.'"

It's also important to think about what you and your partner want from sex. In one 1981 study, researchers interviewed fifty married couples, most of whom were happily married and reported good sex lives. But men and women reported very different reasons for initiating sex. Women said they were seeking "love, intimacy, and holding." Men said they wanted sex for sexual release.[65]

As relationship researcher Elaine Hatfield explains:

> Women basically wanted to be approached in the classical romantic vein—candlelight, wine, music, and romantic settings with time standing still for love and wooing. They did not want a quick grope or a rushed sexual encounter that takes place in bed the last thing at night, but rather a slow, sensual approach with tender, loving caresses, embraces, kisses, and nonsexual body touching or massage with only occasional aggression. The women wanted to be courted, to be spoken to, and to verbally share with their partners their ideas, thoughts, and feelings about nonsexual topics. They wanted to laugh and play and to enjoy their spouses outside of bed. They sought verbal appreciation of themselves as human beings as well as sexual beings. Coitus evolved slowly out of this setting and occurred because the women felt loved.

A significant minority of men, 40 percent, said they also liked a soft approach to sex that included caressing, massage, and seductiveness. The remaining 60 percent wanted their wives to ask them directly for sex and liked it when their wives were aggressive and showed a lack of inhibition. Men often said they wanted to feel "irresistible," and deeply desired by their wives.

In a series of studies, Dr. Hatfield interviewed men and women about how they wanted their partners to behave during sex.[66] Both men and women wanted their partners to be more direct and tell them exactly what they wanted from sex. At the same time, both men and women were often too self-conscious and admitted that they found it difficult to be that direct with their partners in describing their own needs and desires.

But in the research setting, the participants finally were willing to disclose what they desired. Men and women both had very specific sexual wishes they wanted from their spouse.

You don't have to be in a university sex study to find similar answers about your own marriage. Every couple can replicate this experiment by writing down the five things they want from their partner during sex. The lesson from the research is that couples have far more sexual desires in common than they realize. They just have to be willing to talk about it.

Sit down with your spouse and take the following test.

The *For Better* Quiz #5: What Do You Want from Your Partner?

Think about five things you'd like your husband or wife to say or do during sex. Try not to focus on specific acts or positions. The goal here is to determine general behavioral changes that would give you more pleasure in bed. Perhaps you want your partner to talk more, be more loving, be more experimental or adventurous, or be more specific about his or her wishes. Write down your answers.

During sex, I wish my husband would:

1.

2.

3.

4.

5.

During sex, I wish my wife would:

1.
2.
3.
4.
5.

Compare your answers to those of your spouse. It may surprise you that many of your answers match. Pay attention to how your answers are different as well, and what you could be doing to make your partner happier.

Now see how your answers compare to those of other couples who were asked the same questions. Here's what the couples from Dr. Hatfield's research had to say about what they wanted from sex:

What Husbands Wish Their Wives Would Do

1. Be more seductive.
2. Initiate sex more often.
3. Be more experimental.
4. Be wilder and sexier.
5. Give more instructions.

What Wives Wish Their Husbands Would Do

1. Talk more lovingly; be more complimentary.
2. Be more seductive.
3. Be more experimental.
4. Give more instructions.
5. Be warmer and more involved.

What's striking about the research is how much men and women had in common when it came to sex. Both men and women wanted a partner who was more seductive. They both wanted a partner who was more direct and willing to give instructions. And surprisingly, both were looking for a partner who was willing to experiment.

Where men and women differed was also telling. Men wanted their wives to initiate sex more often and be wilder and sexier in the bedroom.

But women's desires were fueled by behavior both inside and outside of the bedroom. They wanted their partners to be warmer and more involved in their lives. They wanted their husbands to speak to them more lovingly and give them more compliments.

The importance of sex to a marriage can't be underestimated. Too many couples believe steep declines in their sex lives are inevitable after marriage, and when the passion begins to wane, they just accept it as something that happens to everyone after many years of being together. But the lessons from the scientific study of sex and marriage teach us that regular sex should be and can be part of a good marriage, and that even though sexual activity may decline over time, it doesn't have to disappear.

So many men and women I've heard from over the years tell me that while sex isn't the most important aspect of their marriages, it's definitely the glue that holds them together. Sam, a seventy-year-old married man whose wife is sixty-three, says he and his wife still have sex at least once a week, sometimes more.

"We laugh a lot, have kept ourselves as fit and attractive as possible for one another, love each other deeply in many ways," he says. "Sex is just a part of our total relationship, but such a wonderful part."

And while more and better sex is certainly a laudable goal for couples who want to rekindle their love lives, there is an added motivation as well. Having an active sex life is a strong indicator of overall physical health and a way couples can stay tuned into each other's physical well-being. In fact, sex, health, and marriage are inextricably linked.

CHAPTER 5

In Sickness and in Health:
How Does Marriage Impact Your Health?

I wish for you good health in each other's arms.

—AUTHOR UNKNOWN

At some point between the walk down the aisle and the first kiss of marriage, many couples make the promise to stay together "in sickness and in health." What many of us don't realize is just how meaningful those words really are. From the moment we say, "I do," the act of getting married has a profound influence on our health and well-being.

Marriage is associated with better health for both husband and wife compared to people who are single, divorced, or widowed. And married people, on average, tend to live longer than unmarried people. This doesn't mean single, divorced, and widowed people are destined for ill-health. What it suggests is that marriage offers significant benefits—ranging from caregiving to financial security—that can lead to better health.

Even so, studies show that marriage alone isn't enough to protect your health. The quality of relationship also matters. Increasingly, studies are showing that good marriages are good for you, but if you're in a bad marriage filled with conflict and unhappiness, it may be better for your long-term health to be single again. In fact, a bad marriage takes a profoundly negative toll on your well-being—some studies show a bad marriage results in physical changes to the heart similar to those caused by smoking.

Even a good marriage can affect your health in unexpected ways. While marriage can be a great source of emotional support, marriages can also reinforce bad habits—like overeating. Studies now show that obesity in a marriage can be contagious. Your partner's conflict style—and how you react to it—has a measurable effect on your health. And whether your partner snores can make a difference in the quality of your sleep, your long-term health, and your hearing as you age.

The Marriage Advantage

Why would being married improve your health?

One reason is that marriage essentially doubles your resources. Higher income is associated with better health as compared with those who have low income or live in poverty. Not only do you typically gain more income with marriage, but you also gain new sets of family members and friends. The benefit to your health can come in the form of emotional support, such as the hand holding and stress relief provided by both your spouse and the friends and family he or she brings to the relationship. Relationships also offer practical support—friends, family, and spouses can care for children when you're sick, pick up a prescription, or take you to the doctor, and care for you as you recover from an illness. A spouse also may be the first to notice when health problems set in—like erectile dysfunction linked with heart disease, snoring that could mean a dangerous condition called sleep apnea, or excessive thirst that could signal diabetes.

Studies show that married people are less likely to get colds, cancer, arthritis, or heart attacks. Married women have stronger immune systems than unmarried women.[67] And people in happy marriages have lower blood pressure. Swedish researchers have shown that marriage at midlife may lower risk for dementia as we age.[68]

And if you feel like you just might die without your spouse, marital health research shows you may be right. During any given period, married people are less likely to die than unmarried people. A major study of death and marriage records in the Netherlands looked at more than two dozen causes of death and found that the unmarried had far higher mortality risks than married persons, in virtually every category—ranging from violent deaths like accidents and homicide to several forms of cancer.[69] Married men have life expectancies that are about seven years longer than those of men who never marry, while married women outlive women who never marry by about three years, according to Canadian statistics.[70]

These data are far from conclusive. Some of the studies point out that many of the early deaths are among young gay men at risk for HIV and AIDS, a fact that may skew the data in favor of marital health.[71] In addition, people with chronic disease or other health problems are less likely to get married, or may experience divorce as a result of their health struggles. Despite these concerns, a large body of research has consistently shown a strong link between marriage and better health.

The results are different for men and women. When a man marries, his risk of dying drops immediately; for women, the marriage advantage doesn't show up for several years. The theory is that men benefit immediately because marriage typically stops some of their more risky behaviors —such as excessive drinking, staying out late, and running around with a bad crowd.

For men, marrying typically leads to stronger social ties that were neglected during his single years. That's because women tend to nurture and maintain relationships with friends and family—keeping in touch with parents and siblings, arranging social events, and sending out holiday cards. All of this translates into social support that has been linked with better health. In addition, women bring health care connections to a relationship. Women are more likely to go to the doctor, schedule appointments, and manage the family's health. Finally, women do a lot of the housework, cooking, and cleaning—all of which benefit a man's long-term health: He may finally be eating better and more regularly than he was before.

Because women often already have strong family and social networks before they marry, for them, much of the health benefit of marriage seems to be related to financial gains. Marriage gives them a higher household income, better access to health care, improved nutrition, better housing, and possibly a more secure job. These improvements don't necessarily lead to immediate gains in health, but over the long term, a married woman has better health than an unmarried woman.

Wives: Gatekeepers of Family Health

One of the often-overlooked benefits of marriage for men is that women are often more tuned in to potential health problems than men are. Several years ago, I interviewed Phil and Rachael, a San Jose, California, couple who had two young kids and a third on the way. Phil felt lousy most of the time, but assumed it was because family demands and excessive work travel had left him tired and jet-lagged. He was remodeling his home and had just, perhaps unwisely, decided to give up coffee. And he was forty-nine years old. Of course he was tired!

But his wife, Rachael, would have none of it. What she saw was that her normally active and energetic husband wasn't just a little sleepy. He was fatigued and exhausted, drinking lots of water, and losing weight. She suspected diabetes. He suspected she had been watching too many medical shows.

Rachael couldn't force her husband to see a doctor, but as the mother of two children and a baby on the way, she was often at the doctor for one reason or another. Two weeks after her baby was born, she talked to her child's pediatrician about her husband's health. Pediatricians and gynecologists say it's not at all uncommon for women to discuss other issues of family health during a visit. Fortunately for Rachael and Phil, their family pediatrician was wise to the fact that men put off going to the doctor and offered a compromise. He handed the new mother a batch of home test strips that her husband could use to check his blood sugar on his own.

When she returned home, she told her husband about the home test. As she expected, he refused to try it. But as he was packing for an out-of-town trip, she slipped the test strips into his briefcase, pleading with him to take the test at his hotel.

Despite Phil's protests, his wife's concerns were finally getting to him. Recently, a colleague had told him he'd appeared nervous during a presentation at work. He actually hadn't been nervous for the talk—but what the co-worker had noticed was that he'd been taking regular gulps of water. As he unpacked later at the hotel he saw the test strip and decided to take the test. To his amazement, it clearly showed he had high blood sugar. He called a doctor, who agreed to see him in two weeks.

But his wife's intervention didn't stop there. She got back on the phone and convinced the doctor's office to see her husband immediately. Sure enough, the checkup showed that Phil's blood sugar was dangerously high, and he was diagnosed and treated for adult-onset diabetes.

"There's an old Jimmy Buffett song where he tells his girlfriend, 'You treat your body like a temple. I treat my body like a tent,'" Phil told me. "It gets back to the value of marriage. If I had been a single guy without someone deeply invested in my life, I'm not sure what would have happened. For lack of a better word, I was nagged into doing something."

Doctors say that the experience of Phil and Rachael isn't at all unusual. It's common for a wife to begin pushing her husband to visit the doctor long before a man thinks he needs to go. Surveys show that men are far less likely to have a personal physician than women. And even when prenatal visits and trips to the pediatrician are excluded, women are still twice as likely as men to visit the doctor.

Even once men get to the doctor, they resist opening up about their health. Physician Harvey Simon, editor of the *Harvard Men's Health Watch* newsletter, says it's common for men to "blame" their wives when they finally do visit a doctor. "When men will finally come in, they are often mute for a while," says Dr. Simon. "And then they pull out a paper and say, 'My wife told me to ask about this.' They still feel the need to hide behind their wife's questions."

A woman becomes remarkably persistent once she begins to worry about the health of her husband. Ridwan Shabsigh, director of urology at Maimonides Medical Center in Brooklyn, New York, told me that one of his own friends refused to see a doctor. The friend's wife had begun to notice signs of erectile dysfunction and was worried about her husband's heart. Tears, tantrums, and threats to withhold sex didn't work. But she didn't give up. At tax season, she saw her opportunity and refused to sign the couple's joint tax return unless her husband went to the doctor. It worked,

and her husband returned with prescriptions to treat high cholesterol and high blood pressure.

Doctors say wives are in a unique position to persuade their husbands to seek medical care. Because erectile function is an important barometer of a man's health, a wife often is the first to notice
subtle changes that could signal a health problem like heart disease.
And because women typically have regular contact with the pediatrician and their own obstetricians and gynecologists, they can ask
for advice and referrals to the right doctors, even if their husbands
won't.[72]

The Benefit of Hand Holding

Wives don't get all the credit for improving a partner's health. One
study revealed that when your husband holds your hand, he's doing
more than just showing you affection. He's lowering your stress
level.

That's what James A. Coan, assistant professor of psychology
and neuroscience at the University of Virginia, found as he studied the effect hand holding had on stressed-out women. Dr. Coan
recruited sixteen married women who had scored high on a marital
satisfaction quiz. The goal of the study was to determine whether
a comforting gesture from a husband could lower a woman's stress
levels. In the lab setting, the stressor was a mild electric shock
administered while the women were undergoing magnetic resonance imaging scans of their brain.

The researchers looked at the women's brains under three sce-
narios. One scan showed the woman experiencing the shock without any comfort from another person. The next two times they
delivered the shock, the woman was holding the hand of her husband or the hand of a stranger.

The brain scans showed that any form of hand holding offered comfort and reduced the appearance of stress on the MRI images. But the biggest gains were seen when the woman was holding her husband's hand.

Hand holding, in general, essentially quieted certain parts of the brain related to the stress response. But when a woman was holding her husband's hand the brain scan showed additional calming in the region of the brain that controls emotional response. The scientists saw further differences when they compared women in the study with the highest marriage happiness scores. Among those women, spousal hand-holding had an even greater effect, calming regions of the brain associated with pain, much as an analgesic drug would do.

The study shows that when someone else is helping you cope, the brain doesn't have to work as hard. Unfortunately, the researchers didn't study whether hand holding has the same effect on a man's brain as it does on a woman's.[73]

Can Marriage Make You Fat?

Our physical effects on each other also stem from the way each person's habits influence those living with them. Given that 60 percent of the adult population is overweight or obese, we can't blame marriage for all our weight gain. But as researchers sift through the data on marriage and health, the link between marriage and weight gain is getting a lot more attention these days. Married people are more likely to be overweight than nonmarried people. A six-year study in Finland found that people who got married gained weight, but they lost weight if a spouse died. Three U.S. studies showed that men and women gained weight after they got married and lost weight when marriage ended.[74]

A lot of unhealthy and risky behaviors stop when we get married. Marriage settles us down and we often drink and smoke less, use fewer illegal drugs, eat more regular meals, and sleep more regular hours. But marriage has another interesting effect. We eat more, exercise less, and smoke less: all behaviors associated with weight gain.

- Having someone to help you cook and shop and to spend time at the dinner table with all translates into extra pounds and inches around the waistline.
- Some studies suggest people exercise less when they get married—particularly men. It may be that we are spending our free time with a spouse rather than taking a spinning class with friends or grabbing a game of pickup basketball, or it may be that men feel less need to stay in shape in order to look good to attract a mate.
- Smoking is linked with lower body weight, and two studies have shown that married people are more likely to quit smoking. Single, divorced, and widowed people smoke more than married people.

What to do about it? We can influence each other positively and negatively. Studies show that couples who diet and exercise together also have a higher success rate in achieving their weight loss and fitness goals.

Sex Life, Aging, and Health

While married couples do have more sex than anyone else, health issues can get in the way of a robust sex life, especially as we age. Erectile dysfunction and menopause can bring out deeper issues. About one in three men between the ages of forty to seventy suffer from some significant level of erectile dysfunction. Most of them, about 80 percent, never seek treatment.

Erectile dysfunction can take a damaging toll on your relationship. Men who suffer from ED often grow distant. Not only does sex decline, but he stops all physical contact with his wife, worried that it might lead to yet another unsuccessful sexual encounter. "I didn't want to hold hands or put my arm around her at the theater," said a fifty-two-year-old Irving, Texas, man, who spoke to me for a story about erectile dysfunction. "When you can't perform, you stop doing all those things."

There are three erectile dysfunction drugs—Viagra, Levitra, and Cialis—and all work about the same. The man I interviewed began using an ED drug and almost immediately regained the intimacy that had been lost between him and his wife. "Yes, the sex is there," he told me. "But the neat thing is we're not afraid to touch or hold hands."

While stories in the popular media suggest that Viagra leads to infidelity and divorce, the more likely story is that people who are generally unhappy in their marriages are at risk for infidelity and divorce, regardless of whether they use Viagra. For people who want to rekindle their sex lives, erectile dysfunction drugs can be relationship savers. In one study of Viagra, researchers looked at couples where the man suffered from erectile dysfunction. They asked both men and women how often they quarreled and how they rated their relationships in terms of tenderness and togetherness. After treatment with Viagra, the men reported improvement in their overall relationship, with less conflict and more tenderness and togetherness. Their female partners also reported meaningful improvements in tenderness and togetherness.[75]

There are other reasons for couples to seek professional help for erectile dysfunction. A man's erectile function isn't just a "lifestyle" issue but an important indicator of his overall health. Changes in erectile function can be an early warning signal of a potentially serious health problem. An Italian study showed that in two-thirds of patients with both heart disease and ED, the erection problems showed up, on average, three years before other more obvious symptoms, such as chest pain.

"The penis is a barometer of the health of the vascular system," says Andrew McCullough, director of male sexual health and fertility at New York University School of Medicine.[76]

The reason erectile function is so closely linked with heart and vascular health is that the penis is sustained by two main arteries. If a man has vascular disease that causes narrowing of the arteries or plaque buildup, the damage often shows up first in the small penile arteries rather than the larger arteries leading to his heart. ED is particularly common among men with one or more cardiovascular risk factors, such as high blood pressure, and strongly associated with lack of exercise.

A couple's sex life is also challenged when the wife goes through menopause, a time when a woman's hormone levels fluctuate wildly and she experiences a number of vexing symptoms. Hot flashes and sleep problems can leave women feeling exhausted and uninterested in sex. Vaginal dryness can make sex painful. Weight gain common during menopause can make a woman self-conscious and dampen her enthusiasm for getting naked. And all the other challenges of midlife—aging parents, graduating teenagers, and job demands—can all increase stress and lower interest in sex.

But your sex life during menopause isn't entirely dictated by your hormones. The Melbourne Women's Midlife Health Project found that one of the biggest determinants of sexual function during menopause is a woman's sexual function prior to menopause. If you have an active, satisfying sex life before menopause, chances are you will continue to do so despite all the physical challenges of menopause.

However, the Melbourne study found that menopause is associated with a significant increase in the percentage of women reporting sexual dysfunction. Early in menopause, about 42 percent of women have sexual dysfunction. As estrogen levels decline, that number jumps to 88 percent. As women become postmenopausal, they report less interest in sex, less sexual responsiveness, and more vaginal dryness and pain. Women's feelings toward their partners also become more negative as they pass through menopause.

Women with mediocre sex lives before menopause were more likely to be pushed toward sexual dysfunction by the hormonal changes they experienced during this life transition. If you have hang-ups about sex, if you're in a bad relationship, or if you just weren't that sexually active during your reproductive years, then things will stay pretty much the same or get worse during menopause unless you resolve the underlying issues that are hampering your sex life. A woman's personal sex history is the biggest factor in her sex life after menopause.[77]

Sleeping Well, Sleeping Together

One of the defining characteristics of a marriage or a long-term relationship is that the partners share a bed at night. And for happy couples, a lot more goes on in bed than just sex. The bed becomes a safe haven to escape children and job stress, catch up on the events of the day, share intimate conversation, and enjoy physical contact, hugs, and caresses that not only lower stress levels and anxiety but reinforce the bonds of the relationship. In fact, various sleep studies have shown that married people seem to enjoy better sleep than unmarried people. Getting more and better sleep is not only linked with having a happier marriage, it's associated with better overall health. People who don't sleep well are at higher risk for diabetes, heart disease, and more.

University of Pittsburgh researchers found, during an eight-year study of nearly 2,000 women, that women who are married or who have stable partners appear to sleep better than women who have never married or have lost a partner.[78] Feeling happy and content in marriage lowers risk for sleep problems, while marital stress increases risk for poor sleep. The main exception was among newlyweds. Couples appear to undergo an adjustment period before they grow accustomed to sleeping with a partner. Women who were single at the start of the study but gained a partner had more restless sleep than women who were already married.

A University of Arizona study found that when men get better sleep, they report more positive feelings about their partner the next day. And women who report having problems in their relationship often also report getting poor sleep. Researchers say couples endure a "vicious cycle" of sleep problems affecting their relationship and relationship problems affecting their sleep.[79]

Brant Hasler, a clinical psychology doctoral candidate at the University of Arizona, said the data suggest that sleep and relationship happiness are closely linked. The lesson for couples, especially those who are struggling with relationship and conflict problems, is that paying attention to sleep habits may help solve those issues. Dr. Hasler said couples should work to resolve problems before bedtime and avoid discussing difficult topics when one or both have not slept well, or at the end of a long day when one or both are tired and perhaps edgy from lack of sleep.

But many married couples have real problems sleeping together, a fact that takes a toll on both their marriage and their health. One of the most common sources of sleep problems in a marriage is snoring, often due to sleep apnea. Obstructive sleep apnea occurs when the tissue in the back of the throat collapses and blocks the airway. The result is a pause in breathing that can last ten seconds or more, and can recur several times an hour. Sleep apnea sufferers end up with alarmingly low levels of oxygen in the blood and are at risk for high blood pressure, stroke, and heart problems.

But as risky as sleep apnea is for the snorer, the snoring, choking,

and gasping through the night is also loud, unpleasant, and sometimes debilitating for the bed partner. In a telephone poll of more
than a thousand adults, 67 percent said their bed partners snore.
About one in three people say that they use a separate bedroom or
earplugs to cope with their bed partner's sleep problem.[80]

Snoring and sleep problems in a marriage don't get a lot of study.
But now some researchers say that in addition to the myriad health
risks that apnea patients face, they also are at higher risk for divorce.
In a small study of ten couples, doctors at Rush University Medical
Center in Chicago found that wives of men with sleep apnea and
snoring were also suffering from sleep deprivation. The problem
is more than a mild annoyance. The lack of sleep can put a severe
strain on the marriage, researchers say.[81]

In one of the couples studied at Rush, the husband's snoring was
waking up his wife several times an hour. Earplugs didn't help, so
she eventually began sleeping alone, which put a heavy strain on the
marriage. After the husband began using a special home machine
to quiet his sleep apnea at night, the wife's sleep also improved. And
the couple's marital satisfaction scores nearly doubled.

Often, snoring problems are laughed off by the snorer, who
doesn't take the complaints from his or her long-suffering spouse
seriously enough to seek medical help. But little attention has been
paid to the collateral damage of snoring and sleep apnea on the
spouse or bed partner. Research shows that people who sleep next to
snorers may wake up as often during the night as people with documented sleep disorders. One Mayo Clinic study found that spouses
of snorers awakened, at least partially, an average of twenty-one
times an hour, nearly as often as the twenty-seven times the snorers
were awakened by their documented sleep problem.[82]

It's not clear just how deleterious the effects of secondhand snoring
really are. Spouses of snorers and people with sleep apnea complain

of excessive daytime sleepiness and fatigue, which can affect relationships at both work and home. At the Mayo Clinic's sleep-disorders center in Scottsdale, Arizona, fifty-four patients with documented sleep apnea were studied, along with their spouses. The patients and spouses were given quality-of-life assessments and sleepiness tests. In the surveys, the spouses reported more pain complaints compared with national averages, although it's not clear why. Interestingly, the spouses of snorers initially showed the same quality-of-life scores as national norms. Researchers think the spouses simply accepted the snoring as part of daily life. Once the sleep apnea and snoring were treated, the spouses' quality-of-life scores jumped significantly, showing that they had been suffering more than they realized. And the spouses' sleepiness scores improved by 20 percent once the problems were treated.

"What the study showed is the entire quality of life was reduced in these people . . . and it did increase significantly when [the spouse] was treated," says James M. Parish, medical director of Mayo's center in Scottsdale. "We have to take into account that this affects the spouse to a significant degree along with the patient."[83]

The *Journal of Otolaryngology* published a pilot study of just four snorers and their bed partners conducted by researchers at Queen's University in Kingston, Ontario. They found that the bed partners all showed a significant amount of noise-induced hearing loss. The four patients all had slept next to a snorer for fifteen to thirty-nine years, and the damage was limited to the one ear that was most exposed to the snoring.[84]

Snoring can reach levels as high as 90 to 120 decibels. For some people, sleeping next to a snorer is the sound equivalent of "sleeping next to an industrial machine for ten years or fifteen years," says study coauthor Andre Tan, who heads the Department of Otolaryngology at Queen's University. In the workplace, workers who are exposed to noise that exceeds 85 to 90 decibels for eight hours or more are generally required to use ear protection.[85]

While earplugs are an option, many people don't want to risk sleeping through an alarm clock or any nighttime emergencies. The longer-term solution involves treating the snoring or apnea problem itself. For some patients, losing weight can result in the most significant improvement. Some problems can be treated with a dental appliance that helps open up a sleeper's airway. Surgical techniques, using radio-frequency heat, lasers, injections, or tiny implants, can reduce the size of the soft palate and open the airway, or help firm up tissue that vibrates during snoring. It's not clear how well the surgical methods work or how long they last, but about 80 percent of patients report at least some improvement in snoring levels. The most serious sleep apnea problems can be treated with an airflow mask that the sleeper wears at night.

So why am I spending so much time talking about sleeping and snoring in marriage? If national polls are any indication, at least one-third of couples regularly leave the marital bed because of sleep problems. Couples who are irritable and fighting a lot need to step back and ask if their problems may stem from sleep issues at night rather than frustrations during the day. They may just be cranky and overtired instead of genuinely angry with each other.

To determine how sleep may be affecting your relationship, do your own marital sleep assessment. Is one partner a snorer? Do you schedule bedtime to avoid your partner's snoring? To determine just how much a partner's snoring might be affecting you, take a two-week "sleep vacation." Make a temporary move into another room at night for two weeks, and see if you notice a difference in your sleep, daytime fatigue, or irritability. Sleeping in a separate room isn't a good long-term solution for couples, but it will help both partners recognize how serious and disruptive the sleep problem really is. If you are the snorer in the relationship, seek help for the health and well-being of your spouse and your marriage.

When Your Spouse Makes You Sick

The stress of an unhappy marriage takes an insidious toll on your health. Unlike money stress or work stress, stress in a marriage seems to be particularly hazardous to your health because it's so personal.

"You can't escape marital stress the way you can other types of stress," says Annmarie Cano, assistant psychology professor at Wayne State University in Detroit. Dr. Cano has researched the link between chronic pain and marriage stress, showing stressed-out spouses suffer more pain than those in happier marriages.[86]

"Most people think of marriage as a comfort zone and a place where you can relax," says Dr. Cano. "But when that is stressed, there is no safe haven."

Scientists at Ohio State University have conducted dozens of studies documenting the pronounced toll that marital stress can take on the immune system. Some of the most surprising research on marital stress has focused on a group of newlyweds who scored high on marital happiness tests and seemed, according to the researchers, "gloriously happy" with each other.

In these studies, the couples were asked about their marriage, and researchers measured individual personality differences and problem-solving behaviors. To begin the study, the couples were asked to discuss a topic that normally caused conflict in their relationship, and the interaction was videotaped and coded to gauge levels of negativity and contempt that predict marital strife. Blood samples were drawn hourly for a twenty-four-hour period to measure levels of various stress hormones.

Ten years later, the researchers checked back in with the couples. They found that 19 percent had divorced. But looking back, the hormone blood tests conducted in the early stages of these marriages had already predicted who would split and who would stay together. Three of the stress hormones measured during the conflict studies—epinephrine (adrenaline), norepinephrine, and ACTH—were consistently and significantly elevated in the couples who ended up divorcing.[87]

Janice Kiecolt-Glaser of Ohio State notes that the individuals with elevated hormone levels weren't typically those who were hot-headed in other situations. And at the beginning of the study, marital happiness tests taken by all the couples showed that the couples who eventually divorced weren't any less happy as newlyweds than couples who stayed together. "They were very happy in what they were saying, but what their hormones are telling us is that some part of them was very uneasy," says Dr. Kiecolt-Glaser.

The Ohio State researchers have conducted similar studies measuring the effect marital stress has on the body's immune system. They found that the stress a couple experiences during an ordinary half-hour argument depresses their immune system in meaningful ways.

One study focused on forty-two married couples that had been together for at least twelve years. Over a two-month period, each couple agreed to two overnight stays at the lab. During each visit, both the husband and wife submitted to a small suction device that left eight tiny blisters on their arms. Another device was placed over the wounds to protect them and allow researchers to withdraw fluids that would normally fill the blisters.

The goal was to study how marital interactions influenced wound healing, a measure of the strength of the body's immune system.

The couples took part in two types of discussion. During the first visit, couples talked, in a supportive and positive way, about a quality or behavior each would like to change about the spouse. During the second visit, the couple talked about a source of regular conflict that often elicited an emotional reaction from one or both spouses.

The study showed that after the emotionally charged discussion, the pressure wounds took a full day longer to heal than after the earlier supportive discussion. Among couples who showed high levels of hostility toward each other, wound healing took two days longer than among couples who showed little animosity during the talk.[88]

Blood samples showed that hostile couples also had an immune system response that has been linked with a range of health problems, including heart disease, cancer, and diabetes.

"Marriage stress is unique because it basically takes what should be your primary source of support and makes it your primary stress," says Professor Kiecolt-Glaser.

Other studies have compared the effects of marital stress and job stress on health, finding that marital distress was linked with a thickening of the left ventricle of the heart, as seen on an echocardiogram, just as was smoking and excessive drinking. But job stress didn't have the same effect.[89]

How much you interact with your spouse in a good or bad marriage can also influence your health. The same study found that among people in unhappy marriages, those who spent less time with a spouse had lower blood pressure than those who had lots of contact. Among those in good marriages, people who spent a lot of time with their spouses had even lower blood pressure.

The Health Effects of Marital Loss

If marriage leads to better health, can we hold on to those gains even if the marriage ends? As it turns out, the loss of a marriage is much more than an emotional one. When married people become single again, they often suffer a decline in physical health from which they never fully recover, even if they remarry.

In one national study of nearly 9,000 people, men and women who had experienced divorce or the death of a spouse reported about 20 percent more chronic health problems such as heart disease, diabetes, and cancer, compared with those who had been continuously married. Previously married people were also more likely to have mobility problems, like difficulty climbing stairs or walking a meaningful distance.[90]

The study does not prove that the loss of a marriage causes health problems, only that the two are associated. It may be that people who don't exercise, eat poorly, and can't manage stress are also more likely to divorce. Still, researchers note that because the effect is seen in both divorced and widowed people, the data suggest a strong association between any kind of marital loss and poor health.

One reason may be changes at the cellular level during times of high stress. High levels of stress affect us at a genetic level, causing chromosomal damage that can mean flipping on a switch to reproduce bad genes. In one study, the stress of caring for a person with Alzheimer's resulted in telomere (what protects the reproductive ends of chromosomes) damage associated with a four- to eight-year shortening of life span. The stress of divorce or widowhood might take a similar toll.

While remarrying led to some improvement in health, the study showed that most married people who became single never fully recovered from the physical declines associated with marital loss. Compared with those who had been continuously married, people in second marriages had 12 percent more chronic health problems and 19 percent more mobility problems. On the other hand, the researchers also looked at depressive symptoms and found that a second marriage did appear to heal emotional wounds: Once a person remarried, the level of depressive symptoms was similar to those who had been continuously married.

While these data don't suggest that people should stay married at all costs, the findings do show that marital history is an important indicator of health. If a person finds himself or herself newly single, either by divorce or the death of a spouse, he or she should be especially vigilant about health issues over which an individual has some control, such as stress management, diet, and exercise.

Other research suggests that the end of a marriage has different effects on men and women. Just as men reap an immediate health reward when they marry, a man's marriage advantage also disappears as soon as the marriage ends.

Divorced and widowed men face the same level of mortality risk in a given period as before they were married. The reason may be that divorced and widowed men quickly return to the unsettled life of their bachelor days, and they lose the household management skills of their wives. The result is less attention to their own health, poorer eating habits, and an increase in smoking and drinking and other risky behaviors. Given that wives often prod husbands to see the doctor, divorced and widowed men are also believed to be less likely to seek medical care when they need it. The same does not hold true for women.

Personally, I've been surprised at how these scientific observations reflect my own experiences with friends, co-workers, and family members. Several divorced men I've known have immediately purchased motorcycles after the marriage ended—their wives had banned the hobby as either too dangerous or too time consuming. Other men increase marijuana use or alcohol consumption after divorce, and begin spending more time socializing in bars. But divorce is often a very different experience for women. Divorced women typically remain the primary caregivers of children, so even if they might want to, they don't have the option of returning to the partying (and less healthful) ways of their premarriage days.

Even so, women also experience immediate declines in health following divorce. All the health gains a woman reaps from marriage also disappear when her husband rides off on his new motorcycle. But importantly, it's only divorced women who lose the marriage advantage. Women who lose their husbands to death have a different experience. Their health remains about the same and resembles that of currently married women.

Why would the death of a spouse be easier on women than divorce? It may go back to the fact that for women, the marriage benefit tends to be more financial than emotional or behavioral. In widowhood, women may be more likely to retain the family home and their husband's assets. Divorced women often lose their house and at least half of the family income and assets.

Lessons for Staying Healthy and Staying Married

Marriage alone isn't enough to protect your health, and the prospect of better health certainly isn't reason enough to choose marriage. What really matters is the quality of your relationship. It's too simple to say that marriage is always good for you. The truth is, only a *good* marriage is good for you. A troubled marriage filled with stress, conflict, and struggle can take a dramatic toll on both mental and physical health. A soured or irreplaceably harmed relationship is most definitely not offering you a marital health benefit, and in terms of personal health, you are better off single.

Conflict is an inevitable part of marriage, and many couples can fight without its taking a toll on their health. But certain styles of argument can result in high levels of stress and are associated with serious health problems.

In one study of 4,000 men and women, participants were asked whether they typically vented their feelings or kept quiet in arguments with their spouses. About one in three men and one in four women said they typically bottled up their feelings during a marital spat.[91]

In men, keeping quiet during a fight didn't have any measurable effect on health. But women who didn't speak their minds during fights were four times as likely to die during the ten-year study period as women who always told their husbands how they felt. It didn't matter if she thought she had a good or bad marriage. Her risk was the same.

The tendency to bottle up feelings during a fight is known as self-silencing, said Elaine Eaker, an epidemiologist in Gaithersburg, Maryland, who was the study's lead author. In a marriage, women, in particular, need to learn how to express their feelings of frustration and anger in a constructive way, not only to protect the marriage but to protect their long-term health. "This doesn't mean women should start throwing plates at their husbands," says Dr. Eaker. "But there needs to be a safe environment where both spouses can equally communicate."

Other studies led by Dana Crowley Jack, a professor of interdisciplinary studies at Western Washington University in Bellingham, Washington, have linked the self-silencing trait to numerous psychological and physical health risks, including depression, eating disorders, and heart disease.

Keeping quiet during a fight with a spouse is something "we all have to do sometimes," Dr. Jack said. "But we worry about the people who do it in a more extreme fashion."

While self-silencing doesn't take a toll on men, husbands are still affected by the emotional tone of an argument.

Utah researchers have videotaped 150 couples to measure the effect that marital arguing style has on heart risk. The men and women were mostly in their sixties, had been married on average for more than thirty years, and had no signs of heart disease. The couples were given stressful topics to discuss, like money or household chores, and the comments made during the ensuing arguments were categorized as warm, hostile, controlling, or submissive. The men and women also underwent heart scans to measure coronary artery calcium, an indicator of heart disease risk.[92]

The researchers found that the style of argument detected in the video sessions was a powerful predictor for a man or woman's risk for underlying heart disease. In fact, the way the couple interacted was as important a heart risk factor as whether they smoked or had high cholesterol, says Timothy W. Smith, a psychology professor at the University of Utah.

For women, whether a husband's arguing style was warm or hostile had the biggest effect on her heart health. Here are two examples from husbands in the study who both were having arguments with their wives about money.

Husband 1: "Did you *pass* elementary school math?"
Husband 2: "Bless you, you are not so good with the checkbook, but you're good at other things."

In both exchanges, the husband was criticizing his wife's money management skills, but the second comment was infused with a level of warmth. In the study, a warm style of arguing by either spouse lowered the wife's risk of heart disease.

Arguing style affected men and women differently. The level of warmth or hostility had no effect on a man's heart health. For a man, heart risk increased if disagreements with his wife involved a battle for control. And it didn't matter whether he or his wife was the one making the controlling comments. An example of a controlling argument style showed up in one video of a man arguing with his wife about money. "You really should just listen to me on this," he told her.

"Disagreements in a marriage are inevitable, but it's how you conduct yourself," Dr. Smith said. "Can you do it in a way that gets your concerns addressed, but without doing damage at the same time? That's not an easy mark to hit for some couples."

For couples who are struggling in marriage, the data on health and marriage show that the stakes are higher than many people realize. Not only will a better marriage make you happier, it can make you healthier. Married people, on average, live longer, healthier lives. They are less likely to have headaches and back pain. They are less likely to smoke, or drink to excess, and they are more likely to exercise. Married people sleep better and receive more logistical support when serious illness strikes.

Doing nothing and allowing marital problems to fester doesn't help your marriage and may be taking a serious toll on the health of both you and your partner.

Summing Up the Benefits of Marriage

By now, hopefully, you are feeling pretty good about the "for better" part of your marriage vows. There's a lot to like about marriage.

Social and economic changes over the past four decades mean couples today are waiting longer to marry, and the result is that modern marriages appear to be more resilient and lasting than the marriages of earlier generations. Divorce is getting less common with each passing decade, and by delaying marriage and choosing like-minded partners, men and women are entering relationships that have greater potential to stand the test of time.

The decision of whom and when to marry is obviously influenced by a variety of factors. Psychologists tell us that we typically marry people who have the same ethnic and socioeconomic backgrounds. We choose mates who have similar levels of physical attractiveness, intelligence, and education. It's no surprise that we like to be with people who have a similar sense of humor, similar political views, values, and long-term goals.

Relationship science also teaches us that brain chemicals, hormones, and biological urges all guide us in the selection of a lifelong mate. Cultural values, social pressures, and personal experiences all influence the way we think, feel, and behave in romantic settings. In a landmark cross-cultural study, University of Texas researcher David Buss asked 10,000 men and women from thirty-seven countries what characteristics they sought in potential mates. Worldwide, women and men wanted mates who were intelligent, kind, understanding, dependable, and healthy.[93] In the end, the decisions we make about when to marry and whom to marry are the result of a complex interplay between our genetic and evolutionary history and our personal and cultural experiences, with a big dose of serendipity mixed in.

Studies consistently show that marriage is good for us, resulting in more sex, better sleep, and better mental and physical health, among other things. But that doesn't mean it's not a struggle. Marriage has changed dramatically over the past fifty years, and couples today have extraordinarily high expectations for their relationships. This has made modern marriage a surprisingly high-maintenance enterprise. Getting married is relatively easy. But maintaining the high standards we set for ourselves in marriage is where the hard work comes in.

And while it's often clear when things aren't going well in a marriage, we really don't know where to start to begin making things better. Is conflict always a sign of marital strife? Or are there times when fighting with your husband or wife is actually good for your marriage? Will children bring a couple closer together, or does starting a family create an entirely new and challenging dynamic within a marriage? What do money worries and housework battles tell you about the overall health of your relationship? Relationship researchers have put marriage under the microscope and closely studied many of the biggest problems couples face. They have discovered new ways to diagnose the health of your marriage and identified the patterns of conflict that can signal a healthy marriage or one doomed to fail. Whether it's the challenges of parenting or battles over housework and money, a vast array of studies by marital researchers now offers simple, practical advice for making small changes that can lead to big improvements in your relationships.

So what should couples do when "for better" becomes "for worse?" The answers, which we'll explore in the next section, may surprise you.

part ii

For Worse (But You Want It to Be Better)

CHAPTER 6

The Science of Your Marriage: Diagnosing the Health of a Relationship

A successful marriage requires falling in love many times, always with the same person.

—MIGNON MCLAUGHLIN

So do you think you can spot a good marriage? One of the most important lessons from the scientific study of marriage is that many of us are focusing on the wrong things when it comes to trying to evaluate and improve the quality of a relationship.

Noted marriage researcher Robert Levenson, now at the University of California–Berkeley, conducted a fascinating experiment to determine whether there are any obvious signs of a good or bad relationship. He put together a videotape of ten couples talking and bickering about routine topics and hot-button issues. At the time the tapes were made, all the couples were married, but Dr. Levenson knew that five had eventually divorced. The researchers studying these men and women had caught their interaction on tape long before the couples themselves even knew the relationship was doomed to fail.

He asked some 200 people to review the tapes and guess which couples had ultimately divorced. The video watchers included college students, recently divorced people, those who had been married a long time, pastors, marriage therapists, and relationship scientists. Overall, the video reviewers guessed right only about half the time. They would have done just as well by flipping a coin.

Although nobody did better than chance at predicting divorce, there were two types of people who did a slightly better job at identifying marriages where one or both of the partners was unhappy. People who had just recently experienced a divorce and long-married couples scored above average in identifying dissatisfied relationships. People who have recently experienced troubled relationships may have learned how to spot a bad relationship when they see it. And long-married couples who have mastered the art of relationships have also figured out a thing or two about what makes a marriage work.

But for most of us, marital appearances can be deceiving. Dr. Levenson's experiment showed that the difference between a good marriage and a bad marriage isn't as obvious as you might think.

Consider a couple who seem to fight a lot. Fighting, anger, and negativity sound like symptoms of a bad marriage. But studies consistently show that how often a couple argues doesn't predict divorce risk. Some studies even suggest that conflict is a good sign, showing a couple's willingness to solve problems rather than let them fester. In fact, research shows that how often you fight with your spouse and what you argue about really don't matter all that much. It's the quality of the argument and *how* you argue that count toward marital happiness.

At the same time, a smiling, joking couple looks like a good bet for having a happy marriage. But studies of how couples in crisis interact show that humor isn't always a positive thing. Sometimes laughter and smiles show up to relieve tension and cover up deeper problems.

The fact is, the typical marriage is comprised of a number of complicated emotions, interactions, and events. And most of what goes on between couples isn't a reliable indicator for measuring the quality of their relationship. But what marriage researchers have learned is that there are some simple and powerful indicators that can diagnose marital strife long before the relationship hits the skids.

So, is your marriage showing signs of good health or trouble ahead? Here's a look at a few ways you can diagnose the health of your relationship.

The Story of How You Met

How did the two of you meet? Was it love at first sight? Did you date for a long time or was it a whirlwind romance?

Newlyweds and long-married couples often are asked to recount the details of their first date, their courtship, or even the wedding proposal. Perhaps you were high school sweethearts or maybe you met through an online dating service, at the grocery store, or through a blind date arranged by friends. First-date stories are almost always interesting, whether they are funny, poignant, or steeped in serendipity.

But what does a story of how you met years ago have to do with how you are getting along with your spouse today? Relationship researchers are keenly interested in hearing how couples met as a way to gauge the quality of their relationship now. But the actual details of the story are far less important than *how* the two of you tell it. Your personal romantic narrative, as told by you or your partner, is filled with clues about the state of your relationship today and can predict whether trouble looms ahead.

It was the work of Pulitzer Prize–winning author Studs Terkel, known for capturing the oral histories and insights of people from the Great Depression and World War II, that spurred the interest of two marriage researchers, Lowell J. Krokoff and John M. Gottman. Based on the approach Mr. Terkel used to get people talking, the relationship researchers developed an oral history interview for married couples, asking men and women about their dating and marital history, their philosophy of marriage, and how their marriage has changed over time.[94]

Since then, studies show that each couple's backstory is particularly revelatory about the present state of their relationship. One of the earliest studies of the value of a couple's "how-we-met" story was published in 1992. Dr. Gottman and his colleagues at the University of Washington took oral histories from fifty-two couples, and their stories were then coded and deconstructed. The couples also took part in laboratory-based discussions in front of cameras and strapped to body monitoring devices. Based on all the evidence the researchers had collected, they already had a pretty clear idea about which couples were happy and those who were headed for divorce.

Three years later, the researchers checked in with the couples again. The researchers had been virtually perfect in their assessments. The how-we-met story had predicted, with 94 percent accuracy, which couples would break up and who would stay together.[95]

The how-we-met story is useful but slightly less predictive in newlywed couples—the relationship is still evolving and couples have yet to settle into a pattern. Even so, talking to a couple about their early romance, even when they are still in the midst of it, can identify potentially troubled relationships. In one study, the researchers collected how-we-met stories from ninety-five newly-weds, and then they checked in again at different intervals for the next nine years.

At the four-to-six-year interval, the how-we-met story had been 86 percent accurate in predicting who would still be together. By the end of the nine-year study, the accuracy of the how-we-met story had slipped to 81 percent.[96] Among the seventy-nine couples who were still married up to nine years later, the researchers had correctly predicted sixty-eight of them would still be together. And the how-we-met story had correctly predicted thirteen of sixteen divorces.

Consider what this means. The how-we-met story, whether told at the beginning of a marriage or several years later, serves as a crystal ball of sorts, peering into the state of the marriage as far as nine years into the future. It shows that how a couple views their relationship very early in the marriage is a strong indicator for how the couple will still be getting along years later.

The *For Better* Quiz #6: The Story of How You Met

Below are some of the questions researchers use to get couples talking about their how-we-met stories. Before you read any farther, go through the questions and then write down your answers. You don't have to answer every question—just pick a question or two that gets you talking. The goal here is to document your recollections of the earliest days of your relationship.

It's important that you answer these questions now so you won't be influenced by the researchers' findings, which are described after the questions.

1. Do you remember the time you first met? What were your first impressions?

2. How long did you know each other before you got married? What types of things did you do together?

3. How did you decide to get married? Was it an easy or difficult decision?

4. Of all the people in the world, what led you to decide that this was the person you wanted to marry?

5. What do you remember about your wedding? Your honeymoon?

6. When you think back to the first year you were married, what do you remember?

7. What moments stand out as really good times in your marriage?

8. What moments stand out as the really hard times? Why do you think you stayed together?

9. Why do you think some marriages work and others don't?

10. What were your parents' marriages like?

The questions seem simple enough, but the answers are loaded with insights. Why is the how-we-met story so important? Typically, the early days of a relationship are the most romantic and the most love-struck. Put us in a brain scanner when we are in the early days of romantic love and we will look like we are crazy or on drugs. The parts of the brain that involve critical thinking are shut down—that's why we aren't troubled by obvious flaws like a filthy apartment or lavish spending habits. Meanwhile, our brains are awash in a dopamine surge and we feel dizzy and exhilarated by love. All of the memories we are creating during this time are tinted by the rose-colored glasses of the newly in love.

And when we are happy in our relationship, we remember the

early days with pretty much the same rosy-tinted optimism. But once we become dissatisfied with our partnership, at some point perceptions shift. It's not that we make up problems that never existed. It just becomes far easier to recall the negatives than the good times. And we end up recasting history to reflect our current state of discontent.

Is the story of your early courtship filled with nostalgia and optimism? Or is it tinged with negativity and regret? Do you remember getting lost in the rain together on your first date? Or do you just remember the fact that he refused to stop for directions?

Spouses who are in happy marriages often recount the early part of their relationship with laughter, smiles, and nostalgia—even when talking about difficult times like a job loss or financial struggles. Unhappy couples, however, tend to recast their past times together in a decidedly negative light.

For instance, imagine a couple telling the story of the first time a wife visited her future husband's filthy apartment.

"My goodness, the place was a wreck! Socks everywhere, empty beer bottles. It was definitely a bachelor pad."

Or she might remember it this way:

"It was disgusting. Even back then, he was a complete slob."

It's the same story about the same messy apartment, told two different ways. But it's clear which wife is happier in her relationship.

Consider my own how-we-met story from my first date with my husband in Austin, Texas. In the early days of my marriage, I would have recounted it this way:

"After dinner, he suggested we take a walk around the Capitol building. I had just had surgery on my foot, but I was having such a good time I didn't care. I didn't want to ruin the moment so I went along, hobbling around the Capitol grounds."

But later, when the relationship began to sour, I sometimes told the story this way:

"After dinner, he suggested we take a walk around the Capitol building. I had just had surgery on my foot. Of course he didn't even notice that I could barely walk."

Even though I would often laugh while telling the story, I'm sure an experienced therapist would have clued in to my negativity long before I was even aware of it. And that's the value of the how-we-met story. In addition to having your partner tell your how-we-met story, listen to yourself and how *you* tell the story of your early courtship. What you learn will provide a useful snapshot of the state of your marriage today.

Here are some of the clues to look for in the retelling of your marital narrative.

DISAPPOINTMENT AND DISILLUSIONMENT

When the University of Washington researchers analyzed the how-we-met stories of the fifty-two couples they studied, they discovered that the most powerful predictor of divorce was whether the husband expressed feelings of disappointment or disillusionment in recounting his narrative. Here's an example of disillusionment:

"I wish we had waited longer before getting married because no one told me how hard it would be. It was an emotional decision and not very rational."[97]

As the researchers interviewed the men and women in the study, some of the men would offer various insights about marriage that suggested disappointment or disillusionment with their current situation. A man would say he had never really seen an example of a good marriage. Or he might mention that he'd had unrealistic expectations about marriage when he and his wife were starting out. Sometimes, he would offer advice to the interviewer that included subtle signs that he felt regret about many of his own choices. Here's an example of comments that are tinged with personal disappointment.

"Before you get married, make sure you've gotten all your traveling and fun out of your system."

"I had no idea what I was getting into when I got married. My parents had a terrible relationship, and I'd never known how a happy couple behaved."

In the study, it was only the husband's disillusionment that was predictive of divorce. This doesn't mean the husband ultimately is the reason the marriage is in trouble. It just means that by the time the husband begins recasting the early days of courtship with a sense of disillusionment, the relationship likely has reached a serious point of deterioration.

PRONOUN CHOICE

Happy couples say "we," "us," and "our" when telling their stories. Their how-we-met story is filled with togetherness. The University of Washington researchers called it "We-ness." Unhappy couples often avoid all first-person plural pronouns, sticking with "I," "me," "mine," and "you" and "yours."

Here's an example of We-ness:

"We took a hike in the mountains and got terribly lost. We were so distracted by the scenery," she said.

"We never went hiking again, but that was still one of our best trips together," he replied.

Couples who don't think of themselves as "we" often are living parallel lives and don't feel connected to their spouse. Imagine this type of couple telling the same hiking story.

"You lost the map that day, and it took hours to get back home. I was exhausted," she said.

"You never really liked hiking much anyway," he said.

FONDNESS

It's obvious when you're in the company of a man and a woman who are incredibly fond of each other. They show empathy and often compliment each other or tout the other's accomplishments:

"It was super. Midge has never been so pretty as she was when she walked down the aisle in her white dress."[98]

While complimenting your wife in her wedding dress may not seem like much of a stretch, it captures feelings of fondness that don't show up in every wedding-day story. In the study, men who scored low for "fondness" didn't show affection toward their wives during the interview. In the retelling of their how-we-met story, couples who scored low on fondness didn't reminisce about, compliment, or express pride toward their spouses.

EXPANSIVENESS

Happy spouses often repeat or expand on the story. In one example, a woman might make the point that it took her husband forever to decide whether to get married. He expands on the thought in a positive way.

"Yeah, it was good quality time. Even now it's good quality time. Being cautious really paid off for us."[99]

If your partner doesn't want to talk about the early days of a relationship, it can be a sign of withdrawal, a risk factor for problems.

"You know I don't like talking about that sort of thing."

RECOUNTING THE STRUGGLE

It's possible that the narrative of your early days together includes some difficult times. Perhaps you struggled financially or maybe even had doubts about your own relationship. Even if hard times are part of your early romantic narrative, happy and unhappy couples will tell the story of struggle in very different ways. Unhappy couples often report "chaos" in telling the story of early struggles. Happy couples "glorify" the struggle. Here are two examples. Think about the use of "I" and "we" pronouns and the positive or negative tone of each example:

"Life was rough during those years. I spent all my energy trying to keep food on the table."[100]

"Life was rough during those years. Sometimes we struggled to keep food on the table, but we got through it."

While the how-we-met story has proved to be a useful tool for diagnosing the health of a marriage, it's important to remember it's not 100 percent reliable. Remember that in the study of newlyweds, there were fifteen couples who seemed quite troubled based on their how-we-met story, but nine years later, they were still married. In addition, three couples who seemed happy in the way they recounted their early love still divorced anyway.

Pay Attention to Pronouns

A surprising amount of scholarship has been devoted to the study of our word choices and pronouns in general. Freud started it with the study of "parapraxes"—those slips of the tongue that betray a person's deeper feelings. Various researchers have studied how word choice reflects a person's neediness and even whether the person might have bipolar disorder or other medical problems. Computer technology has had a huge impact on the study of language. A program called Linguistic Inquiry and Word Count categorizes the words we write and say into more than seventy "psychologically relevant" categories. The computer can identify words that convey negative or positive emotions, pronouns, prepositions, and other words.

One of the leaders in the field, James W. Pennebaker, a University of Texas at Austin linguistic researcher, notes that when the computer program was first introduced, academics used it to focus on the content of our conversations and writings, such as death, religion, or money. But the study of language and word use shows that everybody develops a personal linguistic style, no matter what they're talking about.

The powerful messages we send by the words we choose is particularly apparent in crime investigations. For instance, in 1994, a mother named Susan Smith reported that her two young children had been kidnapped. She told reporters, "My children wanted me. They needed me. And now I can't help them."

FBI investigators made note of this. The fact that she spoke in the past tense suggested she knew her children were no longer alive. Most parents speak of a missing child in the present tense. It was soon discovered that Ms. Smith had drowned her children in a lake.[101]

Word choice is telling, and notably, it's often the little words, not big or descriptive words, that seem to tell us the most. The articles, pronouns, prepositions, and conjunctions we use create a number of patterns. And one of the richest sources of information about a person's psychological and even physical health is the pronoun. In a fascinating paper called "What Our Words Can Say About Us," Dr. Pennebaker outlines some of the findings related to pronoun use.[102]

- When writing about college experiences, students who use more first person pronouns are more likely to be depressed.
- Poets who commit suicide tend to use more first person singular in their poetry. They also make fewer references to other people, suggesting social isolation.
- Widespread social trauma increases the use of the word "we." An example of this was seen after the death of Princess Diana. In chat rooms, the use of the word "we" jumped 135 percent while the use of the word "I" dropped by 12 percent.

In another study, researchers conducted a number of lying experiments, in which students intentionally lied about their views on abor-
tion, the feelings about people they like and don't like, or about whether
they took a dollar bill left inside a book. Analyzing hundreds of conversations and writings, the researchers found a notable trend. When
people lie, they are less likely to use the first person singular. It appears
a person, when lying, tries to distance him- or herself from the untruth
by avoiding the use of the pronoun "I." In fact, the researchers concluded, using the word "I" is one of the best predictors of honesty.[103]

In other work, studies show that people have different patterns
of pronoun use when they are sick compared to when they are
healthy. Sick people use fewer first person pronouns, perhaps as
a way to distance themselves from their illness. When a person's
health begins to improve, they increase the mix of first person plural and singular pronouns they use.[104]

Given the importance of pronouns in understanding a person's
psychological health, motives, and well-being, it's no surprise that
pronouns would be particularly interesting to relationship researchers. Remember the how-we-met story? The use of words like "we,"
"us," "our," and "both" is particularly important, evoking what
researchers call "We-ness," and suggests that the couple is thriving
in the partnership of marriage.

One study, from the University of Pennsylvania and the University of North Carolina–Chapel Hill, looked at the use of "self" and
"other" pronouns among fifty-nine married couples. These couples
weren't typical, because one partner had a diagnosis of obsessive-
compulsive disorder or panic disorder. But the group was of particular interest because half the patients and 40 percent of the spouses
reported being unhappy in their marriages.

Looking at transcripts of the couples discussing various problems, the researchers found trends in pronoun use. Use of first
person pronouns—both "I" and "we"—was associated with better

problem-solving skills. However, couples who regularly used the pronoun "you" when discussing a problem appeared to have more negativity in their conversations, less skill at problem solving, and less marital happiness.[105]

Next time you have a disagreement with your spouse, listen to the pronouns. Try to avoid phrases like "you always" or "you never." In fact, try to avoid the word "you" altogether when having an argument. Try to stick with the first person "I" or "we," and avoid the accusatory "you."

Consider a couple arguing over a messy apartment. Here's one way to start the discussion:

"You're such a slob. You never pick up your things."

And here's an alternative:

"I'm really frustrated by how messy the house is. We've really got to figure out a way to keep it clean. I need some help."

While it may sound like a small change, anyone who has ever been on the receiving end of "you" accusations knows how unpleasant and confrontational that small word can be.

What Eye Rolling Says About Your Marriage

Sometimes the best information about the state of your marriage is written all over your face. Facial expressions can be a powerful predictor of your feelings even when the words you are choosing sound neutral or pleasant.

But figuring out which facial expressions matter the most to a marriage hasn't been easy. In general, scientists have found the face surprisingly difficult to study. The smile is particularly complicated. It can convey happiness, pride, embarrassment, love, or even contempt.[106] One 1950s review of the facial expression science called the face "a researcher's nightmare."

More than a hundred years ago, the French physician Guillaume

Duchenne found a way to detect a genuine smile of happiness. A Duchenne smile, as it's now called, involves muscular activity around both the mouth and eyes and occurs when people are really enjoying themselves. A smile that involves only the mouth muscles is often viewed as less sincere, and may occur when people are trying to mask unhappiness or deception.[107]

But the breakthrough came when researchers stopped trying to study expressions and started studying individual muscle movements. In the 1970s, an anatomical facial coding system was developed that assigned numbers to describe the thousands of potential combinations of facial muscle movements. Raising or lowering of the brow, puffing the cheeks, wrinkling the nose, squinting the lids, parting the lips, dropping the jaw, nostril flares, blinks, closed eyes, wide eyes, and lip puckers were all coded. Notably, most of the action in the face occurs around the mouth, with lots of help from the brow, eyes, and nose. But the early incarnation of this system was unwieldy and time consuming. With further research, a new facial coding system was developed that focused only on the brow, the eyes, the middle portion of the face, and the mouth. This allowed researchers to more quickly code emotions with just as much accuracy as the more complicated coding system.

In one of the earliest studies to code facial expressions of married couples, researchers studied a sample of seventy-nine couples from Bloomington, Indiana. The men were, on average, thirty-two years old; the women were twenty-nine. They had been married an average of about five years.

The couples took part in the standard oral history interview together, at home. Then they stayed apart for eight hours and met up again in the laboratory. They were strapped into body sensors and placed in front of video cameras. (It sounds daunting, but study after study has shown couples quickly forget about their surroundings and are just as happy to bicker in the lab as they are in the privacy of their own homes.) The men and women were then asked to talk for fifteen minutes about the general events of the day (work, kids, errands, the weather), followed by a five-minute quiet period. This gave researchers a sense of how the couple normally interacted.

Then there were fifteen more minutes of discussion about a major area of disagreement in their marriage (money, in-laws, sex), followed by another five minutes of silence. Then they spoke for another fifteen minutes about a mutually agreed-upon pleasant topic (a family vacation, home renovations, the family pets).

Four years later, most of the couples returned to the lab for a follow-up study. The researchers found that facial expressions that had appeared even during seemingly benign conversations between the couples four years earlier had predicted later unhappiness. The facial expressions that matter the most relate to anger, disgust, contempt, sadness, and fear. The type of smile used in conversation also matters. A genuine smile that produces "crow's-feet" wrinkles around the eyes is a good sign. A smile that engages only the lips is a sign of "unfelt" happiness and often predicts trouble ahead.

The complexity of this coding system can't be underestimated. Seemingly dull conversations about the family dog or the in-laws are translated into rows of numbers that create a numerical blueprint for the couple's relationship style. Data from heart monitors, electrodes, and other sensors are synchronized with the video coding. A woman on the videotape may be saying something positive, she may even be smiling, but an astute coder sees the smile is strained and doesn't involve the eye muscles. The body sensors show the woman's heart rate is surging, suggesting she's far less happy than she appears.

All of this information is fed into a complex equation that allows relationship researchers to objectively study how couples interact. But while all these data are fascinating—and exceedingly useful for research purposes—married couples can't be expected to videotape their fights and subject them to complex coding systems in order to identify their trouble spots.

Fortunately, most facial expressions don't matter all that much. In fact, there's just one that matters a lot and you don't have to be an academic researcher to spot it. It's eye rolling.

Researchers say that one of the clearest signals of a problem in your relationship is when you partner rolls his or her eyes in reaction to something you've said or done. Eye rolling is often accompanied by a smile and laughter, so it doesn't always come across as a negative. But eye rolling is a painfully obvious sign of contempt, and it's a powerful predictor that your relationship is in serious trouble.[108] For many couples, this small bit of information is revelatory. In videotaped sessions of couples, the conversations seemed pleasant enough. Voices weren't raised, harsh words weren't used. But researchers watching the exchanges broke down the conversations and "coded" every gesture, expression, and word as a positive or negative sign. What emerged were all the signs that one spouse held the other in contempt, and the strongest evidence for this was a roll of the eyes after the other would speak. How many times has your partner rolled his or her eyes when you start speaking? Or are you the eye roller in the relationship?

Lessons for Assessing the Quality of Your Marriage

Decades of studying relationships have taught us that a few key indicators can give valuable insight into the state of a marriage. It is important to remember that a marriage is more than just a collection of memories, pronouns, and facial expressions; but paying attention to these particular indicators is a first step toward focusing on ways to improve the way you communicate and interact with your spouse. It's also a way for you to identify hidden resentments and frustrations that you yourself may not even be aware you have.

None of these indicators, however, will be the final word on your relationship. Even if your how-we-met story sounds great now, don't stop telling it. Listen for subtle changes that could signal trouble ahead. And if your how-we-met story is filled with warning signs, don't despair. Many of the strategies and steps outlined in the following chapters will help you mend your relationship and ensure that your story, ultimately, has a happy ending.

And next time you argue, listen to yourself and your spouse. Consistently using the pronoun "you" in listing your complaints about your husband or wife is a sign that your argument isn't productive. A partner who regularly rolls his or her eyes, even when it's in jest, is sending a silent signal of contempt that suggests your problems go well beyond the topic you are fighting about. Of course, this doesn't mean you can't ever use the pronoun "you" in a conversation with your partner. But if you and your partner are using a lot of togetherness words like "we" and "us," that's a sign that the two of you are on your way to solving a problem, rather than creating one.

In his workshops with married couples, John Gottman often suggests a quiz to take the emotional temperature of a relationship. He calls it a "love map" that helps you explore your partner's inner world.

The *For Better* Quiz #7: How Well Do You Know Your Partner?

1. I can name my partner's best friends.

   Ⓐ yes   Ⓑ no

2. I know what stresses my partner is currently facing.

   Ⓐ yes   Ⓑ no

3. I know the names of some of the people who have been irritating my partner lately.

    (A) yes   (B) no

4. I can tell you some of my partner's life dreams.

    (A) yes   (B) no

5. I can tell you about my partner's basic philosophy of life.

    (A) yes   (B) no

6. I can list the relatives my partner likes the least.

    (A) yes   (B) no

7. I feel that my partner knows me pretty well.

    (A) yes   (B) no

8. When we are apart, I often think fondly of my partner.

    (A) yes   (B) no

9. I often touch or kiss my partner affectionately.

    (A) yes   (B) no

10. My partner really respects me.

    (A) yes   (B) no

11. There is fire and passion in this relationship.

    (A) yes   (B) no

12. Romance is definitely still part of our relationship.

    (A) yes   (B) no

13. My partner appreciates the things I do in this relationship.

     Ⓐ yes   Ⓑ no

14. My partner generally likes my personality.

     Ⓐ yes   Ⓑ no

15. Our sex life is mostly satisfying.

     Ⓐ yes   Ⓑ no

16. At the end of the day my partner is glad to see me.

     Ⓐ yes   Ⓑ no

17. My partner is one of my best friends.

     Ⓐ yes   Ⓑ no

18. We just love talking to each other.

     Ⓐ yes   Ⓑ no

19. There is lots of give and take (both people have influence) in our discussions.

     Ⓐ yes   Ⓑ no

20. My partner listens respectfully, even when we disagree.

     Ⓐ yes   Ⓑ no

21. My partner is usually a great help as a problem solver.

     Ⓐ yes   Ⓑ no

22. We generally mesh well on basic values and goals in life.

     Ⓐ yes   Ⓑ no

Your score: ____

15 or more "yes" answers: You have a lot of strength in your relationship. Congratulations!

8 to 14: This is a pivotal time in your relationship. There are many strengths you can build upon, but there are also some weaknesses that need your attention.

7 or fewer: Your relationship may be in serious trouble. If this concerns you, you probably still value the relationship enough to try to get help.

Source: Copyright © 2000-2007 by Dr. John M. Gottman. Distributed under license by The Gottman Institute, Inc.*

Obviously, a high score on Dr. Gottman's quiz doesn't guarantee a good marriage, nor does a low score mean you're doomed. But the "no" answers give you a clear indication of what aspects of your marriage need extra attention right now.

---

* The Love Map quiz was written by Dr. John Gottman and is reprinted from the Web site of The Gottman Institute. Dr. Gottman is a world-renowned researcher in the area of couples and family relationships. For further information on couples workshops and private therapy, training programs for therapists, and relationship books and DVDs, visit www.gottman.com.

CHAPTER 7

The Science of Conflict:
Marital Spats and the Rules of Engagement

Never go to bed mad. Stay up and fight.

—PHYLLIS DILLER

Over breakfast at a gathering of relationship and family researchers in Chicago, I was speaking with Philip and Carolyn Cowan
of Berkeley, two noted marriage researchers who have devoted both
their marriage and their careers to the study of families, couples, and
children. I asked them why men and women seem to struggle so much
in their relationships. I was surprised by Carolyn's answer.

"We need to learn to tolerate a little more conflict in our relationships," she said. "Take time to disagree."

More conflict? I was shocked. I spent my entire marriage trying to *avoid* conflict. I saw other couples fighting and bickering
about nonsensical things, and found myself relieved that my husband and I rarely argued. My own parents, married for forty-three
years before my mother's death, argued constantly, although they
professed to love each other a great deal. I started shaking my head

as I mulled her advice. "The last thing I want," I told Dr. Cowan, "is a relationship with conflict."

She admitted that she doesn't like to fight with her husband either.

"But there is some stuff you need to struggle with," she said sagely.

Many couples measure the state of their relationship by the level of conflict they have with their spouse or partner. When they are not arguing, the marriage feels more solid. When they are fighting, they often feel distressed. When it comes to relationships, one thing men and women often agree on is this: The less conflict, the better.

But that's not always true. The scientific study of marital conflict shows that couples need to rethink the role that conflict plays in their lives, and the opportunity it presents to improve their marriages. If you think about what you want from marriage—a soul mate, personal fulfillment, partnership—it makes sense that such ideals can be achieved only through a little negotiation, discussion, and argument.

Marriage researcher John Gottman has a fascinating theory about conflict in a relationship. Just as predators and prey play a role in maintaining nature's ecosystem, he believes positive and negative interactions both play an important role in the ecology of a marriage. He believes a certain amount of conflict is necessary to help couples "weed out" problems that can harm a marriage in the long run. In his own research, he discovered that the "temporary misery" of conflict can be healthier long-term for a marriage. He checked in with couples early in their relationship, finding that peaceful couples reported more marital happiness than couples who bickered. But three years later the peaceful couples were far more likely to be headed for divorce or already divorced. The bickering couples, meanwhile, had worked out the kinks in their relationships and were more likely to be in stable relationships.

"For a marriage to have real staying power, couples need to air their differences, whether they resolve them in a volatile, validating, or minimizing style," writes Dr. Gottman in his book *Why Marriages Succeed or Fail*. "Rather than being destructive, occasional anger can be a resource that helps the marriage improve over time."[109]

The notion that anger can be a positive resource to help a marriage improve is tough to accept, but numerous researchers who have studied conflict have all come to the same conclusion. This doesn't mean all conflict is the same. Violence is always a problem. Hostility, negativity, and contempt during an argument, such as name calling, swearing, sarcasm, and threats, are never healthy. But during most marital spats, what matters to the health of the relationship is whether couples follow some basic rules of engagement that result in a fair and productive resolution to a dispute.

In fact, the main lesson from decades of marital research is that much of the conventional wisdom about marital conflict is simply wrong. The goal of conflict research isn't to eliminate marital spats entirely. Instead the hope is that by understanding what we fight about and how we fight, couples can learn to harness the power of anger and conflict to strengthen a relationship. That means learning how to start a conflict discussion, how to prevent it from escalating, and what part of the argument counts the most.

Why Do Couples Fight?

Determining the reasons couples argue is a tougher study problem than you might think. Conflict is influenced by a variety of social and cultural factors, and couples can come up with a myriad of possibilities for things to argue about. In a groundbreaking series of studies from the 1980s, researcher David Buss, now at the University of Texas at Austin, set out to identify exactly what causes conflict between men and women.

Dr. Buss interviewed a total of 600 men and women for his

studies, including people who were dating, newlyweds, or unhappily married. He began by asking 107 psychology students to list four things that women and men do to "upset, hurt, anger, or irritate" a member of the opposite sex.[110] After eliminating obvious redundancies, Dr. Buss was left with a surprisingly large number of complaints—the students offered 147 distinct sources of upset between couples. The complaints covered the gamut, from "He left the toilet seat up" and "Burping loudly" to "She cut me down in front of others" and "She yelled at me."

Armed with so many potential sources of conflict. Dr. Buss recruited another 317 students, about evenly divided between men and women. He added a second sample of 214 newlyweds, recruited through public marriage records. They were given the list of 147 items of conflict with five extra spaces they could fill in if a common source of conflict wasn't listed. The assignment: Highlight those annoyances that each respondent had personally experienced in the past year. From this part of the study, Dr. Buss determined that the complaints men and women have about each other typically fall into one of fifteen groups. They are:

- Condescending (He/she treated me like I was stupid or inferior.)
- Possessive-jealous-dependent (He/she demanded too much of my attention.)
- Neglecting-rejecting-unreliable (He/she did not tell me he/she loved me.)
- Abusive (He/she slapped me or called me names.)
- Unfaithful (He/she lied to me or went out with another person.)
- Inconsiderate ((He/she did not help clean up or yelled at me.)
- Moody (He/she acted "bitchy" or planned everything for me.)
- Self-centered (He/she acted selfishly.)
- Physically self-absorbed (He/she talked too much or spent too much money on clothes.)

- Disheveled appearance (He/she did not groom him/herself well.)
- Insulting of partner's appearance (He/she told me I was ugly or insulted my appearance.)
- Sexually withholding (He/she refused to have sex or led me on.)
- Sexually aggressive (He/she used me or demanded sexual relations.)
- Sexualizes others (He/she talked about how good-looking another woman/man was.)
- Abuses alcohol/emotionally constricted (He/she drank too much or hid emotions to act tough.)

The findings showed clearly that some sources of conflict transcend gender issues. Men and women agreed that certain behaviors, including being unfaithful, abusive, condescending, and neglectful, are upsetting to both sexes.

Other behavioral issues seemed to bother one sex more than the other. In particular,

Women are bothered by men who:

- Impose sexual demands, making her feel used or trying to force sex
- Hide emotions to act tough, or drink or smoke to excess
- Are thoughtless and unmannerly, for example, leaving the toilet seat up

And men are bothered by women who:

- Refuse to have sex or are unresponsive
- Are moody and act out-of-sorts
- Are self-absorbed, fussing over appearance or spending too much on clothes[111]

While the findings may seem obvious, the reason the data are so important is that the researchers documented, more precisely than ever before, the points of conflict that arise between men and women. You can see some interesting patterns. Sex—wanting it too often or not enough—is a regular source of conflict for men and women. Mood often causes a partner to become frustrated—whether it's hiding emotions to act tough or showing your emotions too often. And isn't it fascinating that women want men to think more of *others,* while men want women to think less about *themselves?*

The data show that conflict often breaks down along gender lines, helping to explain why some problems seem so intractable. While the knowledge of these problems won't result in the toilet seat being put down or your partner spending less on clothes, it suggests that many sources of relationship conflict are culturally and perhaps even biologically entrenched.

The research is limited by the fact that many of the respondents were relatively young and issues of money and child rearing likely hadn't emerged as important in their lives.

More recently, researchers evaluated nearly 4,000 men and women from Framingham, Massachusetts. These findings are interesting because they aren't based on college students, psychology majors, or people who knew their relationships were being studied. Instead, this was an ongoing study of cardiovascular health among a group of adults whose health habits and lives had been tracked for years to measure a number of health issues. These men and women were also asked to list the top reasons for arguing with a spouse. The differences were striking. Look at the top three issues for women versus men:

WOMEN	MEN
Children	Sex
Housework	Money
Money	Leisure

Since men and women are fighting with each other, shouldn't they be arguing about the same things? In some ways they are. Both men and women list money as one of the top three sources of conflict. Both sexes show that issues surrounding how they spend nonwork time—whether it's sharing in housework or enjoying leisure—are important to both sexes.

The top reason for conflict was children for women and sex for men. Think about what these two issues have in common. Children require a lot of time and attention from parents. Sex also requires time and attention for your partner. Both issues ultimately are influenced by how much time partners have for each other. In the end, the conflict data from the Framingham study show that issues of money and time are the main sources of conflict for most couples, issues that we'll explore in future chapters on the role that money and housework play in a marriage.

The *For Better* Quiz #8: What Do You Fight About?

How are the battle lines drawn in your home? During a peaceful moment with your partner, rank the following six categories to identify which issues are most likely to cause conflict in your relationship. Compare your answers to your spouse's and to the average response from the couples in the Framingham study.

	HER RANKING	HIS RANKING
Children		
Sex		
Housework		
Money		
Leisure		
Alcohol		

In the national study, this is how men and women ranked their top reasons for fighting.

	WOMEN	MEN
Children	1	4
Sex	2	1
Housework	3	6
Money	4	2
Leisure	5	3
Alcohol	6	5

Finding out your own sources of conflict can help couples understand each other better, but it doesn't necessarily mean disagreements will ever be resolved. Marriage researchers say that

70 percent of the time, the conflicts that arise between couples are never resolved. In one study, couples who were tracked for a decade were still fighting about the same things they had been arguing about ten years earlier.[112]

While this may be disheartening, it's important to accept that different individuals may care about different things. The research into couples and conflict has led to a change in the advice many therapists now give couples. Often they will tell husbands and wives to accept their areas of disagreement as well as the fact that most issues—whether about housework or shopping trips—will never be resolved.

And the truth is, they don't have to be. While it's good to try to get along and improve a relationship, reaching agreement on everything is not essential to marital happiness and it's probably not even possible. How many people do you know who agree on everything, all the time? To expect your husband or wife to agree with you on all things is an unrealistic burden to place on a marriage.

The Myth of Compatibility

During my marriage, my husband and I had a tremendous amount in common. We both had careers in journalism and came from similar families with long-married parents. We had both majored in the liberal arts and worked at our student newspaper. We loved food, wine, and art, and we were great travel partners and saw the world together. Our circle included several other long-married couples, including some with whom we vacationed. Eventually, we shared two cats, owned a home, and had a child together.

Despite our having so much in common, if you asked my husband today to explain the divorce, he would tell you, "We just weren't compatible."

So what exactly does it mean to be compatible? Does it mean

liking the same things, like skiing or cycling, as your spouse? If one of you gets injured and can no longer participate, does that mean you're not compatible anymore?

Or does compatibility mean having several things in common? If that's the case, then why do seemingly compatible couples with children, a home, shared friends, and a lifetime of togetherness still end up getting divorced?

The lesson, say a number of noted marriage researchers, is that compatibility is overrated.[113] In fact, focusing too much on the issue of compatibility may be in and of itself a sign of trouble, notes Ted Huston, University of Texas psychology professor, who runs the PAIR project, a longitudinal study of married couples. Dr. Huston's research shows that in terms of likes and dislikes, happy couples are no more or less compatible than unhappy couples. But a telltale sign of an unhappy relationship is when one spouse or the other starts to fret about not being compatible or begins to overstate the importance of compatibility to a good marriage. When a man or woman says that he or she is "just not compatible" with their spouse, what they are really saying, notes Dr. Huston, is that they just aren't getting along.

The truth is, compatibility comes and goes and there is no such thing as a couple who is compatible all the time. Sometimes couples get along. Sometimes they disagree about money, sex, kids, and time. Good marriages aren't about being compatible all the time. People in a good marriage know how to manage their differences.

Fighting the Good Fight

So now that you know what you're fighting about, consider this: One of the most important discoveries of marital research is that *what* you fight about just doesn't matter. What matters—and what's predictive of the health of your relationship—is *how* you fight.

Whether it's about sex, in-laws, or housework, the details of your disagreement don't offer any insight into how the two of you are really getting along. What counts is your approach. How do your fights begin? How do the two of you react as you are discussing difficult topics? What facial expressions and body movements do you display? How well do you work to repair the damage of an argument? Do your fights get out of hand or does one of you work to calm the situation?

As with much in marriage research, appearances during an argument can be highly deceiving. Someone who is red faced or crying during an argument may have a healthier argument style than someone who is calm—it all depends on what they are saying and how they are saying it. And how often you fight with your partner also isn't an indicator of the quality of your relationship or whether you're at risk for divorce.

To determine what does matter, various researchers have conducted dozens of studies, during which they videotaped couples talking about difficult topics—money, sex, housework—any number of things that can stir up a fight. At the time, couples are also attached to blood pressure and skin monitors—every body rhythm, facial tic, and movement is recorded, while computer programs help observers code various words and expressions used during the exchange.

The research shows there is a hidden level of communication between couples that goes far beyond the words, tears, or anger that are the most obvious signs of distress during an argument. When we argue with a spouse, we are sending distinct signals about our feelings toward each other, how much we value the relationship and whether we are satisfied or disillusioned with our marriage. So how do we figure out what these signals are? Who starts the fight, the way it starts, and the way the argument is expressed are all indicators of the quality of your relationship.

WHO STARTS THE FIGHT?

Studies show that women tend to initiate about 80 percent of fights. This doesn't mean women are to blame for causing all the trouble in marriages. It just means they are more willing to take the emotional risk of trying to resolve problems. Somebody has to start the conversation, and women, typically, are most willing to do it.

There's a biological explanation for the fact that women appear more willing to shoulder the emotional burden of conflict. In studies of stress, men and women react very differently. A man's cardiovascular system seems to react more quickly to stress and recover more slowly when compared to a woman's. Studies show that when men and woman are startled—say due to a loud noise or crash—a man's heart will beat faster and his blood pressure will stay high longer compared to a woman's.

Dolf Zillmann, a psychologist at the University of Alabama, studied how certain stressful or upsetting situations can affect men and women differently. In a series of experiments, men and women are strapped to body monitors and told they are part of some experiment. The experiment is just a ruse. In reality, researchers are studying them as they interact with the examiner, who is disagreeable and exhibits rude behavior. The examiner then leaves the room, and the participant is told to relax for twenty minutes. For men, the twenty-minute break has almost no effect. Their blood pressure surges and stays elevated. It only begins to fall when the man has a chance to "retaliate." In the experiment, the study subjects are allowed to fill out performance reviews of the rude questioner— and the opportunity to retaliate with a negative review helps calm the man down. In contrast, women in the same situation generally calmed down during the twenty-minute break, suggesting they are physiologically more capable of self-calming during conflict.[114]

The fact that conflict is physiologically so draining for men could help explain why men often don't initiate conflict discussions. It also suggests why things can quickly spiral downward, as a man begins to get defensive, then negative, and feels a need to retaliate as a way to relieve the stress of marital discord.

THE FIRST THREE MINUTES TELL YOU EVERYTHING

In one important study, Dr. Gottman and research scientist Sybil Carrère tracked 124 couples who had been married for less than nine months. Researchers watched and "coded" positive actions or words indicating interest, validation, affection, humor, and joy. And they also looked for more troubling signs, including contempt, belligerence, disgust, domineering, anger, fear, tension, defensiveness, whining, sadness, and stonewalling.

The study showed that the nuanced first few minutes of an argument can set the tone for the entire fight, determining whether the discussion will be productive or harmful to your relationship. In fact, in the University of Washington study the researchers demonstrated that just watching the first three minutes of the conversation helped them predict which couples would stay married and who was headed for divorce during the next six years.[115]

Consider what this means at the most practical level. If your marriage is struggling, you don't necessarily need to dramatically overhaul every interaction with your spouse. The most important part of an argument between couples is the beginning, the start-up. Couples who engage in a harsh or brusque start-up—leveling harsh words and spiteful criticisms—are headed for trouble. Couples who launch conflict discussions carefully and gently are more likely to have a productive argument that strengthens, rather than weakens, their relationship. If you get the *first three minutes* of a fight right, you're a long way toward improving the entire relationship.

Marriage studies show that one of the main differences between a good fight and a bad fight is whether it begins with a *complaint* or a *criticism*. Sometimes the two can be hard to tell apart.

Here is an example of a complaint versus criticism over the issue of housework.

"I was upset last night when I came home and the dishes were in the sink and the floor wasn't swept." (complaint)

Versus

"Why can't you be bothered to do the dishes and clean up after the kids the one time I have a meeting? You never think about pitching in when I'm busy with other things." (criticism)

Or sex.

"I wish we had sex more often." (complaint)

Versus

"You never want to have sex. You're always too tired. What's happened to you?" (criticism)

Or child care.

"I really need more help juggling the kids' schedules on the weekend. I'd like some time for myself too." (complaint)

Versus

"All you think about is yourself. Why would it never occur to you that I might need some help with the kids or there might be something I want to do today?" (criticism laced with sarcasm)

Understanding the difference between a complaint and a criticism can go a long way toward improving the quality of your arguments. Couples are entitled to be unhappy, even annoyed, with each other. In fact, it's inevitable. The key is to focus on the upsetting behavior rather than launch into a general attack on the person. It's a sign of serious trouble when the opening to your discussion begins with criticism, contempt, or sarcasm. Not only will you not win the argument, you will end up unhappy, dissatisfied, and with a dose of negativity that can jeopardize your relationship.

The difference between a complaint and a criticism can be subtle, so it's important to pay attention to your word choices. In his book *Why Marriages Succeed or Fail,* Dr. Gottman explains that complaints are specific, criticisms are global and include blame, and contempt adds insult to criticism. The phrases "you always" or "you never" are a telltale sign that your complaint has morphed into a broader criticism of your partner. Do your best to avoid the word "you" when having an argument with your spouse. Try to stick with the first person "I" or "we," and avoid the accusatory "you."[116]

Even worse than criticism is contempt, says Dr. Gottman. While criticisms are painful, contempt can be cruel. One manifestation of contempt discussed earlier is eye rolling, a dismissive gesture that suggests what the other person is saying is not important. Dr. Gottman notes that contempt is hierarchical, and is used to minimize the person on the receiving end of the barbs. Calling someone a name or tossing out a personal insult is a way to express contempt, and it's one of the strongest indicators that a marriage is in trouble.

The For Better Quiz #9: Are You Complaining or Criticizing?

Take this quiz to help you decipher the differences between conflicts, complaints, and contempt. Circle the letter that best describes the statement, and then check your score below.

1. I am upset that you didn't call to say you'd be late.

    Ⓐ Complaint   Ⓑ Criticism   Ⓒ Contempt

2. You can't be trusted.

    Ⓐ Complaint   Ⓑ Criticism   Ⓒ Contempt

3. You play too rough with the kids.

    Ⓐ Complaint   Ⓑ Criticism   Ⓒ Contempt

4. You never want to have sex.

   Ⓐ Complaint   Ⓑ Criticism   Ⓒ Contempt

5. I feel like you take me for granted.

   Ⓐ Complaint   Ⓑ Criticism   Ⓒ Contempt

6. You're just like your mother!

   Ⓐ Complaint   Ⓑ Criticism   Ⓒ Contempt

7. I wish you would initiate sex more often.

   Ⓐ Complaint   Ⓑ Criticism   Ⓒ Contempt

8. I'm upset you didn't help clean up after the party.

   Ⓐ Complaint   Ⓑ Criticism   Ⓒ Contempt

9. You're such a slob.

   Ⓐ Complaint   Ⓑ Criticism   Ⓒ Contempt

Answer Key:

1. Complaint 2. Contempt 3. Criticism 4. Criticism 5. Complaint 6. Contempt 7. Complaint 8. Complaint 9. Contempt.

The Role Men Play in Conflict

Although women are more likely to initiate conflict discussions, that doesn't mean men don't share responsibility for the tone of an argument.

In one study, researchers Bob Levenson and John Gottman asked couples to get together and take part in a how-was-your-day discussion after the partners had been away from each other for eight hours. They found that the negative patterns that are so clear between men and women in conflict discussions also were showing up in this seemingly benign conversation recounting the day's events. For instance, one man said to his wife with contempt, "Why don't you go first? It won't take *you* very long."[117]

It wasn't a fight, but it was a not-so-subtle putdown and a harsh beginning to a conversation. In one sentence, he had broken two cardinal rules of couples communication. He'd used a harsh start-up and he'd shown contempt for his partner.

In the study, women who were more likely to begin fights with a harsh start-up also had husbands who were uninterested or negative in the how-was-your-day conversation.

Which came first? The wife's negativity or the husband's lack of interest? It's not clear, but Dr. Gottman says the work illustrates how the negative emotional currents in a marriage flow both ways. If one partner doesn't put a stop to the pattern, it usually means big trouble looms ahead.

What Is Your Body Language Saying?

Marriage researchers have identified a few key body movements that can occur when couples argue that suggest trouble in the relationship. As we have discussed, eye rolling during an argument suggests serious problems in a relationship. In fact, in videotaped studies that track facial expressions during conflict, making any kind of unpleasant face during an argument shows a general level of negativity. While some negativity during conflict is inevitable, consistently making faces while a partner is speaking is a sign of trouble, particularly if it's the wife who's making faces.

Movement in general, shifting in the seat, walking around, also suggest agitation and aggression and are signs that the fight may be spiraling out of control. Think about your own conflicts. Fights that don't matter can happen while you're sitting down having a meal. Larger fights often involve one person getting up, walking around with arms flailing, or walking out.

Body language can also indicate whether one person is shutting down. Withdrawal, particularly by the husband, is a common problem during conflict, and it's closely linked with declines in marital satisfaction. Body language that suggests withdrawal includes avoiding eye contact, folded arms, a stoic face with few expressions, and a rigid neck. Another sign of withdrawal is a lack of sounds or of any small body movements. Even when a person doesn't want to engage in the argument, he or she usually will offer up a grunt, hmmmm, or harrumph as the other person is speaking. Head nods or rubbing of the temples at least suggest a person is still engaged. When grunts and these small body movements disappear, it's a telltale sign of withdrawal.

Lessons for Fighting Well

The key to fighting productively is to recognize when a disagreement is going in the wrong direction and to take steps to calm things down and repair rifts.

One of the most important elements of healthy marital conflict is the ability to "de-escalate" a fight. It's an essential ingredient in a happy marriage. Sometimes only one spouse is a de-escalator, but in many healthy relationships both couples take on the role, depending on the circumstances.

De-escalation is a common principle taught among business coaches for resolving conflict at the office, and the lessons also can help couples contain a fight before it burns out of control. Here is some basic advice for how to de-escalate conflict.

- Speak in a slow, quiet voice. (No gritted teeth or seething tone.)
- Look your partner in the eyes. Keep legs and arms uncrossed. Make sure you are sitting or standing at the same level as your partner so neither one of you has to look up or down.
- If needed, take a time-out to collect your thoughts. No storming out. Just make it clear that you're upset and you want to calm down and schedule a time to talk about it later.

Here are some key phrases and words that can help you de-escalate any argument:

- Clarification phrases: "It sounds like you're saying . . ." Repeating someone's words back to them makes it clear that you're listening, even if you don't agree with them.
- Nonthreatening words: Starting sentences with words and phrases like "Maybe . . ." "What if . . ." "It seems like . . ." "I wonder . . ." or "Perhaps . . ." allows you to disagree by asking the person to open his/her mind to another possibility.
- Affirmations: "I know this is hard for you too." "I hear what you're saying." "I'm glad we're trying to resolve this."
- Open-ended questions: "What are your thoughts?" "What are the next steps for us?"

The ability to de-escalate an argument is a skill, and it may take some practice to begin using nonthreatening words, clarification phrases, and open-ended questions. In the heat of an argument, it can be tough to remember exactly how to de-escalate, so it's useful to just pick one or two phrases with which you are comfortable. The point is to pay attention to the fight and not let it spiral out of control. When things are getting tense, when voices are rising and when tempers are flaring, do whatever it takes to calm it down. Sometimes just a simple statement like "I hate it when we fight" offers a break in the action and gives both sides an opportunity to ratchet down the conflict.

Another way to stop an argument from getting out of control is to use humor. Marital conflict studies also show that the happiest couples are skilled at repairing damage with affection and humor, both in the middle of an argument and after a fight. Taking time-outs—stopping the argument to give both sides a chance to calm down and recover—and displaying affection in the midst of the conflict are important tools as well, for turning a bad fight into a good fight.

The bottom line is that nobody likes to fight with their husband or wife, but conflict in a marriage is inevitable. Just because you fight with your spouse doesn't mean you have a bad marriage. In fact, regular spats can be a sign of a healthy relationship. The key is to find a way to make conflict work for you rather than against you by fine-tuning your argument style to fight fairly and productively.

The most important lesson from the scientific study of conflict is that you don't need to worry about what you fight about or how often you fight. Instead, just focus on the first three minutes of your argument. Improving the way you and your spouse start a conflict discussion will ultimately change the tenor of the entire fight and better your chances for resolving the dispute. Soften your approach to conflict and attempt to de-escalate a fight when tempers flare. Learn the difference between a complaint and a criticism, and pay attention to your words and body language during an argument. Fighting is never easy or enjoyable, but learning how to fight fairly will allow you and your partner to air your differences without damaging your relationship. When couples learn to fight well, in the end it doesn't matter what they are fighting about.

CHAPTER 8

The Science of Parenting:
How to Care for Your Marriage and Your Kids

My husband and I are either going to buy a dog or have a child.
We can't decide whether to ruin our carpet or ruin our lives.

—RITA RUDNER

When a mother I know read a newspaper article about parenting and marriage, she scoffed. The article reported that nearly 70 percent of couples experience a significant drop in marital contentment after their first child is born. "Seventy percent?" she said in amazement. "That's *all*?"

Everybody knows that being a parent is a hard job. But what is so surprising to many couples is how hard children can be on a marriage.

It's not how we expect it to be. When couples decide to have children, they typically think of the joy that a baby will bring into their home. Of course, there will be sleepless nights and a lifetime of responsibility, but there is hope that a new baby will give couples a shared sense of purpose and bring them closer together.

Alas. One of the more troubling conclusions by marriage researchers during the past few decades has been the surprising toll that
children appear to take on marriage.

Childless couples excited by the prospect of raising a family
together are often surprised by such cynicism. But when researchers look at marriages before and after children, numerous studies show that children are an enormous source of strain. Since the
early 1980s, more than two dozen studies have found that marital
happiness and relationship quality plummet when couples become
parents.[118]

A major report from the National Marriage Project at Rutgers
University recently noted that many Americans believe the most
satisfying years of adulthood happen *before* kids arrive and *after*
they've left home. Parents often view the years a child lives at home
as disruptive, and children are seen as getting in the way of marital
happiness rather than improving a relationship.[119] In fact, the data
suggest that it's only when children finally leave the house—and
your nest is empty—that couples can return to their earlier levels of
marital happiness.

But if children are in your future—or already in the house—
don't despair. The arrival of children brings both joy and turbulence
to a marriage, and the challenge is to make sure you're equipped to
navigate the stormy waters. All parents know that having a child
increases the stress and challenges of everyday life. The result is that
couples often have less time for each other, less money, and more
housework—all of which can lead to a marked decline in marital
happiness. While the broad data are discouraging, buried in the
numbers is the fact that a significant minority of couples—about
20 percent—cope well with parenthood. They remain happy in
their marriages or even report higher levels of marital happiness
after children arrive.

What are their secrets? We all have much to learn from these couples, and we'll explore how they successfully navigate both parenthood and marriage later in this chapter. But it's important to know that there are no easy answers. Parenting and marriage are both challenging pursuits, and the combination of both can be daunting. But if the quality of your marriage was high to begin with, chances are you can survive the stress of parenthood. And researchers also have found that how couples embark on their journey into parenting may predict how well a marriage survives it.

Parenting clearly adds a new and sometimes difficult dimension to marriage, but evidence shows that stressed-out parents and struggling couples should hold out hope for better times. Simply knowing that the arrival of a baby creates new challenges in a marriage can help you better focus your efforts as you care for both baby and spouse. How much time you spend with your children compared to each other, and even issues like sex and housework after a child arrives, all influence the effect of parenting on your relationship. For couples who are working hard to ensure the happiness and health of their children, the science of parenting offers important insights into how they can also work to protect the happiness and health of their marriage.

The Changing Patterns of Parenting

The notion that children and marriage don't mix is certainly counterintuitive.

From an evolutionary standpoint, having children within a marriage makes a lot of sense. It provides a socially stable relationship in which to reproduce, raise offspring, and guarantee the survival of our genetic material.

And in many cultures, marriages are formed for the sole purpose of producing children. The connection between marriage and reproduction is so strong that in some cultures not having children is reason enough to trigger an automatic divorce. In other societies the preference is to get pregnant and then marry—that way a reproductively successful marriage is guaranteed.

But while our parents and grandparents fully expected child rearing to dominate their lives and relationships, modern couples often define marriage differently. Rutgers researcher Barbara Dafoe Whitehead argues that marriage is no longer "child centered." As recently as 1990, 65 percent of Americans said that children are very important to a successful marriage. But in 2007, the number of adults who agreed with that statement had dropped to just 40 percent, according to a survey by the Washington-based Pew Research Center.[120]

The decline of child-centered relationships can be measured in many ways. In 1960, 71 percent of married women had their first child within three years of marriage. By 1990, only 37 percent had children that soon. Women clearly are waiting longer before starting families. In the 1970s, nearly 75 percent of women in their mid- to late twenties had already become parents. But in the year 2000, fewer than half the women in that age group had begun raising a child.[121]

Changing birthrates are a global phenomenon. Phillip Longman, a senior fellow at the New America Foundation, says, "Fifty-nine countries, comprising roughly 44 percent of the world's total population, are currently not producing enough children to avoid population decline, and the phenomenon continues to spread. By 2045, according to the latest UN projections, the world's fertility rate as a whole will have fallen below replacement levels."[122]

And because women today are having fewer children, it means that couples are finished with parenting sooner. Consider this: If your parents had four children over the course of ten years, they spent twenty-eight years of their marriage raising children, assuming the last child left home at the age of eighteen. Now, say you and your partner have decided to have just two children, spaced a few years apart. Your nest will be empty after just twenty years—you'll gain nearly a whole decade of child-free time in your marriage compared to your parents. Factor in data showing that life expectancy rates are improving, and it's clear that today's couples enjoy longer lives and shorter stints as parents. That means the percentage of our lifetimes that we devote to parenthood is shrinking. As adults, we get a lot more "me" time than our parents ever did.

The reasons behind all these trends are complex. But the reality is that marriage today is far different from the child-centered relationships that many of our parents or grandparents experienced. Complicating matters is that modern couples also have higher—some might say unrealistic—expectations for their marriages. In surveys, researchers have asked couples what qualities are most important in their relationship. Consistently, things like "emotional support" and "friendship" rank higher in importance to a relationship than "child rearing."

Because today's high-maintenance "soul mate" marriages require so much work and attention to sustain, they are also fragile. A high maintenance marriage is particularly vulnerable during the child rearing years.

"Like babies, soul mate marriages have to be nurtured and coddled in order to thrive," says Dr. Whitehead. "When a real baby comes along, much of that nurture has to be devoted to the child. This can be especially threatening to parents who expect the same level of time and attention in their relationship to continue after the baby arrives. This is not to say that couples should neglect each other during the child-rearing years, but it is to suggest that their expectations for sustained intimacy may be disappointed—leading some new parents to feel lonely, resentful, and uncared for."[123]

When Three Is a Crowd

An ongoing theme of marriage research is that couples today appear to be struggling more in marriage than their parents and grand-parents. Juggling demands of marriage and parenting today is harder for couples than it used to be because couples today expect far more out of marriage.

To compare differences between couples today and those from our parents' and earlier generations, researchers led by San Diego State University psychology professor Jean Twenge reviewed 148 studies of marriage and children that date back as far as the 1950s. They discovered that couples who became parents in the 1990s and early 2000s experienced a drop in marriage satisfaction twice as large as that reported by parents in the 1960s and 1970s.[124] There is a variety of explanations for this. Couples today often live far from extended family and don't have parents and siblings close by to help out, potentially adding to their stress level and unhappiness after children arrive. Or it could be that soul mate marriage coming back to haunt again: Couples today have far higher expectations for their marriages than past generations. When children arrive, the loss of quality time with a spouse is more traumatic because it was more valued.

It will come as no surprise to any new mother that the study found infancy to be the most challenging time for women. In the analysis, mothers with infants experienced the largest drop in marital satisfaction of any group in the study. While 62 percent of women without children reported being very happy in their marriages, only 38 percent of new mothers felt a sense of high marital satisfaction.

In fact, studies show that the arrival of a first baby is a particularly vulnerable time for couples. Marriage researcher John Gottman tracked 130 young families for thirteen years. He found that during the first three years of a baby's life, 67 percent of the new parents were reporting less satisfying marriages than before the birth of the baby. New parents also had eight times the number of arguments as nonparents.[125]

Researchers from Vanderbilt and Florida State universities looked at another indicator of parental happiness: depression. That study of 13,000 U.S. adults showed that parents are more likely to be depressed than nonparents. The study, based on data collected in 1987 and 1988 from the National Survey of Families and Households, is important because one-fourth of the respondents didn't have children, giving investigators a chance to compare random samples of parents and nonparents. As a group, the parents were significantly more likely to suffer from depression than nonparents, even after controlling for variables like income and social status. There was also no difference by gender: Fathers were just as likely as mothers to be more depressed than their childless peers. The finding was particularly notable because most major adult milestones—like marriage and employment—appear to protect people from depression. But parenthood doesn't.[126]

All of these data confirm what parents already know: Raising children is an incredibly challenging task. As comedienne Roseanne Barr once joked: "When my husband comes home, if the kids are still alive, I figure I've done my job."

Kids Mean More Work, Less Time, and Less Sex

The arrival of children clearly changes a couple's romantic life. But kids also take a toll in more mundane ways. They create financial troubles, more housework, and less time for parents to spend with each other—all of which are stressors that influence the happiness of a marriage.

Remember sex? If you're not having as much sex after kids as you would like, you are not alone. Sex after parenthood presents a host of practical and logistical challenges for both men and women. The decline in sexual encounters and sex drive after parenthood has been well documented by several marital health researchers. A 1984 study found that only about half of women studied had resumed sexual intercourse by the seventh week after delivery.[127]

Another study of 570 women and their partners found that a month after the baby's arrival, the vast majority of couples had yet to venture back into the bedroom (at least not for sex.) In that study, the average time for resuming sex was seven weeks and two days, but there was wide variability: 19 percent of the couples had resumed intercourse within the first month after birth, and 19 percent did not resume until four months after the birth or later. Notably, about 10 percent of couples still weren't having sex a year after the baby was born.

One important finding of this study was the toll that breast feeding can take on a couple's sex life. There were marked differences in sexual satisfaction among breast-feeding couples compared to couples who were giving their baby a bottle.

There are important biological reasons for this. Estrogen production is suppressed during lactation, resulting in less vaginal lubrication and therefore uncomfortable sex. Prolactin levels are elevated during breast feeding and testosterone levels are lower— both of those factors dampen a woman's sex drive. Researchers say that men and women need to understand the very real hormonal effects of breast feeding so that they don't conclude that the lack of sex suggests a larger problem in their relationship. The loss of desire is normal, and while it may be slow to return, it will be back.

There are other factors influencing the lack of sexual satisfaction when the mother is breast feeding. The fact that a woman who breast feeds has all of the waking and feeding responsibilities when a baby arrives is also no small factor. When a breast-feeding woman says she's too tired for sex, she really is.

Another more complicated issue is the fact that breast-feeding women are doped up on the feel-good hormone oxytocin. This is the cuddle hormone—the same hormone a woman experiences after orgasm, in fact. The reality is that a breast-feeding mother is gaining a lot of happiness and warmth and intimacy from closeness with her baby, and she may be less inclined to seek it from her partner.

Some mothers "at least have their needs for intimate touching met, by breast feeding, and therefore show less interest in sexual expression with their partners," writes study author Janis E. Byrd and colleagues. "Men, in contrast, do not receive this satisfaction from the baby and continue to seek sexual intimacy with their less interested wives, leading partners of breast-feeding women to report less sexual satisfaction than partners of non-breast-feeding women."[128]

The proof of this is in the numbers. At one month after a baby's arrival, nearly one-third of non-breast-feeding women had resumed sex with their partners. Only 15 percent of breast-feeding moms were having sex, and those women reported more frequent lack of sexual desire.

Not surprisingly, there are distinct gender differences influencing a couple's sex life after children. A Gottman Institute study tracked sexual attitudes among couples who had been parents three years or less. On average, women reported feeling sexual desire about once a week, while men said they felt desire about once a day. Women said they would be happy to have sex once every few weeks, but men said three or four times a week would be nice. Mothers also typically feel less sexy than fathers. When asked how sexual they felt, based on a five-point scale, men were bursting with sexual energy, posting an average score of 4.25. Women trailed far behind, with an average score of just 2.95.[129]

Why is there such a strong difference? It's more than just biology. Couples who are frustrated with their sex lives after the birth of a child can take comfort in knowing that when your partner doesn't want to have sex with you, it's not necessarily personal. You have millions of years of evolution working to keep you apart.

Rutgers anthropologist Helen Fisher, who studies how romantic love affects the brain, says that evolution may explain why women lose interest in sex, at least for a while, after a baby is born. She says there is an evolutionary explanation for why passionate love seems to fade when a baby arrives. A woman who was more interested in having sex with her husband than caring for her child wouldn't have had a baby to take care of for very long.

"Romantic love evolved for a particular reason—to initiate the pair bond with somebody, to conceive a child and start the process of creating a family," says Dr. Fisher. "If you were to sustain that very intense romantic love for your partner, you're likely to overlook the baby. From a Darwinian, evolutionary perspective, if Mom's not there to take care of the baby, it will get eaten by a lion."

Dr. Fisher notes that our brain chemistry has evolved to make sure women don't neglect their children. As described above, when a woman is nursing or holding her child, levels of the hormone oxytocin surge, leading to intense feelings of attachment to baby. At the same time, levels of testosterone and prolactin, which fuel the sex drive, start to plummet.

"Mom's not just overly tired and making excuses—she's drugged," notes Dr. Fisher. "Both parents are fighting a basic evolutionary mechanism that evolved to strengthen the mother/infant and parental bond—not the sexual bond."[130]

Dr. Fisher says that while brain chemicals may be thwarting

your sex life after a baby arrives, couples have the power to unleash other brain chemicals to help them reconnect. Her advice: Have sex, lots of it—even if you don't really feel like it. Any kind of sexual stimulation drives up your body's dopamine levels and other feel-good brain chemicals that will help you reconnect with your partner after childbirth.

If you act like you want sex, you eventually really will, notes Dr. Fisher. "If you want to start a very active sex life with your partner, don't wait for your sex drive to get you to the bedroom. Just get to the bedroom," she says.[131]

Surprisingly, a fair number of marital health researchers advocate quickie sex—just to keep your sex life going. The combination of parenting duties, work, and your own slightly dulled romantic feelings make the idea of "gourmet sex," as Dr. Gottman refers to it, less appealing.

Quickie sex obviously isn't a scientific term, but the notion is based in a scientific understanding of the human body. Dr. Fisher notes that all the feel-good chemicals of sex are released whether the sex lasts for hours or minutes. Think of sex like exercise, she says. You do it even when you don't want to, because it's good for you.

The Money Shock

Kids cost a lot more than you think. The U.S. Department of Agriculture reports that it will cost $237,000 for a family with an average annual income of $57,400 to feed, clothe, house, and educate one child from birth to age seventeen.[132] Dr. Whitehead of Rutgers calls it "money shock."

"The task of nurturing, guiding, and preparing children for flourishing adult lives requires higher investments of parental money, time, and attention than ever before," she says. [133]

Dr. Whitehead notes that the estimate doesn't include the cost

of sports, music lessons, camp, or extraordinary expenses for medical care or special needs. And for women, the cost of children
includes lost income and job opportunities if they leave the workforce to raise children. According to journalist Phillip Longman,
author of the book *Empty Cradle*, motherhood imposes a lifetime
wage penalty of 5 to 9 percent per child.[134]

"For many parents today, therefore, the costs of child rearing
mean more debt, smaller retirement savings, and greater exposure
to economic risks and uncertainties than they would otherwise
have," writes Dr. Whitehead. "Indeed, if adults cared only about
their material comfort, they would be crazy to have children when
they could have a more lavish life without children."[135]

Dr. Twenge, the San Diego State University psychology professor, who reviewed 148 marriage studies, also found that a couple's
income level influenced marital happiness after a child arrived.
Surprisingly, wealthier couples seem to have more marital struggles after children arrive than middle class couples. Among the
wealthiest couples, the drop in marital happiness after children was
22 percent, compared to just 7 percent for the middle class.[136]

Dr. Twenge notes that even though wealthier couples have more
money to pay for child care, they may also experience a more dramatic change in lifestyle after a baby arrives, compared to middle
class couples. Having money allows couples to travel, socialize with
friends, dine out at expensive restaurants, and enjoy activities like
boating, tennis, and other indulgences. But every parent knows
extracurricular fun comes to a screeching halt when you have a
baby. Dr. Twenge notes that wealthier couples may experience a
more abrupt change in their lives and the way they relate to each
other. The loss of their previous lifestyle "can be very stressful on
a marriage," she said. Couples with less money couldn't afford all
those fun activities anyway—so they don't feel like they are missing
out after kids come into the picture.

The Stress of Extra Housework

Kids mean more work for everybody, but studies show that when a child arrives, the housework burden shifts disproportionately to mothers, creating a new source of stress in the relationship. After children, housework increases three times as much for women as for men, according to studies from the Center on Population, Gender and Social Equality at the University of Maryland.

Minnesota researchers surveyed 261 fathers and mothers about domestic chores, talking to them during pregnancy and when the baby was six months old. Fathers reported a 37 percent increase in the home workload once the baby arrived. That's a big jump, except it was worse for women. Mothers reported a workload increase of 64 percent after six months of parenting. Women spent forty-nine hours providing child care compared to just twenty-six hours for men. And notably, among parents who were employed, women scaled back at their jobs by eleven hours a week once the baby arrived, but fathers reported an average decline of just twelve *minutes* a week.

The disparity in housework burden is often a source of conflict for parents and may be one explanation for the steep declines in marital happiness when children arrive. The way to resolve it is for couples to take a more egalitarian view of household duties. But as every man and woman knows, that's easier said than done.

Modern Parents Spend More Time with Their Kids

Every parent knows that kids take time, but studies show that today's parents invest far more time in their children than did parents of previous generations.

The sociologists Suzanne Bianchi, John Robinson, and Melissa

Milkie, all from the University of Maryland, compared parenting time by mothers and fathers from 1965 and the year 2000. There was good news. Married fathers today spend twice as much time with their kids than they did in 1965. Surprisingly, married mothers, who are more likely to be in the workforce today than in the 1960s, also spend more time with kids than did moms from earlier decades. Married mothers in the year 2000 spent 20 percent more time with their children than in 1965.

Overall, this translates to a lot of extra hours invested in our children. Another study, by John Sandberg and Sandra Hofferth at the University of Michigan, compared parenting time in 1981 to parenting time in 1997. That study showed that by 1997 children in two-parent families were getting six more hours a week with Mom and four more hours with Dad compared to parents and children studied in 1981.

So where are parents today finding all this extra time for their kids? Mothers, in particular, have dropped some of their housework duties—dads have picked up some of the slack, modern conveniences have made life easier, some parents are using hired help, and some houses are just a little dustier than they would have been in earlier generations. Multitasking is also far more common and a way parents can add hours to their day.

But unfortunately, to find extra time with their children, many parents also are short-changing adult-oriented activities. Extra parenting time has come at the expense of adult time with spouses, friends, family, and personal pursuits. After the birth of a child, couples have only about one-third the time alone together as they had when they were childless, according to researchers from Ohio State.

While it is a wonderful thing to spend time with children, parents have to decide what ultimately is best for family life. More time with children is great, but not if it comes at the expense of the parents' relationship. A stronger, happier marriage is always good for kids, even if it means less time with Mom and Dad. Studies also suggest that parents in happier marriages are more *effective* parents than stressed-out parents in unhappy relationships.

And to assuage your guilt about hiring a babysitter after a long, busy workweek, consider this: In her landmark "Ask the Children" study, researcher Ellen Galinsky surveyed more than 1,000 children, aged eight to eighteen. She found that most children don't want to spend as much time with their parents as parents assume. In the survey, Dr. Galinsky asked the kids a "one wish question," which was:

"If you were granted one wish and you only have one wish that could change the way your mother's or your father's work affects your life, what would that wish be?"

Nearly 60 percent of adults believed their children would wish for more time together. While kids love time with their parents, kids with only one wish asked for something else. "They would wish that their parents would be less stressed and less tired," says Dr. Galinsky.[137]

Are Kids Entirely to Blame When Parents Struggle?

Most studies of children and marital happiness suggest the same trend. Marital happiness drops steeply with the arrival of the first child. The slope continues downward until the kids are teenagers. Finally, the curve begins to shift upward again, right around the time when kids move out.

Brigham Young University professor Richard B. Miller writes about the time when one of his students asked an obvious question. "Why would a couple want to have children when kids mess up a marriage so much?"

Dr. Miller is convinced that the data on parenting and marriage place too much of the blame on the kids for declines in marital happiness. He notes that the roller coaster curve of marital happiness includes a mix of very happy, moderately happy, less happy, and very unhappy couples. The final number averages them all together. Just because the U-shaped curve shows that marital happiness plummets when kids arrive, that doesn't mean every parenting couple is miserable. Just some of them are.

But Dr. Miller points out that the data also suggest that some parents are above the average and sustain their marital happiness or perhaps become even *more* satisfied with their marriages after kids arrive.

"Although the U-shaped curve represents the 'average' of many people's marital satisfaction, it doesn't mean that couples are doomed to experience the same downs and ups in their marriages," writes Dr. Miller. "Research shows that marriage satisfaction is generally quite stable over the life course, with only modest changes. Parenting responsibilities, especially during the early years of marriage, are not the primary cause of negative changes in satisfaction with marriage."

Children clearly are one source of marital stress—but that doesn't mean they are the only source or even the most important source of problems in a marriage. Dr. Miller argues that issues like employment, money problems, help from extended family, and physical and emotional changes unrelated to parenting all influence the happiness of a marriage—but many studies of children and marriage don't fully take those differences into account. Dr. Miller argues that marriages experience "modest, not dramatic, changes over time." The decline after children, he says, "is more like a dip in the road than a pothole."[138]

Just how big a dip in the road is it? Let's compare marital happiness among couples who have children versus couples who don't. Some decline in marital happiness is inevitable for every couple.

Studies show that all married couples experience drops in relationship satisfaction in the early years of marriage, as the idealism of the courtship makes way for the reality of maintaining a daily relationship. The question is: How much of an extra effect do children have on marital happiness?

In the review of 148 marriage studies dating back to the 1950s, Dr. Twenge found that while child-free couples reported higher levels of marriage happiness, the average difference between parents and nonparents wasn't that dramatic. Yes, parents report declines in marital happiness when kids arrive, but nonparents end up experiencing declines in marital happiness for other reasons. Every marriage ebbs and flows, whether or not kids are in the picture. The data showed that couples with children have only about 10 percent less marital happiness, on average, than couples without kids.

Think about what this means. On a scale of 0 to 100, how would you have rated your marriage before kids? If you gave it a 90, then having children might drop your score down to an 81. If your marriage was slightly more troubled—maybe a 70—then kids will bring you down to a 63. The point is that the stress of raising children does present challenges to a marriage, but whether those challenges have any meaningful effect on your relationship depends on the overall strength of your marriage—not just whether you have kids.

Everyone involved in children and marriage research agrees on one important point. Over life, happiness is influenced by a combination of factors—family, children, marriage, career, health, financial success, stress, and numerous other variables. While the parenting studies show that marital satisfaction declines when a baby arrives, overall life happiness does not change. This means that children may steal a little satisfaction from your marriage, but they add happiness in other ways, so your total happiness level is maintained or improved—the balance of good and bad has just shifted around a bit.

Overall, married parents are just as happy in their lives as child-free couples. In surveys, when people are asked what their main source of personal fulfillment is—marriage, family, work, et cetera—the answer that tops the list is children.

"It's important to note that we studied marital satisfaction, not overall satisfaction," said Dr. Twenge. "The message isn't 'Don't have kids,' it's 'Don't have kids to try to improve your marriage.' People should realize that it will be difficult and be prepared for it."[139]

But how do you prepare for it? Researchers have identified several ways couples can cope with parenting stress and still maintain a satisfying marriage.

Lessons on Caring for Children and Your Marriage

Philip and Carolyn Cowan have devoted their academic careers to the study of marriages and family, particularly what happens to relationships when partners become parents. Their professional interest in the topic stemmed from their own experiences and challenges as new parents years earlier. Phil and Carolyn met as teenagers in the 1950s. Like many of their generation, they married young—Carolyn was just nineteen and Philip was twenty-one. A few years after marrying they had the first of their three children. When Carolyn was pregnant with their second child, the family moved away from family and friends in Canada so Philip could take a job at the University of California at Berkeley.

Children, job changes, and moving all took a toll on the young couple. By the time their children were in elementary school, the relationship felt seriously strained. They were stunned when friends and neighbors, many of whom had been married ten or fifteen years, began separating and divorcing. In talking between themselves and with other families, the Cowans realized that in virtually every case, the problems each couple had experienced began around the time the first baby arrived. "It struck us that we weren't the only ones struggling," says Carolyn.

The Cowans began rebuilding their own relationship, paying attention to problem areas and slowly regaining the intimacy that had been lost. With their dual backgrounds in psychology, they also developed a professional interest in the issue, and wondered if something could be done to help couples weather the dramatic changes of parenthood.

At the time, childbirth classes were just coming into vogue. Parents were spending six or eight weeks together learning about pregnancy and what to expect in childbirth. It seemed odd to the Cowans that couples would spend weeks learning about a single day in the child's life, but that they were virtually on their own in raising that child for the next eighteen years. Wouldn't it make sense, they wondered, to offer parenting advice to couples well beyond the birthing day?

The result was a landmark ten-year study that came to be known as the "Becoming a Family Project." It included ninety-six couples, and the Cowans followed them from pregnancy to their child's kindergarten year. The findings have been widely viewed as some of the most important in marriage research and divorce prevention. The findings offer hope to parents who are struggling to regain the relationship they had before children. Here's what they and other marriage researchers have learned about how couples can survive and thrive in parenthood.

THE PATH TO PARENTHOOD MAKES A DIFFERENCE

Some couples plan for children, and even discuss their future roles as parents, how they will divide child care, housework, and paid employment opportunities. Other couples just let their families "happen." It may be because couples don't agree on whether it's the right time to start a family. Often one partner, usually the husband, will give in, either to maintain peace or because he's truly ambivalent about fatherhood.

In the "Becoming a Family" study, couples who were ambivalent about parenthood, disagreed about it, or just "let it happen" were far more likely to be unhappy and were at higher risk for divorce. Couples who planned a baby's arrival or who were equally joyous at becoming parents were far more likely to maintain their marital happiness or even enjoy an increase after the baby was born.

If you've already had children, thinking back to the decision, and whether both of you fully supported it, can give you insights into your relationship now. If you haven't had children yet, make sure you are both equally committed to a new life together as parents. If one of you pushes forward without the full backing of your spouse, chances are you are headed for tough times ahead and your partnership may not survive parenthood.

TRY TO BREAK GENDER ROLES

Often after a baby's arrival, mothers increase housework duties and have to cut back on paid employment. Men increase housework slightly but work the same or even more after a baby is born. The wife resents the husband's lack of involvement and the husband feels trapped, working long hours and missing out on time with family.

It can be difficult to break free of gender roles in any relationship, but at no time is it more important than when you become parents. Fathers need to step out of their safe "breadwinner" zone and recognize there is more to fatherhood than financial support. But even more important, mothers need to relinquish some of their maternal power and give dads a chance at regular caregiving.

This was an important finding of a major study on fatherhood funded by the California Department of Social Services' Office of Child Abuse Prevention, which was trying to find ways to involve fathers more in state family programs. The study was designed to determine how much impact a wife has on the father's role in the family.

In the study, low income couples were randomly placed in one of three groups. Two groups—one with fathers only and one with both parents—received sixteen weeks of parenting counseling. Couples in a control group had a single information session.

The study found that in both intervention groups, the fathers spent more time with their children and helped out with more daily tasks. These dads were more emotionally involved with their kids, and the children had fewer behavior problems, compared to children in the control group.

But notably, the fathers who did best were those who took part in the counseling along with their wives. They had less parenting stress and more marital happiness than any of the other parents studied. What this suggests is that it's not enough to ask fathers to become more involved with their children and share more of the workload. The key fathers do a better job of parenting and helping out when they have support from their wives.

Now you're probably thinking, of course his wife supports his effort to help more around the house. But studies show that's not always the case. A difficult lesson many mothers have to learn is that they are bringing some of the parenting stress upon themselves by not ceding control from time to time. Women often complain that fathers don't help enough, but when they do help, wives often unwittingly sideline their husbands, unintentionally discouraging them by micromanaging the way they wash the baby or change a diaper.

Remember the television show *Jon & Kate Plus 8*? How often

did we see Kate chide her husband for letting the kids play in their dress-up clothes or for putting them in the wrong shoes? Every mother I know can relate to this kind of frustration, but watching it play out on television showed us how discouraging and emasculating that kind of criticism can be for a father. How many mothers have berated their husbands when they've come home and discovered him playing video games with the kids? It's not that video games are banned—the game console is in the house, after all. But maybe the mom would rather see her kids reading or playing outside. Is it really fair to criticize her husband's parenting style just because it's different from her own?

Studies show that the best predictor of a father's involvement with his children is not the way he feels about his kids. The best predictor of a man's parenting is his relationship with his *wife*. When the mother relinquishes her power and lets a father parent his own way, video games and all, he tends to be happier with the mother and is more involved with his children.

DISCUSS PARENTING AND MARRIAGE STRESS
WITH OTHER PARENTS

While this may sound obvious, it's important for parents to know how regular conversations with other parents (as well as gripe sessions, whining, and tears) can make it easier to cope with the demands of parenthood and take some of the stress off your marriage. In the "Becoming a Family" study, group counseling sessions as early as the first few months of a baby's life had a lasting positive effect on the stability of the relationship. Couples who took part in group couples therapy during the last three months of pregnancy and the first three months of a baby's life were far more likely to still be married by the time the child entered kindergarten than were parents who hadn't attended counseling. Later research showed that parent counseling in infancy still had a protective effect by the time the child had entered high school. Even for parents who can't or don't want to attend professional counseling, the study suggests that many parents benefited from the group effect, seeing how other couples were coping and struggling with their dual roles as spouse and parent. New parents shouldn't isolate themselves, but instead seek the company of other new parents. It will quickly become clear that your struggles are universal and not necessarily the result of a specific problem in your relationship. And don't underestimate the importance of venting outside of your marriage. Your husband or wife already knows how tough it is, and complaining at home only adds to the stress. Conversations with other parents can help you work out the tensions and frustrations without triggering a new set of problems in your marriage.

Make time for more than parenting. Chances are you've heard this advice before. I know I did. But when my baby arrived I was simply enthralled with her, and I didn't really want to make time for anything else. I loved being with her, and I had no desire to spend less time with her. But almost without exception, new parents pay so much attention to the child, they forget to pay attention to each other. One of the strongest findings from marriage-and-children studies is that the most successful couples give plenty of time to the relationship and don't spend all of their effort on parenting. "Nobody takes this seriously enough," says Philip Cowan. "Both parents usually are working and they feel guilty if they take even more time out away from their kids."

Carolyn Cowan notes that it doesn't have to be an enormous time investment, and many couples can benefit by just checking in with each other. Ask your partner a simple "How are you?" or even better, she suggests, "How are we doing?" Don't ask these questions as you're walking out the door or herding children to bed. Set aside ten minutes and listen to the answer. This may not sound like much, but amid the hustle and bustle of parenting, especially when there is an infant in the house, these small moments build on each other and ensure that the two of you stay connected or begin to reconnect.

Do it for your kids. The Cowans point out that parents who are truly devoted to their children will sacrifice time with their kids to make time for each other. Studies show that the decision will pay dividends. As part of the "Becoming a Family" study, teachers from eighty different schools were asked to evaluate the children from the families who were studied. An important trend emerged from the teacher evaluations. The kids who received the highest marks for academic performance and social adjustment came from families in which the parents were in happier relationships. Investing time in your partner isn't selfish. Instead, it's one of the best things you can do for the whole family.

HOPE IN THE PRESCHOOL YEARS

While the broad data show that parents' marital happiness doesn't improve until the children move out of the house, there are some findings that suggest marriage and parenting might ease a bit three to five years after a child is born.

A major Swedish study tracked 500,000 women who, among them, had 80,000 divorces. The point of the study was to look at how varying combinations of biological children and step-children influenced a couple's risk for divorce. Overall, divorce risk dropped when the last child reached the age of three, although for certain couples, risk didn't fall until the last child reached the age of six.

In other studies of parents and sex, some data suggest that the "disconnect" in intimacy that new parents experience typically lasts about three years. Another U.S. study of African-American couples supports the idea of a preschool effect on marriage. Parents in that study reported higher levels of marital happiness when kids were preschool age and older than at other times. And divorce patterns in the United States and other countries also suggest that troubles in a marriage begin to ebb right about the time a child hits three or four years old.

Other studies contradict the findings, noting that overall marital happiness typically doesn't bounce back until children leave home. But it does appear that the combination of parenting and marriage gets easier for many parents when a child is three to five years old. To any parent, the trend makes sense. Parenting of children at any age is stressful, but when children are finally out of diapers, able to feed themselves, and particularly when they begin attending school, life gets easier. This isn't to say it will be smooth sailing once kids go to preschool. The data suggest that teenagers create a whole new set of stress and strain on a relationship, and every parent of an adolescent has experienced the logistical nightmare of juggling work and extracurricular activities like football practice, study sessions, and choir rehearsals, not to mention teen dating, curfew violations, and schoolwork.

INSIGHTS FROM THE EMPTY NEST

As I've already explained, study after study consistently shows that marital happiness drops when the first child joins the family, and marital happiness goes back up when the last child leaves home. So what goes on in the empty nest that makes it a happier place? And can we apply some of the lessons to ease parenting stress even when the nest is still full?

To be sure, empty-nest parents clearly miss children who have left home for college, jobs, or marriage. But even though the nest can be a little lonely, husbands and wives also enjoy the greater freedom and relaxed responsibility.

"It's not like their lives were miserable," said Sara Melissa Gorchoff, a specialist in adult relationships at the University of California–Berkeley. "Parents were happy with their kids. It's just that their marriages got better when the kids left home."

Much of the research on children and marital happiness focuses on the early years. To understand the effects over time, researchers at Berkeley tracked marital happiness among seventy-two women in the Mills Longitudinal Study, which has followed a group of Mills College alumnae for fifty years.

The study is important because it tracks the first generation of women to juggle traditional family responsibilities with jobs in the workforce. In the empty-nest study, researchers compared the women's marital happiness in their forties, when many still had children at home; in their early fifties, when some had older children who had left home; and in their sixties, when virtually all had empty nests. At every point, the empty nesters scored higher on marital happiness than women with children still at home. The finding mirrors that of another report presented at the American Psychological Association, tracking a dozen parents who were interviewed at the time of a child's high school graduation and ten years later. That small study also showed that a majority of parents scored higher on marital satisfaction after children had left home.

In studying the women from Mills College, the Berkeley researchers had hypothesized that the improvement in marital happiness came from couples' spending more time together. But to their surprise, the Mills women reported that they spent the same amount of time with their partners whether the children were living at home or had moved out. Despite all the extra time you would think couples would have gained when the kids moved out, empty nesters didn't end up spending more time with each other. What changed in the empty nest was that the *quality* of couples' shared time improved.

"There are fewer interruptions and less stress when kids are out of the house," said Dr. Gorchoff. "It wasn't that they spent more time with each other after the children moved out. It's the quality of time they spent with each other that improved."

This is good news for parents who still have kids at home, because it means you don't necessarily have to find more time in your day for each other. *You just need to make better use of the time you do have together.* Dr. Gorchoff notes that the lesson from the empty nest may be that parents need to work to carve out more *stress-free* time together. "Kids aren't ruining parents' lives," Dr. Gorchoff said. "It's just that they're making it more difficult to have enjoyable interactions together."

The bottom line of the research into parenting and relationships is this: The best way to take care of your children is to take care of your marriage.

It is deceptively simple advice but decidedly hard to implement when you have a crying baby or two kids with a soccer tournament and a dance recital scheduled on the same day. For couples who don't have children, it's tough to describe the chaos and coordination that are part of raising a family. And for parents who delight in the accomplishments and happiness of their kids, it can be difficult to accept or even believe that those bundles of joy and cuteness can take such a troubling toll on their parents' marriage.

There is no way to sugarcoat the fact that children present big challenges to the health and happiness of your marriage. There will simply be days where your relationship gets neglected. There will be days when a woman feels her husband doesn't do enough to help with the kids. And there will be times when a father feels sidelined by his wife's constant micromanaging of household and parenting duties.

But simply knowing that you're not alone, that other couples are struggling with the challenges of combining marriage and parenting, can help ease the burden. One new father I know was confiding to me about how the arrival of his first child had coincided with a time of enormous stress in his marriage. We talked at length about the data on children and marital happiness, which confirmed his own experiences. Instead of being distraught by the bad news, he was relieved. "You have no idea how much it helps," he told me, "just to learn that this happens to everybody." But that doesn't mean we should start expecting less from our marriages once kids arrive or give in to the stress. Smart couples will do their best to sneak in a few minutes here and there for a quick conversation, for a laugh, or even a cry. The goal is to stay connected amid the chaos, grab time together when you can, and make time together as often as possible.

And when all else fails, remember: It really does get better—eventually.

CHAPTER 9

The Chore Wars:
The Science of Housework

Marriage is not just spiritual communion; it is also
remembering to take out the trash.

—DR. JOYCE BROTHERS

A father I know had a spat with his wife, but he wasn't exactly sure why. During a holiday weekend, he had made an extra effort to help out around the house.

"Did you notice how I helped with the dishes?" he boasted to his wife at the end of the weekend.

His wife, a busy mother of three and a community volunteer who rarely saw her husband during the week, was incredulous. The next day he was still confused. Why was she so upset with him? After years of talking to couples, marriage researchers, and my own women friends, I had a pretty good inkling.

"How is it that you're 'helping' her, when all you're really doing is cleaning your own house?" I asked.

He looked sheepish and reminded himself to tell his wife that night how much he appreciated her.

It was a minor spat, but one that plays out in some form every day in households around the world. Housework, whether it's washing dishes, doing laundry, cleaning the toilet, or picking up clothes from the bedroom floor, is one of the most common sources of conflict among married couples. Housework, for all its everyday drudgery, can have a dramatic effect on a marriage.

Couples say an equal division of household labor is essential to a happy marriage. In fact, most say it's even more important to marital happiness than having children, according to a 2007 survey from the Pew Research Center. For 62 percent of respondents, sharing chores was "very important" to marriage, up from 47 percent in 1990,[140] according to the random, nationwide sample of 2,020 U.S. adults.

In 1989, University of California–Berkeley sociologist Arlie Hochschild coined the term that would define the lives of a generation of working women. Her book *The Second Shift* detailed what many working women already knew. A revolution that pushed women out of the home and into paid employment had little if any effect on their domestic duties. Wives were essentially working a second shift, tackling household duties when they returned home after a full day's work. The additional hours that working women put in on the second shift of housework, Dr. Hochschild calculated, added up to at least an extra month of work each year.

Of course, in some households, the roles are reversed and men are the ones doing most of the cooking and cleaning. Research shows that about 10 percent of men feel that the division of labor in their marriage is unfair to them. By comparison, 60 percent of women complain of an unfair housework burden in their homes. Various studies show that on average, women in the United States and around the world tend to shoulder far more of the housework and child care burdens than men.

But men are not entirely to blame for the unequal distribution of household labor. For many women, the source of power in their relationship comes from controlling the home and their children. This "gatekeeping" on the home front could be creating a rift in your marriage.

Both men and women have a lot to learn from the study of housework. Couples who resolve their conflicts about cleaning are typically happier. But the answer isn't necessarily asking your husband to do the dishes or laundry more often. It also means *allowing* him to do it, not trying to control how he does it, and not criticizing him for doing it differently from you. And for men, resolving marital conflict over housework will not only improve your marriage, but it may lead to less stress, better health, and even more sex.

So get out the feather duster and fire up the vacuum; it's time to put an end to the "Chore Wars."

Who Does What and Why?

Researchers from the University of Wisconsin have been tracking housework for decades through their National Survey of Families and Households. It's not surprising that stay-at-home wives do more housework than their working husbands. According to the survey data, women who don't work outside the home spend about thirty-eight hours a week on housework. By comparison, their husbands spend about twelve hours a week on household duties, according to the most current data.

But what happens when both husband and wife work outside the home full-time? Working women typically continue to do the bulk of the cooking and cleaning, spending a total of about twenty-eight hours a week on housework. Husbands of working wives contribute about sixteen hours a week to household chores. That means the dual-career couples spend a combined total of forty-four hours a week on housekeeping, and the wife contributes 64 percent of it. Working husbands and stay-at-home wives spend fifty hours a week cleaning the house, and stay-at-home wives provide 76 percent of the work.

Indeed, studies from around the world show that women typically spend at least twice as much time on housework as their husbands. As women spend more time working outside the home, their time on domestic tasks is declining, while men are picking up more, but not all, of the slack.[141]

According to United Nations data, Canadian, Australian, and Swedish men do slightly more housework than U.S. men. Men in Korea and Japan do the least amount of housework, while men in Latvia do the most.

Researchers at the University of Michigan in Ann Arbor have been studying family income dynamics since 1968, using a representative sample that collects data on the economic, health, and social behavior of the same 8,000 U.S. families. Housework in these studies is defined as the routine and mundane chores involved with keeping up a home—washing dishes, laundry, vacuuming, dusting, cooking dinner, and making beds. The nature of the study allows researchers to track how a person's life changes when they marry.

They have found that for women, getting married results in a 70 percent surge in the amount of time she spends on housework. By contrast, men spend about 12 percent less time on household chores after they marry.[142]

The divvying up of housework duties shifts depending on how many hours a week the wife works. Usually, the more hours a woman works, the more men contribute to home chores.

But what happens when women pursue careers and men stay home? Surprisingly there isn't usually a role reversal, with the man doing most of the housework. Instead, when she has a job and he doesn't, the wife still ends up doing most of the housework, says Sampson Lee Blair, an associate professor of sociology at the University at Buffalo who studies the division of labor in families.[143]

Explaining the Housework Gap

Researchers offer various explanations for why men, on average, contribute far less to domestic chores than women.

BRAIN DIFFERENCES

Some researchers believe that the housework gap results from differences in the male and female brain. Male brains typically don't register details, like color and textures, as well as women's do, notes Michael Gurian, author of the book *What Could He Be Thinking?* As a result, housework is often not an immediate priority for men, because they simply don't notice clothes scattered on the floor or magazines strewn on a table.

The explanation for this may be rooted in the earliest days of human couples. Studies by anthropologist George Peter Murdock, who studied labor practices among dozens of tribal societies, give us a sense of how our earliest ancestors divided domestic responsibilities. In tribal societies, certain jobs were overwhelmingly male— things like hunting, fishing, land clearing, and making weapons. Cooking, water carrying, weaving, and pot making typically were female domains.[144] Men were trained to look out to the horizon; women learned to focus on the details in front of them.

It may be that the division of labor for women was determined by whether a child could safely join in. If you're hunting in a kayak, for instance, "you can't have a bunch of kids hanging off you," notes Roy G. D'Andrade, an anthropologist at the University of Connecticut.[145]

The result may be that natural selection pressures resulted in neurobiological differences related to domestic skill. Women who were skilled at keeping children safe and living areas clean, and at preparing and distributing food, were more likely to pass on their genetic material to healthy, stronger children who could survive into adulthood. Men who stuck close to home for too long would have starved and so would their progeny. The men most likely to pass on their genes were those with big-picture skills like hunting, running, hand-eye coordination, and dexterity.

Today, IQ tests show that women are better at picking out details in pictures than men, and those brain differences may explain housework differences, says Sandra Witelson, a neuroscientist at McMaster University. "I think it's not unreasonable to say that this may be a factor in why a man can open a fridge and not see the bottle of wine at the back. We do that better for some reason," says Dr. Witelson.[146]

Obviously, there are exceptions to the rule. Plenty of men who are neat freaks are married to wives who are slobs. And malefemale brain differences don't get men off the hook from helping to keep their cave clean. It just means there could be a neurobiological explanation for why men may not always feel the same sense of urgency to pick up the house as women do.

CULTURAL NORMS

Men and women reinforce the gender-based division of labor in their children. Studies show that when children are small, there are no real differences in the assignment of household chores. A girl is just as likely as a boy to be asked to feed the family dog. And a boy is just as likely to help in the kitchen as a girl.

But as kids enter adolescence, things change. Adolescent girls do about twice as much household labor as adolescent boys, with girls doing more routine chores like cooking and cleaning, and boys doing occasional outside chores like yard care. Researchers say mothers may end up reinforcing the very gender roles they are complaining about now, by socializing young people to specialize in gender-stereotyped housekeeping roles. This also helps explain why men often feel incompetent completing certain household chores like cooking and laundry—their mothers and fathers never taught them how to do these tasks when they were kids.

"Women are trained better to help with the laundry or cooking," says Esther D. Rothblum, a professor of women's studies at San Diego State University. "When women expect their husbands to share the housework it's an uphill battle, because they are probably partnered with someone who wasn't as focused on housework growing up. And he may have been praised for doing very little, such as taking out the garbage."

REDEFINING HOUSEHOLD LABOR

While it's clear that women are doing more of certain domestic tasks, one problem with housework research is that it's often focused on activities that women value, such as cooking, cleaning, feeding, and bath time. But this can create a skewed view of how much time men really spend contributing to the home. A man may focus his after-work energy on bill paying, for instance, rather than laundry. Or he may run errands during his lunch hour, picking up poster board for a child's science project or getting an oil change. And while he may not pack the lunch box, he spends his evenings hanging out with the kids, reading to them or playing video games. But most of the research designed to study the domestic division of labor doesn't count time hanging out with the kids as a contribution to caregiving.

University of Toronto sociologist Judy Beglaubter interviewed men who considered themselves "involved fathers." She asked them to define what it meant to be an involved father.

"None of them said it was because they did the feeding or the diapering or the laundry," she says. "It was just this idea of presence, of being around, of being animated and excited about their children. A lot of them would say, 'The way I father has a lot to do with the way I grew up. My dad was *not* involved, he was very authoritarian, and I didn't want my kid to grow up that way.' For others, it wasn't even a conscious thing—it was more of a drive to participate, to be involved, to interact with their children."[147]

So in a father's mind, simply spending time in the home, kicking a soccer ball with the kids, or taking extra time at the dinner table to talk to them about school counts as being an involved parent. A mother, however, might define parental involvement as shuttling kids to and from school, packing lunch boxes, and scheduling doctors' appointments.

Beyond the research settings, men and women need to take these findings to heart. Before getting frustrated with a spouse for his or her lack of contribution, the question to ask yourself is whether they really are doing nothing or are they just not doing the things *you* care about? Pay attention to all the little chores your partner is doing—like taking out the garbage, cleaning the cat box, changing lightbulbs, getting the car inspected, shuffling the dry cleaning, or dropping off the tax returns at the accountant. These are things you would have to do if your partner didn't do them. They may not be the top priorities on the list, and they may account for only a small portion of the family chores, but they still count.

When Kids Create More Work

Right after my daughter was born, my husband expressed amazement at how easily I took to parenting. He wrote it off as mother's instinct.

But of course that wasn't the case. Taking care of a baby wasn't instinctive, but it also wasn't entirely foreign to me. Like many women, I had helped with my younger sibling as a child, and as a teen I had been a babysitter for many families. As a young adult, I had oohed and aahed over the babies of friends and relatives, holding, feeding, and changing diapers, while my husband just watched. While I had some real-life experience with other people's children, there was still much I didn't know about parenting when my daughter was born. But I read books, talked to my mom, talked to my girlfriends, and asked questions of the hospital nurses and my pediatrician. Mother's instinct, indeed.

Even so, my husband's notion that I was somehow better wired for parenting stuck. I willingly accepted that I was simply better at it, and he willingly ceded to me much of the daily responsibility. The truth is, I liked having the power over all things involving my child, but I also grew to resent his lack of involvement.

This was a surprise to both of us. Before our daughter arrived, we fully expected to share parenting duties. When Philip and Carolyn Cowan talked to couples about how housework and child care would be divided once a baby arrived, they found that, like my husband and me, couples typically had high expectations for each other. Both husband and wife predicted that most domestic duties would be shared. Both parents expected to be involved with raising their child. But after the baby was born, things rarely turned out as planned. Couples reported that the wife ended up doing a far higher percentage of the housework than before motherhood, and fathers were much less involved in the care of the baby than their wives had predicted.

The Cowans developed a "Who Does What" questionnaire to identify how couples divide domestic duties. Before children arrive, men and women are essentially Jacks-and-Jills-of-all-trades around the house. Sometimes he does the laundry and sometimes she takes out the garbage. But once children arrive, couples tend to get more "specialized." Instead of sharing chores, they divide housework into "his" and "her" jobs. She takes care of the children, does the laundry and the dishes, while he does home repairs, takes out the garbage, and takes care of the car. Even if the workload, in terms of time, is pretty even, it often feels traditional because the work has been distributed along traditional gender lines.

"This leaves some husbands and wives feeling more separate," write the Cowans. "Given their shifting internal identities and their vows to be different from their parents, this separation can feel disappointing, a little frightening, and somewhat lonely."[148]

Women around the world bear most of the child care burdens. A study combining data from Australia, Netherlands, and New Zealand found that when children arrive, domestic labor increases twelve hours a week for women, but adds just two hours of extra work a week for men. U.S. studies show that the wife-to-husband ratio for child care is about five to one.[149]

Even though fathers usually expect to share in child care, there are already signs during pregnancy that mothers will shoulder more of certain responsibilities. In the Cowan study, mothers and fathers expected that mothers would be more involved in responding to a baby's cries, getting up in the middle of the night, doing a child's laundry, and choosing the baby's toys.

But in other key areas, husbands and wives both predicted shared responsibility for deciding what and when to feed the baby, changing diapers, bath time, taking the baby out for a stroll, playtime, scheduling babysitters, and talking to the pediatrician. Despite this, by the time the babies reached six months of age, mothers were shouldering a disproportionate share of those duties as well.

The Cowans also learned that couples weren't happy with how the division of labor was breaking down. Mothers expressed much less satisfaction than fathers about the child care arrangements. But fathers also were unhappy, saying that they wanted to be more involved parents, but just couldn't quite figure out how to make it happen.

Between the sixth and eighteenth month of a baby's life, fathers begin to take on more responsibility. They are more likely to take over bath time, take the baby out, and get up with a child at night. The increase is modest, however, and isn't typically accompanied by an increase in men's or women's satisfaction with the division of child care. In fact, men also scale back on other domestic duties in the second year of a child's life. Eighteen months after birth, men are making fewer meals and taking out the garbage less often, although they are doing more shopping and yard work, ostensibly because those are duties they can perform to and from work or on weekends.

Women and Gatekeeping

Years ago, in a column about the work-family juggling act, I wrote about the laundry habits of my friend David. The bottom line: He wasn't a sorter. Instead, he just threw whites and colors into the same wash load and turned the water to cold. He insisted that the low water temperature prevented the colors from bleeding and everything came out perfectly clean.

Meanwhile, David's wife was an avid sorter (I am too, so I felt her pain). The fact that David didn't sort the laundry drove her crazy. She asked him to separate whites and colors so her clothes and those of her three kids wouldn't be ruined, but he refused. It was more than she could stand. She took laundry off of David's chore list and did it herself.

When I wrote about this, I was flooded with reader mail. I heard from countless women who said they saw right through David's tactics. This wasn't about ideological sorting differences, they said. It was intentional incompetence. By sabotaging the laundry, David was setting himself up to fail so that he wouldn't have to do the laundry anymore.

Meanwhile, I heard from an equal number of annoyed men. This wasn't about whites versus colors, they insisted. This was about control. Women can't ask men to share in the housework and then also expect to control how it's done and criticize when it doesn't meet their arbitrary standards. Good for David, they said, for standing up for a man's right to do laundry the way he wants to.

Marriage researchers call this the "maternal gatekeeper" theory. The theory holds that men don't shirk housework because they have different brains. They don't opt for trash and lightbulb duty because they weren't taught how to cook and clean as kids. Instead, they shun housework because women insist on controlling it. While women claim that they want help with household chores, men say that their wives also want to dictate how the chores are done, such as the way a towel is folded, the way a baby is diapered, or the way a dishwasher is loaded. When the man doesn't do it the "right" way, the wives complain, criticize, or do it over themselves. As a result, men get angry, quit, or do it wrong the next time on purpose so they won't be asked to do it again.

"Housework comes up so often in therapy," says Dr. Rothblum of San Diego State. "The woman wants her husband to do more housework, but in some ways, he tends to sabotage it. He either doesn't do it well or he forgets and has to be reminded. And she says, 'You're doing it wrong,' or 'You're holding the baby wrong.' For whatever reason, women are still taking on the responsibility. They don't want to give up that role."

Kerry Daly, a sociologist and professor at the University of Guelph, says that fathers exhibit "tremendous competency" in child care tasks, but often don't get to prove it. He has studied how parents divide child care tasks in the home and has learned that while men are contributing, their wives often are telling them what to do. This ranges from dictating what clothes a child should wear to scheduling playdates during the time the father is in charge.

"If you're the one doing the delegating and thinking ahead, that comes with a fair amount of power in a domestic relationship," says Dr. Daly. "I think women have, at some level, cherished some of that power."

We've all seen countless examples of this and may be guilty of it ourselves. One woman I know who was leaving town gave her husband a three-page, single-spaced memo about how to care for their young sons. It included everything from how many diapers to pack for day care to detailed instructions about cutting a hamburger into small squares and stroking the kids' backs at bedtime to soothe them to sleep.

Her husband says he wasn't bothered by the detailed list and appreciated some of the instructions. But today his wife admits it was "overkill." "He would've figured it out," she concedes.

Marriage researcher Joshua Coleman, author of the book *The Lazy Husband*, says gatekeeping ends up making husbands lazy and causes them to help less, not more.

Linda Duxbury, of the Eric Sprott School of Business at Carleton University, notes that men don't typically micromanage when a woman picks up one of their chores. Dr. Duxbury, who studies work and family issues, said she even found herself gatekeeping in her own home, describing a time when she told her husband, who was making dinner, how to chop the onions.

"He said: 'Linda, I'm either doing it or I'm not,'" recalls Dr. Duxbury.

"Women have to recognize that in some ways we are the authors of our own misfortune," says Dr. Duxbury. "We like to be martyrs. We like to complain."[150]

Housework and Health

Given how often housework can lead to marital conflict, it's no surprise that it can have a direct effect on stress and happiness levels.

Women who shoulder a disproportionate share of domestic responsibility are less happy in their marriages and more vulnerable to depression.[151] Meanwhile, when men contribute to housework, they are less upset when their wives get emotional and even have lower heart rates during conflict. It may be that the type of man who does housework is just more laid back in general, but the finding may also suggest that when men help around the house, there is less conflict and less stress.

Doing more housework is also associated with better physical health for both men and women. It may be that men who are physically fit help more, or it may be that men who contribute more at home have less marital stress, which can lead to better health.

"When a guy does housework, it feels like he cares about what's important to her," says *Lazy Husband* author Joshua Coleman. "It feels like a partnership."

The Pros and Cons of Hired Help

To solve child care and housework demands, couples often decide to hire help in the form of a housekeeper or nanny. But studies show that farming out domestic duties is not always the right solution.

Researchers at the University of Tennessee surveyed eighty-five men and women, all of whom had attained advanced business degrees, about their career and marital satisfaction. The MBAs, all of whom had an average income above $75,000, were mostly in their thirties and forties and had been married for an average of nine years. They answered questions about career, family, and paid and unpaid help at home, and they took tests used to gauge marital happiness, career satisfaction, and negotiating skills.

Two surprising trends emerged. Paying for outside help actually predicted less marital happiness, not more. Although the reasons for this aren't entirely clear, the researchers speculated that outsourcing domestic chores, particularly child care, can add a layer of financial and emotional stress. Another theory is domestic chores give couples a sense of shared accomplishment and togetherness. Perhaps, the researchers speculated, something fundamental to marriage is lost when domestic chores are farmed out.[152]

Here's one example of why hiring help could lead to more marital stress, not less. A wife needs to work late for a few nights and wants to make sure her husband will be home with their young children. He doesn't want to change his plans, so decides to hire a babysitter. He thinks he's come up with the perfect compromise, but she's furious. She's already feeling guilty about how much time she spends away from her children, and she doesn't want to increase the hours they spend with a babysitter. Now she has to decide whether to cancel her work plans or shuffle her kids off on a babysitter once again. Whatever she decides, she'll be unhappy and resent her husband's choice.

Or consider this scenario: A couple tries to plan a weekend to tackle some landscaping, plant flowers, and create a garden. But then work demands and business travel keep interfering, and soon weather changes will make it impossible to get done. As a result, they hire someone else to do the work. It's a reasonable decision, but it's also frustrating, and a lost opportunity for the couple to spend time together.

The second finding of the research showed that a major source of domestic stress stems from an inability to express your needs and win support from your spouse. Couples who learn to negotiate compromises involving household chores and caregiving are happier in both their marriages and their jobs. In the University of Tennessee study, men and women who scored high on tests measuring negotiating skills also showed the highest level of marital happiness. The research suggests that husbands and wives—particularly wives—should look at whether they have adequately expressed their needs and offered a practical compromise to their spouses for better managing family demands.

Indeed, one of the biggest sources of conflict in marriage is *perceived* unfairness—the feeling that labor, money, or emotional resources are not being evenly distributed. Women are more likely to complain of an unequal distribution of household labor than are men.

But is the inequality because men don't want to help? Or could it be that women aren't negotiating a better deal for themselves?

Studies show that even in the workplace, negotiation is a skill that women often lack. According to economist Linda Babcock, men are twice as likely as women to ask for what they want during job negotiations and four times more likely to ask for a salary increase.[153]

Over the years, I've heard many women complaining that their husbands don't help them enough, but when pressed, they admit they haven't actually asked them directly for more help. "I shouldn't have to" is the common response. But these are typically tough working women who would never expect a business colleague to read their minds. In an office setting, they would make their needs known and negotiate better working conditions. But at home, they don't speak up for themselves.

Housework and Sex

At a dinner party I attended, the husband of the hostess began clearing the table. I offered to help, but his wife waved me off. "My husband can do it," she said. "For him, this is foreplay."

It was more than a funny line. Research studies show that for many couples, the division of household chores can influence a couple's sex life.[154]

"The division of labor in the home is a huge indicator of what the health of the marriage really is," says Neil Chethik, author of *VoiceMale—What Husbands Really Think About Their Marriages, Their Wives, Sex, Housework, and Commitment.*

Mr. Chethik surveyed 300 American husbands and found a consistent parallel between housework and sex. When both spouses were satisfied with the way housework was divided, the couple had sex one more day a month compared to couples in which a spouse was unhappy about housework equity. Men whose wives were unhappy with the division of household labor were more likely to have mulled getting a divorce. And they were more than twice as likely to report being cheated on.

"Men said that if they did housework, their wives were happier with them," says Mr. Chethik. "It's a sign that he is appreciating her, thinking about her and caring about her. Those tend to be things that lead to her warming up to him when it comes to sex."

Mr. Chethik noted that the happier wives were with the division of housework, the happier their husbands were with their sex lives. Housework didn't necessarily have to be split 50-50. The key, he said, was that the wife thought the division was fair. And while men obviously care about living in a clean home, Mr. Chethik notes that a woman may place a higher priority on cleaning because she feels that she, not her husband, will be judged poorly if the house is a mess.

Another hindrance to men contributing more at home is that they have more to lose. The leisure time equation is much more negative for men than women. When housework is redistributed more equitably, women *gain* leisure time, but men *lose* it, meaning they may have to give up some other fun pursuit to make more time for chores at home.

Lessons from the Home Front

The broad lesson from the expansive body of research on housework is that housework is about more than just who cooks, cleans, and does the laundry. The division of labor in a home tells us about the overall dynamics of the relationship and whether a marriage is truly based on partnership. Most studies of housework and marriage show that men need to contribute more to housework and child raising. Women continue to take on a disproportionate share of the domestic responsibility. But sometimes it's their choice. Research also shows that women act as gatekeepers and like to maintain control of the home. For men to contribute more, women also need to back off and allow men to step in and do it their own way, without supervision or criticism. It sounds simple enough but it's a big step. It's difficult for a woman to give up control over her home, in part, because she believes family members and friends typically will judge her housekeeping abilities, not his, if the house is a mess. And often, she is right.

Given that housework is one of the main sources of conflict between couples, focusing on the distribution of labor in your home can lead to dramatic changes in the overall quality of your marriage. And unlike other sources of marital stress—such as in-laws, job worries, or financial issues—housework is something over which you have a fair amount of control. Often small efforts are all that is needed to make a big impact. One woman I know pointed out that she doesn't really need extra help with most of her domestic chores. Her main source of frustration is that her husband doesn't help her get the children ready for school each morning. It's a fifteen-minute investment of his time that would pay huge dividends in terms of improving their relationship. What's important to remember about housework and relationships is that resolving the chore wars with your spouse isn't just going to leave you with a cleaner house. You'll also have a better marriage.

CHAPTER 10

For Richer or for Poorer:
When Money Problems Become
Marriage Problems

The sum which two married people owe to one another defies calculation. It is an infinite debt. . . .

—JOHANN WOLFGANG VON GOETHE

We marry for love (most of the time). But much of what happens in a marriage is also about money.

While that sounds crass, marriage is, at its most basic, a financial relationship. That's not to say love and romance aren't essential. Of course they are. But money is always a factor in relationships. Where we live, how we spend our time, the jobs we choose, how much or little we work, whether and when we have children and how we raise them, and even whether we stay married or get divorced—all of these aspects of marriage are ultimately financial as well as relationship decisions.

Centuries ago, marriage was, indisputably, a financial union, a way for families to build wealth, acquire real estate, and gain or maintain social status. The dowry often was a man's main road to accumulating wealth before his parents died, and it was a woman's main source of survival if something happened to her husband. Sometimes love was part of the marriage package too—but often romance was just a side effect of a strategic economic coupling.

Much has changed in the past century. Now most couples in the developed world marry for love. Even in countries where arranged marriages are the norm, the love-based marriage is increasingly common.

But money still matters. Even when family matchmakers aren't involved, couples still tend to match up under the principle of "positive assortative mating," which means we tend to marry people like ourselves. As a result, highly educated, higher-earning men tend to pair with highly educated, higher-earning women. Less educated and lower-income men tend to pair with less educated, lower-income women.

Even though people of similar economic status tend to marry each other, that doesn't mean they don't fight about money. Studies consistently show that money is one of the main sources of conflict in a marriage. Debt is a biggie. How much debt each individual brings into a marriage is the number one reason newlywed couples argue. Some studies show that Americans spend up to 80 percent of their waking hours focused on some version of a money issue, whether it's earning a paycheck or fretting about how to pay a bill.[155] For couples, financial problems and debt are linked to higher stress and lower levels of marital satisfaction.[156]

The reality is that while marriage is about love and family, it's also about money—managing it, spending it, and accumulating it. Couples grappling with the everyday decisions of marriage are really making choices that can reinforce or weaken both their relationship and their finances. The bottom line: If you solve your money problems, you'll go a long way toward solving—or preventing—marital problems.

The Economics of Marriage

Marriage builds wealth.

Not only can two people live more cheaply than one, but two people also can earn more. It's not just the obvious benefit of combining wages. By sharing domestic chores, people who are married can be more productive in wage-earning tasks. And when one partner stays home, the additional domestic support allows the other spouse to dedicate more time, energy, and resources to earning money.

Ohio State University researcher Jay Zagorsky compared the financial status of 9,055 married and unmarried people. The nationally representative sample focused on people who were in their twenties at the start of the study, and the researchers tracked them for fifteen years, from 1985 to 2000.

Those in the sample who remained single showed a slow and steady growth in wealth, posting an average increase of $11,000 after fifteen years. But those who got married and stayed married posted even bigger gains. Gains in wealth grew to an average of about $43,000 by the tenth year of marriage. Married people built more wealth more quickly than single people.

Dr. Zagorsky, a research scientist at Ohio State University's Center for Human Resource Research, calculated that just getting married (and controlling for other variables) resulted in an average increase in wealth of about 4 percent each year.

Notably, the financial gains of marriage are more than just combining the assets of two single people. And divorce causes a drop in wealth that is greater than just splitting a couple's assets in two, says Dr. Zagorsky.

Getting married essentially doubles a person's wealth compared to staying single. And getting divorced decreases a person's wealth by about 77 percent.

"If you really want to increase your wealth," says Dr. Zagorsky, "get married and stay married."[157]

While some of the wealth of married couples results from their ability to pool their time and resources toward a common good (earning, saving, and investing money), that's not the whole story. Social and legal biases also favor the married.

Studies show that married people receive more money from family members than single people. A married couple is widely viewed as more stable than a single person or even couples who are "just" living together.

Government and employer rules also favor the married. Consider the following financial perks of being married:

Workplace benefits: Most employers offer health and pension benefits to the spouses of workers. And even if a firm offers benefits to a domestic partner, there is still an advantage to being married. In the United States for instance, health coverage for a domestic partner is taxed as income, while the benefit is tax-free for a spouse.

Survivor benefits: A husband or wife typically is entitled to survivor benefits. In the case of U.S. Social Security, for example, a surviving husband or wife receives one-half of their spouse's social security benefits and extra benefits after a spouse dies.

Lower insurance rates: Married people often pay lower rates for auto and other types of insurance than single people.

Estate and inheritance rights: A spouse typically has a legal right to some percentage of a partner's estate, with or without a will. In the United States a surviving spouse has a legal right to at least one-third to one-half of the estate. And unlike people who aren't married, a spouse typically doesn't have to pay estate taxes when money and property is willed to them.

Despite all the financial benefits of marriage, the timing of marriage also matters, particularly for women.

The ability to focus on education and spend long hours at the office early in a career is rewarded, so women who don't have child care or marital demands at home reap gains early in their careers from which they continue to benefit years later. Studies show for every year that a woman delays having her first child, her lifetime earnings rise by ten percent.

But marital finance is about more than just accumulating wealth. It's also about juggling competing needs and desires, providing for family members, and making decisions about how and when to spend money.

The Work-Family Juggling Act

Managing the competing demands of work and family life is a regular source of stress for married couples. He has a meeting, she has a business trip, and the babysitter called in sick. Who picks the kids up from school and shuttles them to soccer practice and dance class? In one national study, 83 percent of working mothers and 72 percent of working fathers reported experiencing conflict between the demands of their jobs and their desire to spend time with their families.[158]

Juggling career and family affects men and women differently. Women in dual-career families are typically less satisfied with their "personal growth" and careers than are men. Studies show women's careers tend to be secondary to their husbands'. As a result, women's career opportunities and chances for advancement tend to be more limited because of conflicts with their role as wife and family caretaker.[159]

However, some research suggests that work-family conflicts are beginning to cause more distress for men than for women. In one study, men and women who were married or had children were asked, "How much do your job and family life interfere with each other?"

In 1977, women clearly were struggling more with the issue—41 percent of women and 34 percent of men reported some or a lot of work-family interference. But in 2002, the same question was posed to working families. Surprisingly, 46 percent of men complained of work-family stress, compared to 41 percent of women.[160]

This doesn't mean husbands are juggling more of the family burdens than women. More likely it reflects the fact that family life has become a bigger priority for this generation of men compared to their counterparts in the 1970s. While women for years have developed support systems and strategies to help with the work-family juggle, it's only recently that men have been expected to take a bigger role at home. As a result, men are still struggling to figure out the balancing act between work and home responsibilities.

When She's the Breadwinner

When I was growing up in the 1970s, my parents had fairly traditional roles. My father was a military pilot and away a lot. A disproportionate share of the parenting duties fell to my mother. But in the early 1980s, my father stopped flying and we settled into life in Dayton, Ohio. With the family's four kids in middle school and high school, my mother had more freedom from family duties and decided to embark on a career in real estate. She did this with my father's full support—he was thrilled to have the extra income.

But what neither my mother nor my father expected was how wildly successful my mother would be at her new career. She gained a loyal following among her clients, who showered her with referrals. Before long she was the top-selling real estate agent at her firm and then in the city. My formerly insecure mother gained confidence. Clients called in the evening, weekends, and on holidays and my mother was devoted to meeting their needs. As a military wife who had moved dozens of times in her life, she had a unique understanding of the stress involved with moving and finding a new home, and I've always believed her empathy with her clients was the secret to her success.

The money she was bringing in created new opportunities for the family, giving my sisters a chance to attend better colleges, allowing my parents to buy a secondhand Chrysler Cordoba for the teens in the family to drive, and we even managed a few family vacations that had never been possible on my father's military salary alone. For the first time in their marriage, my parents didn't worry about money. But it put a tremendous strain on their relationship. My mother wasn't financially dependent on my father. In fact, she was making more money than he was.

Eventually, when my father retired from the air force, he made the decision to take a job in Texas. The pay was better than what he'd earned in the military, but moving would force my mother to quit her career. The overall family income would drop, but my father still insisted on the move.

My mother passed away a few years ago, and my father and I were talking about her life. The subject of her successful real estate career came up, and I asked him why he had uprooted her, rather than finding a job in Ohio. He shrugged his shoulders and admitted that after so many years as the primary breadwinner, it had been difficult to cede the role to her. He was still unable to explain why the whole experience had been so hard on their relationship.

Today, about one in three married women earns more money than her husband.[161] It's widely believed that a woman's financial independence increases divorce risk. But the reality is that as women have made economic gains, divorce rates have dropped. The divorce rate peaked in the late 1970s at 23 divorces per 1,000 couples, but it has dropped to about 17 divorces per 1,000 couples.[162] Typically, the more economic independence a woman gains, the more likely she is to stay married. And in states where fewer wives have paid jobs, divorce rates tend to be higher.[163]

Why would a woman's financial independence keep couples together? When women don't have to marry for financial security, they can be more selective and enjoy more negotiating power once married. The result can be a marriage that is more equitable to both husbands and wives.

But it's not always easy to get there. Some men feel emasculated by a wife's greater earning power and the expectation to do more housework. Many working women find it difficult to cede domestic duties to a husband who doesn't clean or do laundry exactly the same way she would.

The shifting economics of marriage appear to take the biggest toll on older men. Rutgers sociologist Kristen W. Springer has found that among men in their fifties, having a wife who earns more money is associated with poorer health. Among the highest earning couples, a husband of a female breadwinner is 60 percent less likely to be in good health when compared to male breadwinners.[164]

But for many working couples, the biggest challenge centers around who does the *unpaid* work—the cooking, cleaning, and childcare that has traditionally been performed by women.

Lynn Prince Cooke, a professor of sociology at the University of Kent in the United Kingdom, studied couples who first married in the 1980s and 1990s. The couples at lowest risk for divorce were those where the wife earned about 40 percent of the income while the husband contributed about 40 percent of the housework. Divorce risk rises the more a woman earns and the more housework a man does, but the risk is still lower than a traditional male breadwinner-female homemaker marriage. The highest risk couples are those in which the wife earns more than 80 percent of the income and the husband does most of the housework. The findings suggest that an unfair housework burden, whether it's on a wife or husband, puts a marriage at risk.[165]

Since the 1960s, men's contributions to housework have doubled, while the time men spend caring for children has tripled. But even among dual-earning couples, women, on average, still do about two-thirds of the housework. Why are women, who often are working outside the home as much or more than their husbands, still doing most of the housework?

Social scientists speculate that this may be due to men and women engaging in "compensatory" behavior—by doing less housework men are asserting their masculinity as a way to compensate for the fact that they aren't the family's main provider. By comparison, women, sensing the husbands' sensitivity on the issue, may pick up extra home duties as a way to reassure their husbands about their relative family roles.

However, more recent research suggests the trend begins to shift the more money a woman earns. Sanjiv Gupta, professor at the University of Massachusetts–Amherst, has found that the amount of housework a woman performs isn't influenced by her husband's income, but instead is dictated by her own earnings. Among married women who work full-time, every additional $7,500 in wages corresponds to one less hour of housework per week, says Dr. Gupta. Women who are among the highest 10 percent of wage earners perform nine fewer hours of housework a week compared to women on the opposite end of the spectrum, those who are among the lowest 10 percent of wage earners.

Dr. Gupta notes that the findings show the importance that class differences have on housework duties. Women who are low earners do nearly sixteen more hours of weekly housework than their husbands. Higher-earning women also do more housework than their husbands, but they have narrowed the gender gap, performing about five more hours of domestic chores than their partners.

One interesting footnote to Dr. Gupta's research is the fact that overall family income doesn't influence how much housework a woman does. A high combined family income doesn't reduce a woman's housework. It's only when the woman's own income is high that her housework drops—suggesting that only a woman's earnings are used to hire outside help.

"This is surprising, given that the daily work of providing nutrition, clean clothing, and a sanitary environment benefits everyone in a household," writes Dr. Gupta. "It suggests that both men and women still tend to feel that it is the woman's responsibility to organize such chores, though she may use her money to farm them out."[166]

Tightwads Versus Spendthrifts

Early in my own relationship, it became clear that my husband and I had very different values about money. I was a saver and cautious with my funds. I had worked two jobs for nearly a year before college to save for my education and become financially independent of my parents to help me qualify for financial aid, and worked part-time throughout college. My husband, meanwhile, had grown up in a family that regularly took big vacations. He enjoyed dining out and travel and believed that you worked hard so that you had enough money to pay for the fun stuff. I wanted nothing more than to own my own home. He wanted to travel, enjoy museums and theater, and eat at the finest restaurants.

While it sounds like a recipe for disaster, it didn't seem that way when we met. I knew I needed to lighten up and enjoy life more. On our second date, he treated me to a meal at one of Austin's finest restaurants. I still remember the dish—salmon with champagne sauce—because it was nothing like the Red Lobster meals I had grown up with. And he appreciated my skill at saving and bill paying and knew that he needed to plan more for a future. He spent. I saved. Together, it felt like a balanced match.

But neither of us realized how fundamental shared values about finances can be to a good marriage, and once the honeymoon was over, our disagreements about spending began to take a toll. One of the qualities that had drawn us to each other ended up being one of our greatest sources of stress.

New research shows we weren't alone. Although in most cases, men and women gravitate to partners who have qualities similar to their own, in the realm of money, opposites appear to attract. Free-spenders or "spendthrifts," it turns out, are attracted to savers or "tightwads."

Why would a saver be attracted to a spender and vice versa? The authors of the study speculate that people on the extremes of spending and saving often dislike their own attitudes about money. As a result, a tightwad likely would be turned off by a fellow tightwad. In the early stages of courtship, a tightwad would enjoy the free-spending ways of her date. A spendthrift might appreciate being reined in by a woman who is more practical about money than he is.[167]

The problem is that we're not well served by our instincts. Spendthrifts and tightwads are destined for a life of conflict when they marry each other. There is, of course, the opportunity for both sides to meet in the middle, but often, values about money are rooted in family experience and too deeply entrenched to change much. That was certainly the case in my own relationship. Money quickly became one of the biggest sources of stress in our marriage.

Investing in Your Marriage

The data from much of the research on marriage and money suggest that couples who solve their money problems go a long way toward solving their marital problems.

If you find yourself regularly arguing about money, disagreeing how to spend it, or fighting for control over it, it's time to make solving your money woes a priority in your marriage. If you're not sure, answer the questions later in this chapter to determine how dominant the money problems are in your marriage. There is no single formula or one-size-fits-all strategy to determine how much of a risk money problems present to your relationship. It all depends on how much money you make, how much you spend, and how much stress those issues cause you and your spouse.

Couples who feel like money has become a serious problem in their relationship should seek the guidance of a financial planner to help them get to the root of their money problems and develop a plan for extricating themselves.

To Merge or Not to Merge?

Couples commonly ask questions about the logistics of merging finances and managing money. Some couples find it works best to keep separate checking accounts, with each couple contributing a share proportionate to their earnings to a joint account each month. Other couples prefer to pool all their resources in one single account, while others prefer to completely separate accounts. Unfortunately, there are limited data to guide couples about which is the best strategy. A 1993 study by Dr. Lawrence Kurdek of Wright State University found that maintaining separate finances was a risk factor for divorce.[168] A 1995 study in Britain found that equality between husband and wife was greatest where money was pooled and managed jointly.[169] The limited data seem to favor merging a couple's finances. But in the 1993 report, it's not clear whether the decision to keep separate accounts led to a troubled relationship or whether the relationship was already flawed, prompting the man and woman to maintain financial autonomy. In the British study, couples who merged their finances had a more equal relationship, but it may

simply be that couples who view a marriage as an equal partnership
are more comfortable combining their accounts. Whatever system
a couple agrees on, financial planners say both husbands and wives
always need to stay abreast of the couple's overall financial picture.

In another study of money management in early marriage, the
investigators discovered that many couples change their financial
strategies over time.[170] Before the wedding, most couples keep their
money separate, and many continue to keep separate accounts in
the early years. But often, major life decisions like buying a house
or having a child lead to a change and couples begin pooling their
assets. Couples who continue to keep separate accounts often do so
as a way to maintain autonomy. The researchers found that keeping separate accounts was particularly disadvantageous to women
who later decided to reduce their work hours or quit outside work
altogether once children arrived.[171]

While each couple's personal situation will vary, there are two
pieces of consistent financial advice marriage counselors and financial planners will give you.

The first: Maintain a little independence. While it's important
to pool your resources and solve your money problems together,
both partners should have the option of spending money on things
that make them happy, even if their partner frowns on it. If you
focus on your specific spending priorities—maybe it's clothes shopping, a weekly poker game, or tickets to a sporting event—then
it's also easier to share equally in the sacrifice when you're cutting
back. Instead of six games this season, maybe you'll only attend
three. Instead of spending hundreds of dollars on clothes shopping,
maybe you can choose just a few special pieces.

The second priority is important but often forgotten as couples
are sorting out their money troubles. One of the best places where
you can spend your money is on your marriage. This means investing in your time together, planning vacations and fun dates and

evenings out. Depending on your budget and money problems, you may have to scale back—instead of a weeklong vacation in Europe, you may have to settle on driving to a nearby bed-and-breakfast. Research shows that spending time together, traveling and engaging in new activities, is an important way to boost the health of your marriage.

Remember, though, that fights about money often are symbolic—of a power struggle or lack of alignment in values. Facing up to the areas of conflict is always better than not, and can lead to a more engaged relationship—or warn you away from the wrong one.

Lessons on Love and Money

When heart disease researchers set out to study the lifestyle factors that might influence stress and overall health, they discovered what many married couples have always known: Money is a major source of conflict in a relationship. The heart researchers asked 4,000 men and women their top reasons for arguing with a wife or husband. For both men and women, money was among the top three reasons for fighting with a spouse. Financial problems are also among the most-cited reasons when couples get divorced.

Why is money such a big source of marital strife? When people argue about finances, they aren't really disagreeing about dollars and cents. Money conflicts are about values, goals, and priorities, and if you're fighting about money, it means you and your partner aren't in sync about some of the most basic values affecting your relationship.

Building a life together means making plans, setting goals, and heading toward something at least as good as, or better than, what you have now. Money often is a barometer for how close or far we are from those goals. Are you hoping for a bigger home or a kitchen remodel? Do you like to take family vacations once or twice a year?

Do you like to eat out or stay in and cook at home? Will your children go to private school or public? Will you help them pay for an Ivy League education or are student loans in their future? Will your planning allow you to retire early and travel the world together?

In a national study of more than 21,000 couples, David H. Olson, a longtime relationship researcher and professor emeritus of family social science at the University of Minnesota, attempted to identify the signs of a strong marriage. He found that even happy couples disagree more about money than about any other topic. But for troubled couples, money disputes lead to frequent and heated disagreements.[172]

Dr. Olson determined that there are five simple questions that can help you determine whether money is a major issue of conflict in your relationship. Take his quiz to see how your answers compare to those of the couples in the survey.

The *For Better* Quiz #10: Financial Strengths of Happy Couples

Read the following statements and note whether you agree or disagree. Don't rush, and give each question some thought. The answers will help you understand whether money and debt are positive or negative factors in your relationship.

1. We agree on how to spend money.
2. I have no concerns about how my partner handles money.
3. We are satisfied with our decisions about saving.
4. Major debts are not a problem.
5. Making financial decisions is not difficult.

What was your score? The statements are actually a litmus test for the level of happiness in your marriage. Happy couples will agree with at least four of the statements. When couples disagree with three or more of the above statements, they are also far more likely to score low on overall marital happiness tests. Here's how happy versus unhappy couples scored on the national survey.

Among couples who scored high on marital happiness tests:

89 percent agreed on how to spend money.

80 percent said they had no concerns about how their partner handles money.

73 percent were satisfied with their decisions about saving.

76 percent said major debts were not a problem.

80 percent said making financial decisions was not difficult.

Among couples who scored low on marital happiness tests, it was clear that money problems were creating problems in their marriage. Among these couples:

59 percent did not agree on how to spend money.

68 percent were concerned about how their partner handles money.

71 percent weren't satisfied with savings decisions.

65 percent said major debts were a problem.

68 percent said making financial decisions was difficult.

Source: National Survey of Marital Strengths, 2003

My own score on this test would have been highly predictive of a troubled relationship. How many of the statements would my husband and I have agreed with? None of them. But if you'd asked either of us during the course of our marriage, neither of us would have cited money disagreements as our biggest problem.

Debt, in particular, can have a profound effect on a marriage. Indebtedness is a major reason couples delay marriage. Nearly three-quarters of men and women bring debt into their marriage, primarily in the form of credit card bills, student loans, medical bills, and car loans. And studies show debt is the number one source of marital strife for newlyweds and a common reason for delaying children.

Among couples who score high on marital happiness tests, a distinguishing characteristic is that they typically do not have major debt problems. Happy couples have fewer worries about money and agree on the proper amount to save. Stop for a minute and think about what this finding means to your own relationship happiness. *If you solve your debt problems, you will go a long way to solving your marital problems.*

Dr. Olson's survey revealed that most money problems occur because one partner thinks the other should be more careful about spending. The problem is most pronounced when couples have married at an older age, and aren't used to having to discuss financial decisions with another person.

But sometimes spending by one spouse can occur without his or her partner's knowledge. It's called "financial infidelity," and marriage counselors say it breaches trust and ruins marriages. Secret spending is surprisingly common. A survey by the finance company GMAC found that in one-third of 2,800 households surveyed, men and women admitted to hiding at least one purchase from their spouse. Spending on clothes, hobby-related items, and gambling were the most common things spouses admitted to hiding from each other.

Even when spending is under control, Dr. Olson's survey showed that couples struggle to agree about how much to save, setting priorities and power over the purse strings. Here's another quiz that Dr. Olson used to measure how financial conflict affects a relationship.

The *For Better* Quiz #11: How Money Can Hurt Your Marriage

Read the following statements and note whether you agree or disagree. Don't rush, and give each question some thought. The answers will help you understand to what extent money issues are contributing to marital conflict.

1. I wish my partner were more careful in spending money.
2. We have trouble saving money.
3. We have problems deciding what is more important to purchase.
4. Major debts are a problem for us.
5. My partner tries to control the money.

How many of these questions did you answer yes to? If you answered yes to even one, financial worries are likely taking a toll on your marriage. In the national survey, couples who scored low on marital satisfaction tests also were far more likely to be struggling with these financial stumbling blocks.

72 percent wished a partner were more careful in spending money.

72 percent said they had trouble saving money.

66 percent had problems deciding what was more important to purchase.

56 percent said major debts were a problem.

51 percent said a partner tried to control the money.

Source: National Survey of Marital Strengths, 2003

The main money lesson from the 21,000-couple survey is that even happy couples argue about money issues. But the happiest couples are those who have learned to agree on how to spend money and make joint financial decisions, and who are not saddled with debt.

Summing Up Marital Struggle

Even the best marriages have their bad moments, those difficult times that remind you of the "for worse" part of your marriage vow. But the lessons from marriage scientists teach us that identifying the areas of difficulty in your marriage and setting them straight is not as complicated as many experts have led us to believe. Often, couples who are struggling in a marriage are focusing on the wrong things. Every marriage, of course, will include some degree of conflict. The challenge is not to stop fighting, but to learn how to fight with your spouse. Couples who know how to argue are able to use conflict not only to resolve issues but to strengthen, rather than weaken, their relationship. Don't focus on how much you fight or what you fight about. Think instead about the words you use, how fights begin and end, and whether you are being critical, accusatory, and harsh, or are raising legitimate complaints in a nonthreatening manner. Once you learn how to better manage your conflict, you'll have a framework for resolving the main issues about which you bicker—things like parenting, housework, and money.

The good news is that there are ways to improve your odds of solving your problems and staying married. As you'll see in Part III, marriage researchers have identified various risk factors for divorce, and they have also developed several prescriptions for marital health—proactive steps you and your spouse can take to boost the health and happiness of your relationship.

part iii

From This Day Forward

CHAPTER 11

Your Better Half:
Overcoming Gender Roles
and Power Struggles

If you would marry suitably, marry your equal.

—OVID

In a study comparing work and family roles among 150 couples,[173] Mount Holyoke professor Francine M. Deutsch stumbled across two couples with similar career paths. In each case a doctor had married a college professor. In the first couple, the wife was the professor, and both she and her husband had agreed that his job as a doctor was far less flexible than hers.

But in the second couple, the husband was the college professor, and the wife was a doctor. And guess what? They also both agreed that his job, as a college professor, was far less flexible than her job as a doctor.

Many men and women will say they value equality in relationships, but the challenge is making it happen in real life, where husbands and wives often default to traditional gender roles. Why is equality in a marriage such a difficult ideal? What role does gender play in the way couples communicate and divide marital responsibility? Is a 50-50 marriage really desirable or even possible?

For answers to these questions, marriage researchers have turned their attention to two types of couples who have broken the traditional marriage mold. The first group of couples who are offering new insights about gender and relationships may surprise you—they are gay and lesbian couples. Given that same-sex marriage isn't legal in most places, it's hard to believe there's much to be learned from gay and lesbian partners. But a large body of scientific literature on same-sex relationships offers important insights about how couples interact and the husband-wife dynamic in particular. Gay couples, by definition, don't have to deal with gender differences. And when gay couples are studied in the laboratory alongside heterosexual couples, it becomes clear how often gender issues define—and undermine—a marriage.

The second type of marriage under scrutiny by relationship researchers is the 50-50 marriage. These couples are rare and are distinguished by the fact that they truly have a 50-50 division of home, work, and parenting responsibilities that doesn't break down along gender lines. For many couples, practical, social, and logistical reasons prevent them from having this type of relationship, but there are still lessons to be learned from 50-50 couples about issues of gender, equity, and fairness that often get in the way of a happy relationship.

When Gender Isn't Part of the Fight

Longtime marriage researcher Robert W. Levenson, a professor of psychology at the University of California–Berkeley, had spent his career studying how husbands and wives interact. He and his colleague, John Gottman at the University of Washington, had pioneered the use of video recording and the coding of conversations to predict, with surprising accuracy, the stability of relationships.

Many of the patterns that emerged, however, consistently broke down along gender lines.

"There were these very reliable differences between men and women and the way they dealt with negative emotions in particular," says Dr. Levenson. "Women would want to talk about problems and keep on pressing to resolve conflict. Men would want to get far away and didn't seem to be able to tolerate dealing with those issues. It seemed so sex bound."

But was it? How much of these patterns was based in biology and what could be attributed to socialization and cultural gender roles? There was only one way to find out: Study couples in which gender differences were impossible.

Dr. Levenson, Dr. Gottman, and several colleagues embarked on a twelve-year study comparing cohabiting and married couples, both gay and straight. The researchers videotaped and monitored conflict discussions among same-sex couples, just as they had done in earlier studies of straight couples. The same-sex pairs were asked to talk about a routine topic and then later prompted to discuss a topic of ongoing disagreement. As it turned out, many of the findings were unremarkable. Just like straight couples, gay couples in long-term relationships love, parent, disagree, argue, split up, and stay together.

But when the researchers compared the interactions of gay couples with those of straight couples, some of the differences were striking. In video after video it became clear that conflict style is dramatically different when two members of the same sex are involved in the discussion.[174]

When the researchers dissected the video footage, they found that arguments between two men or two women contained fewer verbal attacks, compared to conflicts between opposite-sex couples. And in same-sex relationships, each partner made more of an effort to defuse the confrontation. The use of controlling and hostile emotional tactics, like belligerence and domineering, also were

less common among gay couples. And the same-sex couples were
far more positive, and less likely to be negative, than opposite-sex
married couples. In short, same-sex couples appeared to fight more
fairly than opposite-sex pairs.

Even the physical reactions exhibited by the men and women
in the study were different. Same-sex couples were less likely to
develop an elevated heartbeat and adrenaline surges during arguments, compared to straight couples. And gay couples get over their
fights more quickly, and don't take barbs leveled during arguments
so personally. Heterosexual husbands and wives were more likely
to stay physically agitated after a conflict.

"When they got into these really negative interactions, gay and
lesbian couples were able to do things like use humor and affection
that enabled them to step back from the ledge and continue to talk
about the problem instead of just exploding," said Dr. Levenson.

There was one important area where gay men fared worse than
straight or lesbian couples. This was in the "repair" portion of conflict.
Straight and lesbian couples were better at smoothing over the rough
edges left by a fight. Notably, in heterosexual relationships, women
also tend to be more skilled at repairing these rifts than men.

When Couples Struggle for Power

There was another unexpected finding from the study of same-
sex couples. A common dynamic among married couples is called
the "pursuer-distancer" or "demand-withdrawal" style of conflict
discussion. In these types of marriages, one partner brings up a
problem and begins to demand change. But talking about marital
problems fills the other partner with dread, and he or she resists
talking and escapes by reading the newspaper, turning on the television set, or taking up a mundane household task. The short-term
escape leads to anger about being "nagged." The other partner also

gets fed up and withdraws, and feels resentment for not being listened to. This is a dangerous pattern and is the type of marriage most prone to unhappiness and divorce.

In 80 percent of these types of marriages, the person making the demands or "pursuing" is the woman. She is eager to confront and discuss problems. The man typically is the one to withdraw, avoid confrontation, and assume the "distancer" role. Relationship researchers have long believed this demand-withdraw pattern is rooted in gender. Women have been raised to communicate, discuss, and express their feelings. Men typically are taught to withhold their emotions and retreat from conflict.

But when Berkeley psychology researcher Sarah R. Holley reviewed videotaped conflict discussions among sixty-three straight, gay, and lesbian couples, she discovered that the demand-withdraw conflict style showed up equally among all the couples, whether gay or straight. The finding suggests that gender is not the reason one person in a relationship begins to make demands for change and the other withdraws. The real issue, she says, is power.[175]

Where does power in a relationship come from? Power tends to be gained by the partner who has greater resources. It may be better education, a better job, higher income, and greater social status. Imagine a couple in which one person has a very high income while the other partner has a lower-paying job or doesn't work outside the home. Decisions about how to spend the money, whether to take an extravagant family vacation, and what kind of car to buy may be discussed between the partners, but ultimately the higher earning partner will make the final decision or have veto power. Studies show that among gay men, older and wealthier men had more power in the relationship.[176] The American Couples study showed that income is an extremely important force in determining which partner in a gay relationship will be dominant.

The same is true if there is an imbalance of social status. Imagine

a couple in which one partner is a schoolteacher and one is a politi-
cian, writer, or actor who is better known and has a larger social
circle of equally high-status friends and colleagues. The partner
with the more glamorous job and set of friends will typically prevail
when it comes to making social plans, giving him or her an additional power advantage in the relationship.

Power also can be decided by how much each partner depends
on the relationship for personal happiness. If one partner is strongly
attached, while the other is more ambivalent, then the ambivalent
partner holds the power. An attached partner who "can't live" without his or her partner is more likely to compromise. The ambivalent
partner will hold out for what he or she wants because the consequences of a fight or breakup don't matter as much.

How do you know who has the power in a relationship? One way
to know is to pay attention to a couple's communication patterns.
In conversation, who interrupts? Who gets interrupted? Instances
of conversational dominance, such as interrupting a partner in the
middle of a sentence, are a sign that the relationship has a power
imbalance.[177]

But the main indication of a power imbalance is that one person
is making demands that are ignored or rejected by the other.

"The reason anyone complains in a relationship is because the status quo is not fulfilling them," notes Dr. Levenson. "People who are
unhappy in their relationship nag. And people who are still getting
their way don't have any real investment in giving away their power."

The lesson from same-sex couples research is that couples
shouldn't blame gender differences when they experience this type
of power imbalance. "Like everybody else, I thought this was about
male behavior and female behavior," notes Dr. Levenson. "But what
this study teaches us is that it's not 'just how men are' or 'just how
women are.' So it means there is a lot more hope that you can do
something about it."

Understanding Your Spouse's Point of View

Dr. Glenn Roisman, assistant professor of psychology at the University of Illinois at Urbana-Champaign, conducted a study of 259 couples that was unusual for its inclusion of so many different types of relationships. The study tracked 109 couples who were dating, 50 who were engaged, 40 older married couples, and 60 gay and lesbian couples. Overall, gay couples were just as attached and committed to each other as opposite-sex couples.[178] He also found that lesbian couples were more skilled at resolving conflict than straight couples and male same-sex couples.

But Dr. Roisman added an interesting twist to his research. In studying a couple's communication style, he wanted to know whether gender or sexuality was the distinguishing factor for these couples. He decided to pair off men and women who didn't know each other. In a laboratory experiment, he asked pairs of same-sex and opposite-sex strangers to work together to solve a complex three-dimensional puzzle.

The same-sex stranger pairs worked more effectively together than opposite-sex stranger pairs. Whether or not individuals are romantically involved, they appear to work better with a member of the same sex.

"The advantages that same-sex romantically involved couples have in terms of conflict resolution may stem less from something related to sexual orientation per se, and have more to do with the gender makeup of these couples," said Dr. Roisman. "It may simply be easier to resolve conflict with someone of the same sex."

That doesn't mean opposite-sex couples will always be at a disadvantage when it comes to working out relationship problems. It just means that heterosexual couples need to work harder to see a partner's point of view. Research shows that heterosexuals who can relate to their partner's concerns and who are skilled at diffusing arguments do just as well in conflict resolution as same-sex couples. Perspective, says Dr. Levenson, appears to be the "active ingredient" in stable relationships.

"The best advice is to try to get that perspective, get that kind of understanding, and try to see the conflict through the eyes of the other person," he said. "For heterosexual couples, that might be more work."

The Importance of Outside Relationships

One striking characteristic of same-sex couples is that the individuals involved typically have a strong network of friendships outside the relationship. In many heterosexual relationships, the husband and wife take an insular view, focusing most on each other and their children—often to the detriment of their relationships with extended family and friends. This ends up putting an enormous amount of pressure on husbands and wives to be "everything" to their partner.

But gays and lesbians, perhaps because their own family members sometimes struggle to accept them, tend to develop an extensive network of friends and be deeply involved in their communities.

"Same sex couples, singles, lesbians, and gay men aren't living in a nuclear family," says Dr. Esther D. Rothblum, the professor of women's studies at San Diego State University. "They are very interconnected with their community of same sex friends, they attend film festivals and book readings and any number of events. It's this wonderful sort of web of people. Just being a lesbian gives you an automatic membership in a community. That's something heterosexual couples don't have."

The result, says Dr. Rothblum, is that gay couples often have several outlets to cope with the stress of a relationship. "Heterosexual men tend to say their wife is their best friend or their only friend," says Dr. Rothblum. "If anything happens to the wife, or she breaks up with him, he's lost his entire community. I think it's healthier when you have certain things you do with your friends and people to whom you can complain on the phone. And then you have your partner. It's a more diverse way of dealing with stress when it happens."

Sociologists Naomi Gerstel of the University of Massachusetts–Amherst and Natalia Sarkisan at Boston College have found that married people have fewer ties to relatives than people who aren't married. They are less likely to visit or call their parents and other family members, compared to relatives who are single. Marriage also cuts a couple's ties to the larger community. Married people are less likely to socialize with neighbors or help out their friends. And married people are less likely to be politically active, whether it's attending a rally or signing a petition.[179]

The important lesson from same-sex research is that strong friendships outside the marriage can take the pressure off your relationship, help you work things out away from your spouse, and ultimately protect your marriage from unnecessary stress and discord. Friendships are good for marriage.

When Gender Isn't Part of Parenting

In most marriages, parenting duties also typically fall along gender lines, with women doing most of the child rearing. But same-sex couples can't fall back on gender to divide up parenting responsibility. As a result, studying same-sex parents can help us better understand the roles and challenges that heterosexual parents face.

Philip and Carolyn Cowan, the Berkeley professors who have devoted much of their careers to the study of marriage and children, have developed a survey to study how couples divide household and parenting tasks. It asks partners to indicate "How It Is

Now" and "How I Would Like It to Be." The survey results often capture the dramatic inequity in household responsibilities among opposite-sex couples.

Charlotte Patterson, a professor of psychology at the University of Virginia, offered the survey to lesbian parents, and discovered that their answers were very different from those of straight couples. Lesbian couples showed a far more equal distribution of household labor and far fewer complaints about "how I would like it to be."

Dr. Patterson also looked at work outside the home. She found that straight parents and gay parents all take on about seventy hours of paid work a week. But in heterosexual couples, men take on more of the wage-earning duties, putting in about forty-seven hours of paid work compared to twenty-four hours for heterosexual mothers. Lesbian mothers typically both work outside the home for about thirty-five hours a week each.

For lesbian parents, one of the main sources of conflict is over child care. But while most heterosexual couples fight about one partner (usually the husband) not picking up his share of the work, lesbian couples often have conflict over one partner feeling left out of parenting. Lesbian moms often bicker about not getting enough time with the kids, according to the National Longitudinal Lesbian Family Study, headed by Nanette Gartrell, a psychiatrist with the University of California at San Francisco.

One common source of conflict arises when the biological mother is breast feeding and the other mother feels left out. (It's notable that breast feeding often is a time of struggle and loss of intimacy for opposite-sex couples.) But a hallmark of lesbian relationships is a concerted effort to restore balance, often through lengthy discussions acknowledging one partner's feelings of unhappiness. Lesbian mothers often allow one parent to bottle feed and designate other rituals—like bath time—to the nonbiological parent.

Is a 50-50 Marriage Really Possible?

Several years ago I asked a colleague in the next cubicle for information about his children's soccer league and his daughter's ballet school. He just gave me a baffled look. His wife, a busy banking executive, handled all the kids' after-school activities, even though his job clearly was the more flexible of the two. He shrugged his shoulders, and conceded that the arrangement didn't necessarily make sense.

If you had asked my friend and his wife, they both would have told you that theirs was a marriage of equals. She was even the main breadwinner in the family. But other aspects of their marriage broke down along gender lines. While he certainly "helped" with grocery shopping, meal preparation, and the children, the vast majority of the home duties were handled by his wife.

Many men and women will say they value equality in relationships in theory, but the challenge is making it happen in real life. Dr. Deutsch, the Mount Holyoke psychology professor who studied the two doctor-professor couples mentioned at the beginning of this chapter, notes that many couples who say they want an egalitarian relationship discover that the ideal doesn't match reality.

Part of the problem for working couples is that, regardless of the occupation, men and women often perceive the woman's job as being more flexible. Some of this may be due to the fact that the woman is simply more willing than the man to curtail work hours or leave early to meet the needs of her family. "Gender filters the way we see the world," says Dr. Deutsch. "Women in a job look for ways they can make the job flexible. They negotiate with their employers. My guess is that men do not try to negotiate with employers (work life issues) nearly as much as women. I did find evidence of that in my study." During her interviews, Dr. Deutsch spoke with a male postal worker who said part-time work or a flexible schedule was simply impossible for people in his line of work. Yet during the same interview, he regularly referred to a female colleague who worked a flexible schedule. Dr. Deutsch recounts a similar experience with a male physician who said he had no choice but to exceed a forty-hour workweek, but acknowledged that a female colleague had found a way to work part-time. "The pressure on women to figure out ways to combine work and family means they look at their jobs, and they try to find the cracks where they can get some flexibility," says Dr. Deutsch. "Men just assume there is no way to get flexibility."

Dr. Deutsch acknowledges that asking for flexibility or shifting to part-time work can and does have an impact on a person's career. But the risk isn't just for men.

"Men feel like if they do that they're not going to be taken seriously in their careers," she says. "It may have consequences for both men and women. It's just that women are willing to make that trade-off."

Dr. Deutsch has coined the term "equally shared parenting" to describe these 50-50 relationships. She notes that equality in heterosexual relationships requires the unlearning of gender roles by both men and women, but some of these roles were set long before the couple got married. The decision about whether one or both of you is going to scale back at work after kids arrive, for instance, may be influenced by choices you made years earlier. Perhaps a man wants to take time off to contribute more at home. His wife, however, majored in art history in college. He pursued an MBA. In terms of earning potential and family finances, it's far easier to let her scale back and him continue working full-time because his overall earning power is so much greater than his wife's.

That said, Dr. Deutsch says the challenges of equality in marriage shouldn't be blamed on socialization, because that suggests we have to wait an entire generation before things change. History shows that people who are socialized with one way of thinking—whether it's racism or believing women shouldn't pursue careers—can change in a relatively short period of time. For instance, women who were socialized to be homemakers and who married in the 1950s were inspired by the women's movement to pursue careers.

Dr. Deutsch found that the single most predictive factor of whether a couple shares home and work duties is to look at their friends. Couples with equal relationships typically have friends who have relatively equal relationships.

Other researchers have also discovered that a true 50-50 marriage presents numerous challenges.

During a study of hundreds of married and cohabitating couples, relationship researcher Pepper Schwartz was puzzled when she stumbled across a few dozen couples who stood apart from the rest. These men and women appeared to have bypassed traditional gender roles and, at least on the surface, it seemed, had achieved truly egalitarian marriages.

She began talking to about thirty married couples from the study and discovered that these marriages were based on a mix of both equity and equality. Each partner contributed time and money to the relationship based on what he or she received, and each person had equal status in the household. Husband and wife were equally responsible for economic, household, and domestic duties.

But what struck Dr. Schwartz was that these couples hadn't set out to maximize fairness. Instead they enjoyed relationships of "intense companionship," and ended up sharing chores, responsibilities, and decision making equitably. Dr. Schwartz dubbed this kind of collaborative relationship a "peer marriage."

The *For Better* Quiz #12: Do You Have a Peer Marriage?

A peer marriage is defined by the following four goals. Mark yes or no to determine how closely your marriage resembles a peer marriage.

1. Household duties and child rearing are shared equally or almost equally, with no greater than a 60-40 split.

    Ⓐ yes   Ⓑ no

2. Each partner believes the other has equal influence over important decisions.

    Ⓐ yes   Ⓑ no

3. Each partner feels he or she has equal control over family money.

    Ⓐ yes   Ⓑ no

4. Each partner's work is given equal weight when the couple makes plans.

    Ⓐ yes   Ⓑ no

While answering yes to all four statements may sound impressive, the reality is that these relationships aren't perfect, and often require sacrifices that many couples simply can't or won't make. Dr. Schwartz found that couples in a peer marriage are constantly challenged by social norms that run counter to their personal goals. The constant focus on equality can be emotionally taxing—it takes far less thought to divide household and parenting roles along gender lines than it does to work out a complex system of balance. Peer couples typically can't pursue careers to the fullest extent possible because the relationship is the focus and priority of both partners' lives.

Consider one couple, married for thirteen years. The wife wanted to live in New York to pursue her career in media and be closer to her East Coast family, and the husband wanted to live in San Francisco, where he grew up, to remain near his family. A therapist noted that the only fair solution was to shift cities and breadwinning responsibilities every two years. The couple could live for a few years on the

East Coast and focus on the wife's job and family, and then after two years they would move to the West Coast, and focus on the husband's career and family. It was certainly equitable, but it was also unrealistic and impractical. By focusing on fairness and equality in the relationship, neither partner would be able to gain momentum in his or her career. And in this case, the "fair" solution also would prevent them from maintaining deep ties in either community.

Although peer relationships often involve intense companionship, some peer couples reported having less robust sex lives. One reason may be that sexual tension is often based on masculine and feminine roles. Peer marriages de-emphasize gender roles and place a greater emphasis on friendship and fairness. While that can make for a great partnership, it can also take some of the sizzle out of a relationship.

In addition, many couples have career goals and financial aspirations that would make this kind of relationship impractical. Men and women in peer marriages often scale back career ambitions and choose jobs that give them flexible work hours and don't require extensive overtime or travel. An executive who spends long hours at the office and on the road can't commit to taking on an equal share of housework or of the child-raising responsibility.

Inside a 50-50 Marriage

The truth is, often one or both spouses don't want to tackle the challenges and choices that go along with constructing a 50-50 marriage. But even if your goal is not to create a peer marriage, there are still lessons to be learned from these couples.

One such couple is Marc and Amy Vachon, who have managed to construct a relationship around "equally shared parenting," or ESP. She's a pharmacist, and he works in information technology for a marketing firm. Both work exactly thirty-two hours a week, but neither has a job that the couple values more than the other. The focus on family rather than work means that neither is on an intense career track, forgoing a big income for more family time.

He says he wants a life with balance that gives him time to parent, hang out with his wife, and play tennis with his friends, but he still wants to work outside the home. She says she also wants a balance between work and home life, which for her means not being saddled with 100 percent of family duty like many other mothers. They divide housework and parenting, and share all decisions.

Dr. Deutsch notes that the Vachons represent only one model of equally shared parenting, a model that requires both couples to scale back at work and focus intensely on home life. But another approach to ESP is for both couples to focus intensely on career and outsource more of the home duties rather than adding those burdens to one partner or the other. The third model of marital equality is a combination of both. Both partners focus intensely on career but they also both look for opportunities to increase flexibility, so they don't have to outsource as much child care or other domestic work. "I think it's possible to figure out how to do this without giving up work goals," says Dr. Deutsch. "If men could compromise a little bit, then women wouldn't have to compromise so much."

I met the Vachons during a panel discussion at a Chicago marriage and family conference, where they waxed happily about being "ESPers." During a question-and-answer session, I couldn't help but express my skepticism. I simply haven't met many men who would leave work early to make dinner, who were willing to forgo career ambitions for a thirty-two-hour-a-week average-paying job in exchange for "life balance."

Mark and Amy acknowledge that it can be tough for a man to break gender roles and be as enthusiastic about changing diapers as he is about his career. There is no doubt that men like Marc Vachon are not typical, but he is convinced that more men would embrace the ESP lifestyle if it were more widely accepted by family members, friends, and even wives themselves.

Amy Vachon notes that the biggest hindrance to ESP isn't always the man. In a story she tells often, she explains how on the day she returned to work after four months of maternity leave, she left a detailed list for her husband about the baby's napping and feeding schedule. But when she handed it to Marc, he tore the list in half. He knew perfectly well how to care for his child.

As we discussed earlier in this book, women often have a difficult time giving up control over housework and parenting, particularly when they and their husbands have different standards for cleanliness or child care. Equal parenting means sometimes biting your tongue or turning the other way when one parent doesn't clean or parent the way you would—like the times dust collects or the laundry isn't sorted or the dad plays rough with the kids just before bedtime rather than reading them a quiet story. It means sometimes letting a father pick out a child's clothes, plan birthday parties, and contact teachers about school issues. For women, it also means giving up on the intellectual labor of running a household and, rather than delegating, trusting your partner to remember to pack a lunch for the class field trip or be on time for the dentist appointment. The reality is, many women don't trust their husbands to remember these things.

Catherine Kenney of Bowling Green State University in Bowling Green, Ohio, studied 1,023 couples from twenty large U.S. cities and found that mothers typically protected parenting roles related to caregiving and school, but were willing to cede control to fathers for playtime activities.[180] Sarah Schoppe-Sullivan, an assistant professor of child development at Ohio State University in Columbus, studied ninety-seven couples, and found that fathers were more involved with their babies if the wife or partner actively encouraged it.[181]

"Women say they want this, but sometimes they don't appreciate how much they must let go," says Amy Vachon.

Lessons for Creating a Friendship Model of Marriage

In 1975, Clarence Tripp, a colleague of the noted sex researcher Alfred Kinsey, noted that many people who look at gay relationships try to understand them through a husband-wife frame of reference. When many people look at a gay couple, the ask themselves, "Which one is the husband and which one is the wife?"

Little has changed since then. During a recent *Late Night* monologue, David Letterman talked about a gay marriage law in San Francisco. "So right now, gay men are asking themselves the big question: Who's driving and who nags?" he said.

The problem is that many couples believe that traditional husband and wife roles are the only two roles available in a marriage. But studies of gay relationships show they are based on an entirely different structure—the best-friend model—and it's a model that offers important insights for heterosexual couples.[182]

The American Couples Survey by Dr. Schwartz also found that gay and lesbian couples demonstrated several distinct differences in the way they interacted on a daily basis compared to heterosexual couples. Gay couples, she found, shared more common interests, spent more time together, and divided household chores more evenly. In fact, they looked a lot like the peer marriage couples we talked about earlier.

The equal division of household chores has been a strikingly consistent finding in studies of same-sex couples. Wright State University researcher Lawrence A. Kurdek has conducted several studies comparing gay and lesbian relationships to straight couples. He found that gay and lesbian couples were more likely than heterosexual couples to relate to each other as best friends and aspire to an egalitarian relationship. In a study comparing gays, lesbians, and heterosexual couples, Dr. Kurdek found that, invariably, wives in heterosexual couples did most of the housework, but among gays and lesbians, chores were more evenly divided.

In a later study of straight and gay parents, Dr. Rothblum, professor of women's studies at San Diego State University, found that wives in heterosexual marriages are consistently saddled with the majority of the family's housework duties, performing between eleven and twenty hours of chores a week, while heterosexual fathers contributed about six hours.

But there were no such differences among lesbian and gay parents, who each reported doing between six and ten hours a week of cooking, cleaning, and other domestic chores.

After Vermont legalized same-sex civil unions in 2000, it gave relationship researchers a unique opportunity to study similarities and differences between married couples of the same and opposite sex. Dr. Rothblum, and two colleagues from the University of Vermont and the University of Washington, embarked on a three-year study tracking 65 male and 138 female same-sex couples who had entered civil unions during the first year after the legislation was passed. They recruited 84 same-sex couples who were in the friendship circles of the study group, but who hadn't legalized their relationships. And they also included 55 heterosexual married couples—one member of each married couple was a sibling of one of the gay couples. The advantage of studying siblings is that they, for the most part, will have the same racial and demographic background as the gay couples in the study. All told, 342 committed couples joined the study.

The aim of the research, which asked couples numerous survey questions, was to compare how couples navigate common causes of marital strife, such as housework, sex, and money.

In the heterosexual couples studied, women did far more of the housework. Men were more likely to have the financial responsibility. Men in opposite-sex marriages also were far more likely to initiate sex, while women were more likely to refuse it. And when men and women argued, the woman was far more likely to have started the conversation about problems in the relationship.

But with same-sex couples in the study, of course none of these dichotomies were possible. The partners tended to share domestic burdens far more equally. Each partner helped with housework and managed money at about the same rate. Both partners showed about the same interest in sex, and both partners showed similar patterns of initiating conflict discussions.

Notably, there weren't any measurable differences in how often the couples argued. The gay and lesbian couples had about the same rate of conflict as the heterosexual ones. Even so, gay couples tested higher on relationship satisfaction scores.

What does all this mean to the average married couple? It suggests that conflict is not the reason marital happiness fades. Instead, it appears that gender roles and the inequality typical of opposite-sex relationships may take a significant toll on a couple's marriage. Women in heterosexual relationships tend to initiate conflict discussions because they are the ones who find the distribution of labor and decision making unfair. The wife is typically burdened with more housework and domestic duties and feels less power in the relationship than her husband.

"Heterosexual married women live with a lot of anger about having to do the tasks not only in the house but in the relationship," said Dr. Rothblum. "That's very different than what same sex couples and heterosexual men live with."

The main lesson from the science of same-sex couples and from opposite-sex peer couples is that every couple needs to take a closer look at the source of tension in the relationship. Couples who assume fighting is their biggest problem may discover that the real issue isn't conflict but an imbalance of power and an overall feeling of unfairness in the relationship.

CHAPTER 12

To Have and to Hold:
Assessing Your Risk for Divorce

*In every marriage more than a week old, there are grounds
for divorce. The trick is to find, and continue to find, grounds
for marriage.*

—ROBERT ANDERSON

One of the strongest memories of my own marriage occurred on the day it began. Standing in the foyer of a church in Austin, Texas, I was a twenty-one-year-old bride doing last-minute primping as I prepared to walk down the aisle. But like many brides, I was focused on the minutiae of the moment. I began to scowl as I realized the string quartet was playing the wrong part of Pachelbel's Canon. My distress must have shown in my face because my father, assuming I was nervous about my impending nuptials, leaned over to reassure me and whispered, "You're doing the right thing."

It should have been reassuring, except I didn't hear him correctly. What I heard him say was *"Are* you doing the right thing?"

And then the music shifted, my wedding song began, and my

feet started moving down the aisle, all while my father's misunder-
stood words were ringing in my ears.

"Are you doing the right thing?"

And that's when I realized. I had spent the past several months
choosing the right dress, the right music, the right flowers, and the
right venue for the reception. But I hadn't spent much time at all
on the issue that really mattered at this moment. Had I chosen the
right partner?

As it turned out, there were many wonderful things about the
man I chose to marry, but we struggled as well. We certainly loved
each other, but we also learned the hard way that sometimes love is
not enough. Despite our best efforts, our marriage ended in divorce
more than seventeen years later in a New Jersey courtroom.

In what seemed like a particularly cruel moment, the judge in
divorce court asked us to confirm the date and location of our wedding.
(New Jersey divorce law is oddly anachronistic.) The judge's questions
brought back a rush of memories of that spring day seventeen years
earlier and that confused trip I had made down the aisle. And just as
the court was about to pronounce us ex-husband and ex-wife, my husband and I glanced at each other with sadness, sharing what would
be our last moment of mutual understanding as a married couple.

At the end of my marriage, just as I had at the beginning of it, I
wondered to myself, "Are we doing the right thing?"

The uncertainty of that moment set me on a quest to better
understand where and why it had all gone so terribly wrong. In
doing so, I discovered the vast scientific literature on marriage and
relationships, and was shocked to discover that my risk for divorce
had been apparent from the beginning. If only I had known what
signs to look for, my husband and I might have sought intervention
sooner to save our relationship—or perhaps we would have recog-
nized our irreconcilable differences years earlier, cut our losses, and
had far more confidence in our decision to divorce.

What Type of Marriage Do You Have?

In a sweeping thirty-year study on divorce in America, marital researcher E. Mavis Hetherington identified five types of marriages. Much of what she learned about marriage style revolved around conflict style. Two types of marriages—the cohesive marriage and the traditional marriage—were most likely to be stable over time. However, she identified three styles of marriage—the pursuer-distancer, the disengaged marriage, and the operatic marriage—that put couples at high risk for divorce.[183] Here's a look at the five styles of marriage.

COHESIVE/INDIVIDUATED MARRIAGE

These are couples who seem to balance togetherness and separateness. We've all seen this type of couple. The partners don't spend every waking moment together, but they nonetheless seem bonded. Dr. Hetherington describes these couples as the "cultural ideal" for a good marriage, because they embody "so many baby boomer values." "This marriage could almost be described as an expression of one very primary boomer value, gender equity," she writes. It is characterized by an old-fashioned sense of intimacy and shared responsibilities at home, yet these couples maintain individual differences within "the larger marital 'we.'"

"The marriage functions like a refuge the husband and wife return to at the end of the day for renewal, support, affection, and companionship."

In Dr. Hetherington's research, these couples had the second-lowest divorce rate. They become vulnerable to divorce when one partner begins to put more emphasis on the "individuated" half of this relationship, neglecting the "cohesive" part. As Dr. Hetherington explains, divorce risk increases when one person "begins to put more emphasis on 'me' than 'we.'"

TRADITIONAL MARRIAGE

It's often a surprise when people learn that a traditional marriage, which is marked by the male breadwinner/female homemaker roles, is widely viewed as the most stable marriage. It had the lowest divorce rate in the studies by Dr. Hetherington. But just because these marriages are stable doesn't mean they always are the most happy.

For a traditional marriage to thrive, both partners have to be happy with their individual role, perform it well, and feel respected by the other partner for the contributions they make to the marriage and family. If one partner changes, particularly if the wife decides she wants to work outside the home, the marriage can be stressed, often beyond repair.

THE PURSUER-DISTANCER MARRIAGE

In 80 percent of pursuer-distancer marriages, the pursuer is the woman. She is eager to confront and discuss problems. The man typically is the one to withdraw, avoid confrontation, and assume the "distancer" role.

In a common pursuer-distancer conflict, the wife will bring up a problem. The husband will resist engaging in the discussion by reading the newspaper, turning on the television set, or just staring into space or at his food. Eventually, the distancer gets tired of the "nagging" and gets angry. The pursuer also gets fed up and withdraws into herself. The distancer begins to feel her "cold contempt" and panics at the risk of losing her, but often he is blindsided when his wife walks out. He never saw it coming. Meanwhile, his wife reads his withdrawal as evidence that he doesn't love her.

The sad thing about these relationships is that the husband often feels that his love for his spouse is obvious, and he shouldn't have to do anything to show it. The distancer is often quite happy in the relationship but oblivious to the high level of discontent his partner feels.

Notably, pursuer-distancer relationships are often romanticized. In 2001, Israeli researchers Daniela Kramer and Michael Moore randomly selected a hundred Harlequin romance novels and found that nearly three out of four demonstrated the courtship dynamics of a pursuer-distancer relationship. If you read romance novels, you can only conclude that marriage is "built on this theme of pursuing and evading, without any other healthy role option of two equal partners," wrote the researchers.

Scores of marital research studies have attempted to dissect this type of relationship, which is often called a demand-withdrawal pattern. This has also been called the "rejection-intrusion pattern," "nag-withdraw," or "close-far polarization." It is the highest-risk marriage and the most prone to unhappiness and divorce.

The good news is that couples who find themselves in this pattern have the ability to change their behavior during conflict once they recognize it.

"It's a diagnostic sign, like that red light that comes on in your car, that there's something wrong in the relationship," says Dr. Levenson of Berkeley. "If you're in that pattern where one person is unhappy and the other person isn't willing to discuss and compromise, it can't go on like that. You have to rebalance. The person who is unhappy has to be given something. And the person who is happy with the status quo has to give it."

THE DISENGAGED MARRIAGE

Disengaged marriages unite two self-sufficient individuals, "who fear or don't need intimacy to achieve a sense of well-being." Often these couples lack mutual interest, shared values, and common family backgrounds. Disengaged couples don't argue a lot—in fact, they often don't need each other on a daily basis.

The problem is that the men and women in these marriages

would have pretty much the same lives if they were single, and they lack mutual affection and support. Dr. Hetherington notes that these marriages, which have the second-highest divorce rate after pursuer-distancer relationships, typically end with a whimper as one or both individuals ask themselves, "Is that all there is?"

THE OPERATIC MARRIAGE

This type of marriage is characterized by dramatic highs and lows. These couples are emotionally volatile. Quarreling often leads to sex. In fact, Dr. Hetherington said people in operatic marriages reported the highest level of sexual satisfaction among all of the marriage types studied. The fighting-sex cycle can work, but the danger is in the fighting style and whether one or both partners say hurtful, damaging things during the conflict. Often these relationships end when one partner, typically the husband, decides the passion isn't worth the constant conflict.

How Do You and Your Spouse Communicate?

The hallmark of modern marriage research is its focus on marital interaction. Scientists have video-recorded thousands of conversations between couples and used computer-assisted coding program to deconstruct these interactions down to their most basic elements. What has emerged is the knowledge that a few styles of interaction pose a distinct risk of marital unhappiness and divorce.

AVOIDING CONFLICT

A *New Yorker* cartoon once showed an angry woman glowering at her husband as he watched television. "I said I don't want to fight," she told him. "That's your cue to apologize."

This cartoon captured a troubling risk factor for divorce. Couples who habitually avoid conflict think they are simply choosing a peaceful path, but the reality is that they are putting their marriage at risk. Conflict puts a couple on track for resolving differences. Avoiding conflict means problems don't get solved.

One study followed married couples over just a three-year period. At the beginning of the study, the couples who rarely argued had the highest levels of marital happiness. They equated a happy marriage with low levels of conflict.

But three years later, much had changed. The couples who were arguing a lot at the beginning of the study reported big increases in marital satisfaction. They had resolved many of their differences and were enjoying a contented, productive partnership. What about the peaceful couples? Three years later, many of them were headed for divorce. By staying quiet and avoiding conflict when things bothered them, they had missed important opportunities to cultivate and grow their relationship.

SHOWING CONTEMPT

As we discussed earlier, signs of contempt when couples communicate suggest a marriage is in serious trouble. Contempt can be shown by dismissive comments or actions such as eye rolling. Name calling, swearing, and put-downs also are signs of contempt. Marriage researcher John Gottman has said that contempt is one of the most telling predictors of divorce.

DISILLUSIONMENT AND DISAPPOINTMENT

Feelings that your marriage isn't what you expected or a sense of disappointment about how your life turned out are predictors of divorce. A University of Texas at Austin study of 156 newlywed couples found that disillusionment in the early part of the relationship was a powerful predictor for divorce.[184] One way to determine

if a man or woman is feeling disillusioned is to listen to how they
tell their how-we-met story. (See page 125.)

The *For Better* Quiz #13: Assess Your Relationship Risk

To help couples get a sense of their relationship, University of Denver marriage researchers Dr. Scott Stanley and Dr. Howard Markman offer the following research-based quiz. Dr. Markman says
couples should take the scores seriously but realize that there is a
lot the quiz doesn't take into account about a relationship. He says
high- and medium-high scoring couples should use the results to
help them take a serious look at where their marriage is heading—
and take steps (such as going to one of his couples retreats) to turn
negative patterns around for the better.

Rate how often the following situations occur based on the scale
of 1 to 3 below.

1 Never or almost never
2 Once in a while
3 Frequently

1. Little arguments escalate into ugly fights with accusations,
   criticisms, name calling, or bringing up past hurts.
2. My partner criticizes or belittles my opinions, feelings, or
   desires.
3. My partner seems to view my words or actions more negatively
   than I mean them to be.
4. When we have a problem to solve, it is as if we are on opposite
   teams.
5. I hold back from telling my partner what I really think and feel.
6. I feel lonely in this relationship.
7. When we argue, one of us withdraws, that is, doesn't want to
   talk about it anymore, or leaves the scene.

Calculate Your Score

Add up your points to determine your score. (Include only your scores; do not add to your partner's!) The ranges suggested are based on results from a nationwide, random phone survey of 947 people (85 percent married) conducted in January 1996.

7 to 11 "Green Light"

If your total points are in the 7–11 range, your relationship is probably in good or even great shape at this time.

12 to 16 "Yellow Light"

If you scored in the 12–16 range, it's as if you are coming to a "yellow light." You need to be cautious. While you may be happy now in your relationship, your score reveals warning signs of patterns you don't want to let get worse. You'll want to be taking action to protect and improve what you have. Spending time to strengthen your relationship now could be the best thing you could do for your future together.

17 to 21 "Red Light"

Finally, if you scored in the 17–21 range, it's like approaching a red light. Stop, and think about where the two of you are headed. Your score indicates the presence of patterns that could put your relationship at significant risk. You may be heading for trouble—or may already be there.

Source: Used by permission of PREP, Inc., and adapted from the book *Fighting for Your Marriage,* and available at loveyourrelationship.com.

The "D" Word

In 1980, researchers from three different universities began following more than 2,000 men and women. They kept track of them over the next twelve years as they went through various stages of marriage, divorce, and remarriage.

The researchers discovered a simple and obvious predictor for future divorce. Men and women who had pondered thoughts of divorce in 1980 were nine times more likely to have gotten a divorce by the end of the study. Simply contemplating divorce suggests you're open to the idea, and that makes you vulnerable to it.[185] Once you or your partner starts talking about divorce, either to your confidants or to each other, it's a sign that the marriage is already in serious, perhaps irreparable, trouble.

Infidelity

A landmark study by the Alan Guttmacher Institute sought to identify risk factors for cheating. What circumstances, personality traits, or experiences increase a person's risk of cheating?[186]

The analysis included 2,598 men and women aged eighteen to fifty-nine who had participated in the 1992 National Health and Social Life Survey and who had ever been married or lived with a sexual partner. The researchers collected their data using a combination of face-to-face interviews and written questionnaires asking about social background; health; fertility; and sexual activities, attitudes, and fantasies. Overall, cheating rates were extraordinarily low—only 11 percent of respondents reported infidelity. But the scientists also found that cheating was associated with some specific risk factors.

> *Being a man:* In the survey, men were twice as likely to report infidelity as women. While it may be that women are less likely to admit cheating, most studies support the notion that men are more likely to be unfaithful, if for no other reason than they typically have more opportunities to be away from home.

Thinking about sex several times a day: A person who has sex on the brain all the time is 30 percent more likely to stray than a person who is less distracted by sexual thoughts.

Having a high number of prior sex partners: The more sex partners a respondent had between age eighteen and the time of first marriage or cohabitation, the more likely he or she was to be unfaithful.

Living in the city: Being an urban dweller increases infidelity by 50 percent. It may be that living in the city presents more opportunities to be unfaithful.

Being in a long relationship: Infidelity appears to be a by-product of boredom or disillusionment. For each year couples lived together, respondents became 1 percent more likely to be unfaithful.

Living together without marriage: Couples who haven't tied the knot are twice as likely to cheat on each other.

Having lived together before marriage: Men and women who had cohabited before marriage were 40 percent more likely than others to have been unfaithful. It's not clear what this means. Perhaps the type of person who cohabits before marriage is simply more likely to admit to cheating. Or perhaps it means couples who cohabited were less sure of the relationship in the first place, making them less committed and more likely to stray.

Being unhappy: Couples who aren't happy in the relationship are 30 percent more likely to be sexually unfaithful.

The study also identified some factors that appeared to protect couples against infidelity.

Disapproval: People who stated they thought extramarital sex is wrong were 50 percent less likely to be unfaithful.

Having lots of friends in common: Sharing social networks with a spouse decreased the odds of cheating by 30 percent.

Notably, a couple's religious, educational, and age differences had no significant impact on the odds of infidelity. The likelihood of infidelity was not significantly influenced by sexual opportunities in the workplace or how often somebody went to church.

Another factor influencing infidelity risk is the Internet, which has made it easier for couples to cheat if they want to. Sites like Facebook and MySpace give people more opportunity to flirt and reconnect with old flames—something that makes them vulnerable to affairs during business travel or a difficult period in the relationship. About 20 percent of adults who used social-networking sites in 2008 admitted that they flirt while using the sites, according to a survey by the Pew Internet and American Life Project. Another way the Internet may influence infidelity is the increasing availability of online pornography. This isn't some judgmental warning about the dangers of pornography. But studies show that repeated exposure to pornography can affect sexual attitudes and perceptions of "normal" behavior. While this doesn't mean porn makes people cheat, it might make them more vulnerable to straying. In other words, the easier access we all have to Internet porn may be subtly shaping our attitudes and values. For many people who are routinely exposed to provocative and sexually explicit images, having sex outside of marriage may not seem to be as abnormal or verboten as it may have to earlier generations.

While infidelity is certainly a risk factor for divorce, studies show that a broken marriage vow does not have to lead to a broken marriage. Surveys find the majority of people who discover a cheating spouse remain married, deciding the indiscretion does not warrant throwing away years of commitment. Others ignore their suspicions as a way to preserve the relationship.

For evidence of this, one need look no further than the headlines. We routinely see stories of political wives who weather the public humiliation of infidelity and still choose to stay with their husbands.

(Notably, examples of cheating wives are less common among public figures, but that doesn't mean it doesn't happen. It just means either they haven't been caught or the social stigma of being cuckolded keeps men quiet when a wife strays.) While the experiences of a political couple are certain to be different from those of the average man and woman, the same story of infidelity and forgiveness is repeated countless times among less famous couples.

In any given year, about 10 percent of married people say they have had sex outside their marriage. In one survey, among 1,084 people whose spouses had affairs, researchers found that 76 percent of both men and women were still married and living with that spouse years later. Similar surveys have found rates of about two-thirds and higher.

Why do so many couples appear to survive infidelity? It may be that modern marriages—as high maintenance and difficult as they can be to maintain—are also more resilient when things go wrong. Spouses share history and goals, children, and strong bonds to friends and community.

Health, Violence, and Substance Abuse

Some risk factors for divorce are completely out of one or both spouses' control. Violence and substance abuse put couples at high risk for divorce. Illness poses a special challenge to marriage. A European study found that while most cancers don't affect divorce risk, divorce risk increases if one partner suffers from testicular or cervical cancer. The study compared divorce rates of 215,000 cancer survivors to couples free of cancer. Women with cervical cancer had nearly a 70 percent greater risk of divorce at the age of twenty, a level that fell to 19 percent at sixty. For testicular cancer, the divorce risk was 34 percent at twenty and 16 percent at sixty. Head injuries and mental illness also raise a couple's risk for divorce.

Boredom Predicts Divorce

Marriage researchers from New York, California, and Michigan in 2009 decided to look at the role of boredom in predicting marital satisfaction. They surveyed 123 long-married couples from Wayne County, Michigan, asking them questions about boredom during the seventh and sixteenth years of their marriages. Here's the questionnaire.

The *For Better* Quiz #14: Are You Bored?

1. In the past month, how often did you feel that your marriage was in a rut (or getting into a rut?), that you do the same thing all the time and rarely get to do exciting things together as a couple?

   ⓐ Often   ⓑ Sometimes   ⓒ Rarely   ⓓ Never

2. All in all, how satisfied are you with your marriage?

   ⓐ Very satisfied   ⓑ Somewhat satisfied
   ⓒ Somewhat dissatisfied   ⓓ Very dissatisfied

3. Select the picture that best describes your marriage.

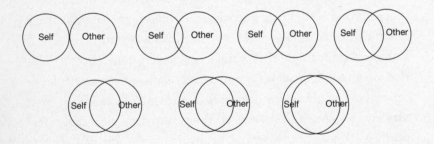

Source: A. Aron, E. N. Aron, and D. Smollan, "Inclusion of Other in the Self Scale and the Structure of Interpersonal Closeness," *Journal of Personality and Social Psychology* 63 (1992): 596–612.

The three questions measured boredom, marital satisfaction, and relationship closeness. The study showed that boredom is an important predictor of marital happiness. Couples in their seventh year of marriage who reported boredom were less likely to be happy or report strong feelings of closeness by their sixteenth year of marriage.[187]

The data are important because they suggest a simple intervention—just adding a little excitement to your daily life—may go a long way to boosting couples' marital happiness and preventing them from growing apart.

Don't do the same old thing. Dine with different sets of friends. Choose different restaurants. Take a pottery class together if you've never done it before. Go on a cooking vacation. In studying the effect exciting activities can have on marital happiness, researchers have found that "exciting" is relative. One couple dining out in New York decided to venture over to the Upper East Side instead of staying on the Upper West Side. While that may not sound particularly daring to most of us, for them, it was different. And studies show doing different things can often help keep the marital spark alive.

If you are bored in your marriage now, chances are you will be unhappy and distant from your partner within a decade. Protect your marriage by adding variety to your life.

Loss of Passion, Intimacy, and Commitment

Most people think the words "I love you" are the three words that matter most in a marriage. But psychologist Robert Sternberg suggests another three-word mantra: "passion, intimacy, and commitment."

When passion, intimacy, and commitment are all sustained at high levels, the ideal pattern—consummate love—emerges. But while consummate love is desirable, it is also extraordinarily difficult to sustain. Most of us, says Dr. Sternberg, don't get there at all. The result is that we typically muster high levels of only one or two of the variables. The resulting combinations of high and low levels of passion, intimacy, and commitment form seven distinct patterns of love, some better than others.[188]

- *Infatuated Love:* This occurs when your passion is high but the relationship lacks intimacy and commitment. Think "love at first sight."
- *Empty Love:* Married couples can be highly committed to each other, but their relationship lacks passion and intimacy. Arranged marriages often begin as empty love, and some long-lasting marriages can begin to feel empty.
- *Romantic Love:* Romantic lovers feel a strong bond and physical attraction—they are passionate and have an intimate knowledge of each other. But the relationship is typically new and hasn't reached the stage of commitment.
- *Fatuous Love:* Some couples end up committing to each other after a whirlwind, passionate courtship. Their passion for each other is high and their commitment is solid, but they discover they know very little about each other, and their intimacy remains low.
- *Companionate Love:* Often a lasting love is based on deep affection and commitment, but typically it's lacking in sexual desire. Commitment and intimacy are high, but the sparks of passion have died down.
- *Liking:* Some of our most intimate relationships are with friends. Some marriages become more like a long-term friendship, with intimacy at a high level, but they lack passion and commitment.
- *Consummate Love:* For most couples, this is the ideal. It's a complete form of love with a high level of commitment, intimacy, and passion.

Dr. Sternberg argues that during the course of a relationship, all three aspects of love can shift to various combinations of highs and lows. Infatuated lovers can become romantic lovers who then become consummate lovers before settling into companionate love. Even the empty love of an arranged marriage can quickly turn passionate and even consummate. But breaking down your relationship in terms of passion, intimacy, and commitment can help you simplify which areas most need improvement.

The *For Better* Quiz #15: Determine Your Love Pattern

Take this quiz to determine your love pattern. Place an X under "high" or "low."

	HIGH	LOW
Passion		
Intimacy		
Commitment		

Lessons to Lower Divorce Risk and Improve Your Odds

Statisticians and relationship researchers have identified several "static" risk factors that are linked with a rocky marriage. These are variables over which an individual has little or no control. If you haven't yet married, it's a good idea to consider these factors to improve your odds of picking the right mate. If you've already married, knowing whether your marriage has a risk factor for divorce in one area should serve as extra motivation to focus on ways to lower your risk for problems in others.

Here's a look at the factors that can influence your odds of staying married:

Marry after the age of twenty-five. Marrying young is associated with a higher divorce rate. Marrying as a teenager is the highest known risk factor for divorce, according to Rutgers marriage researchers. A recent government study found that 59 percent of marriages for women under age eighteen end in divorce or separation within fifteen years, compared with 36 percent of those married at age twenty or older. Those who are married young are less likely to have completed college, which raises your chances for success in marriage. They may be in lower-paying jobs, be dealing with financial stress, or have married because of an unplanned pregnancy. People who marry after thirty have very low divorce rates. This may be due to the fact that such persons are unusually particular and hold out for an ideal mate. Or it could be that the wisdom of years helps one better cope with the stress and challenges of marriage.

Don't marry a college dropout. People with "some college" have higher divorce rates than high school graduates and those who finished college. This may suggest that a person who "drops out" is also more likely to drop out of other commitments like marriage. Or it could be that factors that influenced quitting college, such as emotional problems, alcohol dependency, or financial stress, also influence divorce risk.

Stick it out for at least ten years. The majority of divorces occur in the first ten years of marriage. While there are definitely divorces that occur later in life, the ten-year mark represents an important milestone for most families.

Marry someone with similar interests and background. Having different backgrounds, religions, or political views puts you at risk for divorce. The more similar people are in their values, backgrounds, and life goals, the more likely they are to have a successful marriage. Opposites may attract but they may not live together harmoniously as married couples. People who share common backgrounds and similar social networks are better suited as marriage partners than people who come from divergent backgrounds and have dissimilar social networks.

Marry someone whose parents are still married. When two adult children of divorce marry, they face nearly three times the risk of divorce compared to men and women who both come from intact families. The risk is lower if at least one marriage partner grew up with both parents in the home.[189] One study found that when the wife alone had experienced a parental divorce, the odds of divorce increased by more than half (59 percent), but when both spouses experienced parental divorce, the odds of divorce nearly tripled (189 percent).

Of course, all of these risk factors for divorce are only part of the story. It's never just one thing that determines whether or not a marriage will succeed or fail. Whether it's the age at which you married, your relationship style, or boredom, troubled marriages are usually troubled for a lot of reasons. The little things add up and make it seem impossible to turn back the tide. But even if your marriage ends up in divorce, the factors laid out in this chapter should show that there's rarely any one particular person or trait on which the dissolution can be blamed.

As we've explored throughout this book, most marriages don't end in divorce. Most of us end up in stable, relatively contented relationships that have plenty of room for improvement. But a "good" marriage is in the details, and just as small things can add up in a bad marriage, good marriages can benefit from small, positive steps taken over time.

CHAPTER 13

The Science of a Good Marriage: A Prescription for Marital Health

Chains do not hold a marriage together. It is threads, hundreds of tiny threads, which sew people together through the years.

—SIMONE SIGNORET

The lessons from marriage research show that improving a relationship is not about making sweeping changes. As we've discussed throughout the book, it's the small things that matter most. The words we use in conversation and conflict, how often we offer compliments and affection, and our body movements and facial gestures all make up the fabric of a marriage.

But now that you've taken a closer look at the issues that can cause problems in a marriage—like conflict, children, sex, and housework—you may be wondering what positive steps can be taken to keep a marriage healthy.

After years of focusing on the negatives that can sabotage a marriage, a number of relationship scientists now have shifted their focus to identify the positive interactions that can protect a relationship and promote intimacy and a stronger bond. Just as a doctor might prescribe blood pressure pills or a daily aspirin to keep your body healthy, marriage science also offers a prescription to boost the health of your relationship. Researchers have identified several small, positive changes on which couples can focus that have the potential to reap big rewards in overall satisfaction with your marriage.

"We've found that the positives are more and more important," says Howard Markman, codirector of the Center for Marital and Family Studies at the University of Denver and one of the nation's leading marriage researchers. "It turns out that the amount of fun couples have and the strength of their friendships are a strong predictor of their future."

Dr. Markman notes that helping couples better manage conflict is important to halting the steady negative slide of a troubled marriage. But simply stopping or repairing conflict problems doesn't necessarily lead to a strong, happy relationship. "The couple that is not able to handle conflict, for them things aren't going to work out," notes Dr. Markman. "If they learn to handle conflict well, then they may have an okay marriage but not necessarily a great marriage."

So what's the next step? Couples in lasting, satisfying relationships know that it's not enough to avoid negative behaviors. Good marriages require daily maintenance and positive feedback to help couples stay connected. Here are seven strategies that studies show successful couples use to stay happy and bolster the strength of their marriage.

#1: Celebrate Good News

In the epic poem *Paradise Lost,* John Milton writes: "Good, the more communicated, more abundant grows."

He could be dispensing marital advice. Research shows that

couples who regularly celebrate the good times have higher levels of commitment, intimacy, trust, and relationship satisfaction.

A common thread in both marital and psychological research has been to focus on the negatives. How do couples cope with hard times, conflict, and unhappiness? But research shows that how couples cope with good times is just as important.

Did your wife's meeting go well? Did your husband finally beat his much younger racquetball partner? Did one of you get a raise?

How do you react to the big and small achievements of the person you love? Do you offer a grunt? A smile of support? Or do you pop the champagne cork, order takeout, and give a high five?

In marital science, celebrating the good news is called "capitalization"—a measure of how much couples are "capitalizing" on the positive events in their lives. In simpler terms, it just means that you need to make a big deal out of the good moments of your marriage.

To measure the importance of sharing good news, researchers from the University of California–Los Angeles and the University of Rochester first recruited 154 college students who were asked to document the good and bad things that happened to them over the course of a week. In the life of a college student, things like running out of money and poor test scores ranked high on the list of bad things. The good news included things like high test scores, a phone call from a faraway friend, and receiving a care package from a family member. The students were also quizzed on whether they shared their bad or good news with others, and filled out daily questionnaires that measured their overall life satisfaction and happiness.

Using a complex formula, the researchers were able to determine the effect of the good news on the student's day, as well as the additional effect that *sharing* the good news had on a student's happiness. Students who received good news—and then shared it—reported more happiness than those who just kept the good news to themselves. Good feelings are amplified and reinforced when shared with others.

To see if sharing good news with a partner was associated with relationship happiness, the researchers conducted two additional studies. One involved 59 college couples who had been dating for an average of fourteen months. The second group included 178 married couples who had been together for an average of ten years.

Using various scales, the researchers measured the couples' feelings of commitment, relationship satisfaction, and intimacy. And they also measured "capitalization"—the level at which each partner "capitalized" on the positive events in their loved one's life. Here's a shortened version of the Capitalization test:

The *For Better* Quiz #16: How Do You React to Good News?

Please take a moment to consider how your partner responds when you tell him or her about something good that has happened to you. For example, imagine that you come home and tell your partner about receiving a promotion at work, having a great conversation with a family member, getting a raise, winning a prize, or doing well on an exam at school or a project at work. Please consider to what extent your partner does the following things in response to your good fortune.

1. My partner usually reacts to my good fortune enthusiastically; he/she often asks a lot of questions and shows genuine interest about the good event.
2. My partner is usually silently supportive of the good things that happen to me; my partner says little, but I know he/she is happy for me.

3. My partner reminds me that most good things have their bad aspects as well; he/she points out the potential downsides of the event.

4. My partner seems uninterested; sometimes I get the impression he/she doesn't care that much about something good that has happened to me.

The researchers have identified four different types of personalities based on how they respond to a spouse's good news. They are:

1. Active Constructive responders are those who enthusiastically react to good news.

2. Passive Constructive responders are those who show quiet support. They don't say much, but the spouse feels loved and supported.

3. Active Destructive responders have a negative outlook, always seeing the potential downside of positive events.

4. Passive Destructive responders don't say much because they simply aren't interested.

Not surprisingly, the final two groups—the Active and Passive Destructive responders—were associated with low scores on intimacy, satisfaction, and other measures of relationship happiness.

But the most surprising results came from the Passive Constructive responders. These partners were positive and loving, just not particularly emotive. A husband or wife of a Passive Constructive responder reports feeling loved; they just know their partner isn't the type to be vocal about it. Yet when put to the test, a husband or wife who had a silently supportive spouse also scored poorly on measures of relationship happiness.

In the end, the only couples who scored high on intimacy and daily relationship satisfaction were the Active Constructive group—the couples who make a big deal out of the good things that happen to them. You finally finished your project at work? Let's go out to dinner to celebrate. You ran you first 5K? High five and a hug. Your boss singled you out for praise at the weekly meeting? I'm so proud of you. I'm cooking dinner tonight.

> **THE LESSON:** It's not enough that your partner *knows* that you take pride in his or her accomplishments. You have to show it. Making a fuss over the small, good things that happen every day can boost the health of your marriage.

#2: Know the Mathematics of Marriage

Once researchers came up with a way to study videotapes of couples in conversation, they were able to catalog every nice or negative thing a couple did or said during a discussion. Things like laughing, touching, smiling, or paying a compliment were coded as positive interactions. They also tracked the number of not-so-nice moments—eye rolling, sneers, criticism, defensiveness, anger, and withdrawal.

As University of Washington researchers reviewed the data, a striking pattern emerged. In stable marriages, there are at least five times more positive interactions than negative ones. When the ratio starts to drop, the marriage is at high risk for divorce.

In real life, no couple can keep a running tally of positive and negative displays. There are hundreds of them that happen in any given day. But in a practical sense, the lesson is that a single "I'm sorry" after bad behavior isn't enough. For every snide comment or negative outburst in a marriage, a person needs to ramp up the positives so the good-to-bad ratio doesn't fall to a risky level. Couples in solid, lasting relationships do this naturally. Sometimes the positives are spoken. "You look nice today, honey." "That color looks good on you." "What a great meal." "You're a good dad." Sometimes the positives are gestures—pats on the hand or back, a hug, a tousle of the hair, a kiss for no reason.

THE LESSON: Do marriage math. Even when you make a mistake, tell yourself that you're going to do at least five positive things for your spouse to make up for it, and then do them. And don't wait until you bicker to turn on the charm. Nice gestures and comments go far in a marriage, they are easy to do, and they will help insulate your marriage from being damaged by the inevitable bad days.

#3: Keep Your Standards High

One common theme couples often hear in marital counseling is that they have unrealistic standards and hopes for marriage. If you're unhappy and feeling disillusioned, maybe it's because you were too idealistic about what you expected from marriage in the first place. Often, therapists advise couples to ratchet down their expectations for marriage and from their partners to a more realistic level.

But more recent research suggests that high standards are a good thing. An important study led by University of North Carolina psychologist Donald H. Baucom set out to determine how having high, even idealistic, standards about various aspects of a relationship can affect its quality.[190] Couples filled out questionnaires related to their hopes and feelings about finances, affection, household tasks, relations with family and friends, religion, sex, leisure, career issues, and parenting. They answered questions about how they communicate positive and negative feelings to their spouses.

All told, the survey involved sixty different standards couples have for their relationships. Here's a shortened version of the survey:

The *For Better* Quiz #17: Does Your Marriage Have High Standards?

Use a scale of 1 to 5 to indicate support or disagreement for the following statements:

"When my partner and I disagree on some child-rearing decision, each of us should try to get the other to agree with our point of view."

"Only one of us should have final say on decisions we make about money."

"My partner and I should take part in our leisure activities with each other."

"We should show our love for each other through physical affection."

Now answer the following questions:

"Are you satisfied with the way this standard is being met in your relationship?"

"How upsetting is it to you when this standard is not met?"

The questions were simple enough, but a pronounced pattern emerged. Couples on the extremes—those who expected a lot from their marriages and those who expected very little—tended to get exactly what they asked for.

Dr. Baucom found that people who have idealistic standards, who really want to be treated well and who want romance and passion from their marriage, end up getting that kind of marriage. Men and women with low standards, who don't expect good treatment, communication, or romance, end up in relationships that don't offer those things.

THE LESSON: Husbands and wives who hold their partners to a reasonably high standard have better marriages. If you expect a better, more satisfying relationship, you improve your chances of having one.

#4: Pay Attention to Family and Friends

As we've discussed, one of the reasons modern couples struggle so much is that a soul mate marriage places a heavier burden of personal responsibility on both husbands and wives. Modern marriages tend to be far more insular than marriages of previous generations. Throughout history, family, friends, neighbors, and co-workers have been important sources of social, personal, and financial support to married couples. But today, many people view their husband or wife as the primary person they turn to for support. Many couples even believe that outsiders can interfere with the marital bond, and they distance themselves from close outside relationships.

Sociologists Naomi Gerstel of the University of Massachusetts–Amherst and Natalia Sarkisian at Boston College have found that married people have fewer ties to relatives than people who aren't married. They are less likely to visit or call their parents and other family members, compared to relatives who are single. Marriage also cuts a couple's ties to the larger community. Married people are less likely to socialize with neighbors or help out their friends. And married people are less likely to be politically active, whether it's attending a rally or signing a petition.[191]

"Today we expect much more intimacy and support from our

partners than in the past, but much less from everyone else," notes marriage historian Stephanie Coontz, who teaches history and family studies at Evergreen State College in Olympia, Washington. "This puts a huge strain on the institution of marriage. We often overload marriage by asking our partner to satisfy more needs than any one individual can possibly meet."[192]

Indeed, in the quest to achieve deeper intimacy with a spouse, many couples end up reducing the time they spend with parents, siblings, and friends. In 2006, sociologists from Duke University and the University of Arizona analyzed data from the General Social Survey, one of the nation's longest-running surveys of social, cultural, and political issues. The survey asked about 1,500 respondents about their "core discussion networks," the people with whom they had close personal and social ties.

The *For Better* Quiz #18: Measuring Social Ties

Survey respondents were asked to answer the following question: Looking back over the last six months, who are the people with whom you discussed matters that are important to you?

The study showed that our circle of confidants has shrunk dramatically in the past two decades.[193] Compare your answers to the survey results.

- In 2004, 80 percent of respondents said they talk only to family members about important matters, up from 57 percent in 1985.
- The number of people who depend totally on their spouse to talk about personal issues has jumped to 9 percent, up from 5 percent.
- In 1985, nearly one in three people said they had four to five regular confidants. By 2004, that number had dropped to just 15 percent.

- The researchers also reported a decline in the number of groups that people belong to and the amount of time they spend with clubs and other organizations.

"There is a trend toward smaller, closer social networks more centered on spouses and partners," said Miller McPherson, professor of sociology at the University of Arizona.[194]

Dr. Coontz thinks all this togetherness is not necessarily good for couples. The way to strengthen a marriage, she argues, is to put fewer emotional demands on spouses. This doesn't mean losing emotional intimacy with your husband or wife. It just means that married couples have a lot to gain by fostering their relationships with family members and friends. The happiest couples, she says, are those who have interests and support "beyond the twosome."

THE LESSON: Sometimes, improving your marriage means giving it a break. Increasing your connections with family, friends, and society is good for your marriage.

#5: Don't Expect Your Spouse to Make You Happy

Happiness is an increasingly popular and complex topic of research among psychologists. The good news is that most people are happy most of the time.

What is surprising is that research shows happiness is relatively stable. A major life event (like marriage or the birth of a child) may offer a short-term happiness boost, but studies suggest most people return to their own personal happiness "set point." If you ranked your level of happiness as a 7.5 on a scale of 1 to 10, research shows that most of the time, the events of your life won't change that. You'll pretty much be a 7.5 happy person all your life.

Of course there are exceptions. People subjected to extreme poverty, hunger, or violence, or those suffering from mental health problems, will obviously score differently on a happiness test from the average person. But in general, happiness in life appears to be pretty stable, and largely unaffected by money, education, race, and other variables.

Some fascinating studies have looked at the emotional extremes—the thrill of winning the lottery and the devastation of a paralyzing injury—and the resulting effect on happiness. In a series of studies led by Northwestern University researchers, happiness was measured in winners of the Illinois state lottery, among paralyzed accident victims, and among a control group of people who didn't have any dramatic events to report. Despite the euphoria of a big lottery win, the study showed that the lottery winners weren't any happier than the control group. And people who had experienced a devastating spinal-cord injury were happier than expected.[195] There were limits to the research. It may be that the accident victims who agreed to take part in the study simply were more outgoing and socially active people who started off happier than most of us, so declines in happiness after injury weren't as apparent to the researchers.

But other studies suggest that happiness is an inherent trait. Researchers who have studied twins raised apart have found identical levels of happiness in both twins, even though each twin's life experiences were different. That finding suggests that a person's happiness is genetically determined and intractable, but most happiness researchers say the happiness equation is likely far more complex. However, they do see strong evidence that a person's happiness level is not easily altered.

Given the sense that happiness is relatively stable over time, the question is whether getting married makes people happier. It's clear that marriage can have dramatic effects on our emotional state.

In 1967, psychiatrists Thomas Holmes and Richard Rahe looked at the medical records of five thousand patients to determine the link between stressful life events and illness. The groundbreaking article listed fifty major life events associated with serious stress. It's notable that among the top ten stressors, five of them involved marriage. Getting divorced is listed as worse even than going to jail. Here are the top ten most stressful life events.[196]

1. Death of a spouse
2. Divorce
3. Marital separation
4. Going to jail
5. Death of a close family member
6. Personal injury or illness
7. Marriage
8. Getting fired
9. Reconciling with a spouse
10. Retirement

Several studies have found connections between marital status and happiness. In a sample of 59,169 persons in forty-two nations, researchers found married people around the world reported higher life satisfaction than people who weren't married.[197] But does marriage really make people happy? Or do happier people tend to get married, simply because they are more pleasant and outgoing, which makes them more successful at finding a mate?

Michigan State University psychology professor Richard E. Lucas and colleagues searched for clues about marriage and happiness in a study of 24,000 Germans conducted over fifteen years. Overall, married people were happier than single people. However, the study showed that people who get married and stay married typically were happier than the average long before they walked down the aisle.

Overall, the study showed that, on average, people only got a very small boost in happiness as a result of marriage—measured as one-tenth of a point on an 11-point scale.[198] The increase in happiness came primarily from the early euphoria of a wedding and marriage. On average, most people were no more satisfied in their lives after marriage than they were before marriage.

So does that mean the pursuit of happiness is futile? Not at all. The study showed large individual variations. Some people who got married ended up much happier than they were before marriage, while others, notably, ended up less happy after marriage.

The study did find that people who started off pretty happy didn't have a lot of happiness to gain from marriage. The researchers theorized that happy people already have a rich social network and don't get as much out of the companionship of marriage. A person who is lonely and unhappy with his or her life has more to gain from marriage.

"What determines people's reactions to important life events is not just their personality but also the total circumstances of their life," wrote the study authors. "If a person's life is going very well, he or she has less to gain from a positive change such as marriage. Similarly, if a person's life is going very well, he or she might have more to lose from the loss of an intimate companion, because it is likely that the close companionship was partly responsible for the person's overall subjective well-being. Thus, it is perhaps easier for a deprived person to profit psychologically from a good event and more disruptive for a person with a psychologically valuable resource to lose that resource."

The study data were surprising in how little an impact major marital events seemed to have on a person's overall well-being. The researchers examined a small group of study participants who started the study unmarried, got married, and then quickly got divorced. In that group, baseline satisfaction was almost exactly

average and there were no significant changes in happiness levels
during their marriages. Here is a summary of the findings:

- Individual personality appears to influence overall happiness,
  whether a person is married or not.
- Happier people are more likely to get married.
- Marriage triggers an initial boost in happiness, but after about
  two years, people, on average, settle back to the same level of
  happiness they had prior to marriage.
- Some people experience very high surges in happiness once they
  marry, and the increase often is maintained for years. Often,
  these people were more isolated prior to marriage, so they receive
  a greater benefit from the companionship of marriage.

THE LESSON: Happiness research should offer couples a large dose of
reassurance. While the early euphoria of a new marriage does drop, that
doesn't mean we have become less happy with each other or less happy
in life. It just means that as individuals, we aren't dependent on marriage
as a main source of life happiness. And people who get married are
typically happy people to start with, and marriage doesn't change that.

#6: Just Do It

Sex won't solve all of your marital problems, but it will certainly
help. The simple act of having sex—even when you're not in the
mood—harnesses your body's brain chemistry, unleashing the
chemicals vasopressin and oxytocin. These are powerful bonding chemicals. In studies of monogamous mice, just injecting a
male mouse with vasopressin made him more attentive to a female
mouse, even though he hadn't actually mated with her.

Experts tell low-desire couples to have sex even if they don't want to. After about five minutes of going through the motions, sexual activity will release the bonding chemicals and you are likely to even start enjoying yourself.

This is difficult advice to follow for many couples once they've allowed their sex lives to wane. A woman wrote to me once and told me her marriage became sexless after she had children. She was the one who had lost interest, and the couple had begun discussing divorce. A marriage counselor told her sternly that if she wanted to save her marriage, she needed to start having sex twice a week whether she wanted to or not.

"I hated this advice," she says. "What about my needs? But I followed it anyway. I forced myself, and you know what? I loved it, he loved it, and our marriage loved it."

For couples who are struggling to reignite their sex life, experts have several suggestions. It may just be that you need time away from kids and work stress—scheduling a regular date night might be the answer. Or you may need to start slower, holding hands and cuddling and working to restore intimacy.

A marriage counselor might help you identify the issues that are interfering with your sex life. Some studies show that problems at work can lead to a loss of interest in sex. Unfairness about the division of chores in the home can impact a couple's sex life. A medical checkup might also be in order—a number of health issues ranging from heart disease, depression, diabetes, menopause, and medication side effects, among others, can take a toll on your sex life. Couples retreats are another way for couples to work on their sex lives.

In a study of sixty-five couples who had been married an average of twenty-four years, sex therapist Linda Banner discovered a simple but effective solution. For two out of three couples, the use of educational sex videos was enough to recharge their sex lives.[199]

Over time, regular sex can improve your mood, make you more patient, damp down anger, and lead to a better, more contented relationship.

> **THE LESSON:** Forget the lesson. Put down this book and go have sex with your husband or wife.

#7: Reignite Romance

Most studies of love and marriage show that the decline of romantic love over time is inevitable. While brain scan studies show that some long-married couples do maintain intense romantic feelings, they seem to be the exception. For most people, the butterflies of early romance quickly flutter away and are replaced by familiar, predictable feelings of long-term attachment. There's nothing wrong with the calm, settled feeling of companionate love, and many couples wouldn't trade the deep intimacy and commitment they've achieved for another whirl at passionate romance. But the risk of companionate love is that it might go stale and that, when it does, boredom and discontent will set in, and your hard-won intimacy will fade.

But it doesn't have to happen. Love researchers have come up with a way for long-married couples to rekindle their early feelings of romance. Here's the prescription: Embark on a regular date night, but reinvent it to include new and unusual experiences.

The advice is based in brain science. New experiences activate the brain's reward system, flooding it with the brain chemicals dopamine and norepinephrine. These are the same brain circuits that are ignited in early romantic love, a time of exhilaration and obsessive thoughts about a new partner. And several experiments show that novelty—simply doing new things together as a couple—may help bring the butterflies back, re-creating the chemical surges of early courtship.

Over the past several years, Dr. Arthur Aron and his colleagues have tested the novelty theory in a series of experiments with long-married couples. In one of the earliest studies, the researchers recruited fifty-three middle-aged couples. Using standard questionnaires, the researchers measured the couples' relationship quality and then randomly assigned them to one of three groups.

One group was instructed to spend ninety minutes a week doing pleasant and familiar activities, like dining out or going to a movie. Couples in another group were instructed to spend ninety minutes a week on "exciting" activities that appealed to both husband and wife. Those couples did things they didn't typically do—attending concerts or plays, skiing, hiking, and dancing.

After ten weeks, the couples again took tests to gauge the quality of their relationships. Those who had undertaken the "exciting" date nights showed a significantly greater increase in marital satisfaction than the "pleasant" date night group.

The *For Better* Quiz #19: How to Reignite Romance

First, both you and your partner take the Passionate Love quiz on page 59. Make note of your score. Next, make a list of ten to twenty activities and "date night" excursions that sound fun and exciting that you haven't done together for the past six months. Ask your partner to do the same and compare your lists. Choose ten "dates" that sound fun to both of you and schedule one activity a week for the next ten weeks. After completing the ten-week prescription, retake the Passionate Love quiz on page 59 and compare with your previous score.

Dr. Aron cautions that novelty alone is probably not enough

to save a marriage in crisis. But for couples who have a reasonably good but slightly dull relationship, novelty may help reignite old sparks.

And recent brain scan studies show that romantic love really can last years into a marriage. Bianca Acevedo, a researcher at Albert Einstein College of Medicine in the Bronx, New York, led brain scan research involving ten women and seven men who claimed to be intensely in love with their spouses after an average of twenty-one years of marriage. Brain scans confirmed it, showing increased brain activity associated with romantic love when the subjects saw pictures of their spouses. The images were markedly similar to the brain scan studies of newlyweds.

It's not clear why some couples are able to maintain romantic intensity even after years together. But the scientists believe regular injections of novelty and excitement most likely play a role. Rutgers anthropologist Helen Fisher notes that the new activities couples choose don't have to be time consuming, expensive, or wacky. "You don't have to swing from the chandeliers," she says. Just take a drive, wander around a new part of town, or stop by a local art show or community fair. The key is to share a new experience together.

THE LESSON: Protect your marriage by regularly trying new things and sharing new experiences with your spouse. Make a list of the favorite things you and your spouse do together, and then make a list of the fun things you'd like to try. Avoid old habits and make plans to do something fresh and different once a week.

Of course, it takes more than a pottery class, regular sex, and a few celebrations to make a good marriage. But these seven strategies for strengthening your marital bond can put you on a path to restoring and strengthening the positive connections that brought you together in the first place. The dual ability to stay positive and minimize the negative behaviors is what distinguishes long-married stable couples from those who struggle.

The Science of a Good Marriage

The goal of this book is to recapture the optimism we feel when we first marry and to give couples the tools they need to nurture a good relationship or renew a troubled one. The good news is that the answers are out there. Scores of academic researchers have devoted their careers to studying human relationships, and the results of their work offer evidence-based advice for couples interested in improving their marriages. Some of the lessons—whether softening your approach during the first three minutes of an argument or picking up a bigger share of the housework—won't be learned overnight. In fact, an ongoing theme of the study of marriage is that healthy relationships require time, effort, and regular maintenance. Couples need to find the time to support each other, to talk as friends, to go out on a date, to hold hands, and even to disagree.

Even couples who seem to get along well and rarely fight shouldn't be complacent about the relationship. While a number of couples in stable relationships are not on an obvious trajectory for divorce, these men and women are still at risk, because often they aren't finding joy in the relationship or forming a deeper connection beyond the years they've spent together and obligations like home ownership and children. Dr. Markman calls this the "good enough" marriage.

"These are the marriages where couples don't fight in front of the kids, but they are low conflict and low intimacy," he says. "To protect and restore the positive connections in a relationship is much more of a challenge."

There is no single way to define a good marriage, but scientists have been able to identify the qualities and characteristics of long and stable relationships. Most couples already know they need to spend time together, manage their conflict, and strengthen intimacy. But what they don't realize is that often they pay attention to the wrong things when assessing the health and quality of their marriage.

The main lesson from the science of marriage is that couples often misread the emotional temperature of their relationship, wrongly focusing on the level of conflict and the types of things about which they argue. But what marital science teaches us is that improving a marriage doesn't require sweeping changes. *Couples in good marriages get the little things right.*

For instance, successful couples argue just as much as everybody else. But they know the difference between a complaint and a criticism. They avoid accusatory language and signs of contempt when they have disagreements. Partners in stable relationships know that the first few minutes of a conflict are the key to setting the tone for the argument and the marriage as a whole. Stable couples know how to de-escalate an argument and how to harness the power of conflict to improve the overall relationship. They know that intimacy, sex, and affection are a daily priority.

Couples in good marriages retell the story of how they met and the ensuing courtship with warmth, affection, and humor. And when couples become parents, those who best navigate the chaos of children find ways to share quality time with each other. Successful couples know that making the marriage a priority is not only good for the relationship but good for the whole family. They distribute household labor in a way that feels fair to both partners, and they manage their money and their debt, insulating their marriages as much as possible from financial stress.

Of course, every marriage is unique and remarkable in its own way, and there are some dynamics between couples that even science can't explain. While much of the advice gleaned from marital science is simple, applying it in the real world, to a real marriage—to your marriage—may not always be easy and the strategies outlined here may not be effective for every couple.

But the fact that you are reading this book shows that marriage is important to you, whether you are working on a struggling relationship, strengthening a good one, or trying to decide whether to get married at all. The broad trends of marriage and divorce give us reason to be hopeful. Divorce is getting less common, couples are waiting longer to get married, and once a man and a woman do finally decide to marry, marriage and divorce statistics clearly show that the odds of staying married are in their favor.

Of course, not every marriage can be saved or should be saved. But the vast scientific literature on marriage, couples, and divorce makes a convincing case that the secrets to marital happiness are not nearly as complicated as they often seem. Small, simple changes in our everyday behavior can save a troubled relationship and transform a good-enough marriage into a lasting and satisfying union.

When we get married we promise to accept our partner for better or for worse. But the truth is, we only want it to be better. And the science of marriage shows us that it can be.

ACKNOWLEDGMENTS

As I was finishing this book, my daughter suggested that I dedicate the work "to the fabulous, totally awesome Laney." I offered a compromise. "How about just 'For Laney'?"

Unfortunately, there is limited space to express my feelings for her and the many wonderful people who contributed to this book. I should start with all the marriage researchers who made it possible. They are too numerous to mention by name, but without their dedication to the field of relationship research, there would be no science of marriage. I am amazed and gratified at the generosity and knowledge of the scientists behind the studies cited throughout this book.

My agent, Lynn Johnston, has been a constant source of support, not only in seeing this book to completion, but in all matters related to life, love, work, and parenting. If ever there was a perfect man, it's my friend and colleague Toby Bilanow, a fellow lover of both dogs and blogs. I simply couldn't imagine a workday or any day without him. This book was greatly improved by the wisdom and insight of Larry Rout, my former *Wall Street Journal* colleague and a great, true friend.

I'm grateful to my Dutton editor, Amy Hertz, for her insights, advice, and commitment to this book, and to editorial assistant Melissa Miller for her help. A special thanks to all my colleagues at *The New York Times*, particularly Laura Chang and the Science *Times* staff for their support. And I'd like to send a special shout-out to Jane Curry and Stephanie Lett, for regularly offering play-dates, food, and friendship during the writing of this book. And most important, a heartfelt thanks to my daughter, Laney, for being so fabulous and totally awesome. I love you.

The *For Better* Workbook: Quizzes and Exercises to Help You Rate Your Relationship

No single test can determine if you have a strong relationship. But researchers have developed various quizzes and exercises that they use to assess the state of a couple's marriage. In a research setting, these tools allow scientists to compare couples over time and draw conclusions about the characteristics of both strong and vulnerable relationships.

Although these tests are less predictive when used in a home setting, they can help couples identify the strengths in their relationship as well as the areas that need more work.

On the following pages, you'll find your own personal relationship workbook, filled with the *For Better* quizzes and assessments developed from the various research studies discussed throughout this book. Take them for fun to learn more about yourself, or quiz your partner to get a sense of the good, better, and best parts of your relationship.

Remember, these tests are just for fun. A high score doesn't mean you're guaranteed smooth sailing, and a low score doesn't mean you're headed for bumpy waters. But whatever your answers, the *For Better* Workbook will give you and your partner lots to talk about.

So pour yourself a glass of wine, sharpen your pencil, and get started!

#1: What's Your Flirting Response?

Try to imagine the following scenario as vividly as you can, as if the events described are really happening to you. After the visualization exercise, you will be asked to complete some word puzzles. This is designed to distract your attention from the scene you just visualized. After you complete the word puzzles, you will be asked how vividly you recall the scenario, which is why it's important to imagine it as best as possible.

Now, imagine that you're in a coffee shop and you run into a friend or a co-worker whom you find attractive. Spend some time visualizing the scene and making it as real as possible. The man or woman you run into is really happy to see you, and you are also happy to see this person. The two of you strike up a warm, engaging conversation, and you lose track of time. You realize you need to get home. As you are leaving, the person gives you his/her phone number so you can get together again for coffee sometime.

Now, take a break from the visualization exercise and try to solve the following word puzzles.

1. L O _ A L
2. D E _ _ TED
3. C _ _ M I _ _ E _
4. I N V E _ TED
5. B E _ A _ E
6. T H R _ _ T

THE *FOR BETTER* WORKBOOK

Answer Key: Women are more likely to complete the word puzzles with words indicating commitment or threat, while men are more likely to choose neutral words. The possible puzzle solutions are listed below, with the commitment and threat words listed first, and neutral words listed second.

1. *Loyal, Local* 2. *Devoted, Deleted* 3. *Committed, Committee* 4. *Invested, Invented* 5. *Beware, Became* 6. *Threat, Throat*

#2: Passionate Love

Answer the following questions to test your level of passionate love. Think of the person you love most passionately now and respond by circling the appropriate response. Answers range from (1) not at all true to (9) definitely true. Then, add up your scores and check the scale below to see how hot your love fires burn.

	UNTRUE . . . TRUE
I would feel deep despair if my partner left me.	1 2 3 4 5 6 7 8 9
Sometimes I feel I can't control my thoughts; they are obsessively on my partner.	1 2 3 4 5 6 7 8 9
I feel happy when I'm doing something to make my partner happy.	1 2 3 4 5 6 7 8 9
I would rather be with my partner than with anyone else.	1 2 3 4 5 6 7 8 9
I'd get jealous if I thought my partner was falling in love with someone else.	1 2 3 4 5 6 7 8 9
I yearn to know all about my partner.	1 2 3 4 5 6 7 8 9
I want my partner physically, emotionally, and mentally.	1 2 3 4 5 6 7 8 9
I have an endless appetite for affection from my partner.	1 2 3 4 5 6 7 8 9

For me, my partner is the perfect romantic partner.	1 2 3 4 5 6 7 8 9
I sense my body responding when my partner touches me.	1 2 3 4 5 6 7 8 9
My partner always seems to be on my mind.	1 2 3 4 5 6 7 8 9
I want my partner to know me—my thoughts, my fears, and my hopes.	1 2 3 4 5 6 7 8 9
I eagerly look for signs indicating my partner's desire for me.	1 2 3 4 5 6 7 8 9
I possess a powerful attraction for my partner.	1 2 3 4 5 6 7 8 9
I get extremely depressed when things don't go right in my relationship with my partner.	1 2 3 4 5 6 7 8 9

PASSIONATE LOVE SCALE SCORES

106–135 points—Extremely passionate. Your love is wild and reckless.

86–105 points—Passionate. The fires of passion still burn, but not as intensely.

66–85 points—Average. Contentment, with occasional sparks

45–65 points—Cool. Tepid, infrequent passion

15–44 points—Extremely cool. The fire is out.

#3: Defining Your Love Style

Answer True or False to each question. Even if you feel a question doesn't quite describe your feelings, you must pick an answer.

Ⓣ Ⓕ   1. I believe that "love at first sight" is possible.

Ⓣ Ⓕ   2. The first time we kissed or rubbed cheeks, I felt a definite genital response (lubrication, erection).

Ⓣ Ⓕ   3. We kissed each other soon after we met because we both wanted to.

Ⓣ Ⓕ   4. Usually the first thing that attracts my attention to a person is his/her pleasing physical appearance.

Ⓣ Ⓕ   5. At the first touch of his/her hand I knew that love was a real possibility.

Ⓣ Ⓕ   6. Before I ever fell in love I had a pretty clear physical picture of what my true love would be like.

Ⓣ Ⓕ   7. I like the idea of having the same kinds of clothes, hats, plants, bicycles, cars, et cetera, as my lover does.

Ⓣ Ⓕ   8. I did not realize that I was in love until I actually had been for some time.

Ⓣ Ⓕ   9. You cannot have love unless you have first had caring for a while.

Ⓣ Ⓕ   10. I still have good friendships with almost everyone with whom I have ever been involved in a love relationship.

Ⓣ Ⓕ   11. The best kind of love grows out of a long friendship.

Ⓣ Ⓕ   12. The best part of love is living together, building a home together, and rearing children together.

Ⓣ Ⓕ   13. Kissing, cuddling, and sex shouldn't be rushed. They will happen naturally when one's intimacy has grown enough.

Ⓣ Ⓕ   14. It is hard to say exactly when we fell in love.

Ⓣ Ⓕ   15. The best love relationships are the ones that last the longest.

Ⓣ Ⓕ   16. When things aren't going right for us, my stomach gets upset.

Ⓣ Ⓕ   17. When my love affairs break up I get so depressed that I have even thought of suicide.

Ⓣ Ⓕ   18. Sometimes I get so excited about being in love that I can't sleep.

Ⓣ Ⓕ   19. When my lover doesn't pay attention to me I feel sick all over.

Ⓣ Ⓕ   20. When I am in love I have trouble concentrating on anything else.

Ⓣ Ⓕ   21. I cannot relax if I suspect that my lover is with someone else.

Ⓣ Ⓕ   22. Even though I don't want to be jealous I can't help it when my lover pays attention to someone else.

Ⓣ Ⓕ   23. At least once when I thought a love affair was all over, I saw him/her again and the old feelings came surging back.

Ⓣ Ⓕ   24. If my lover ignores me for a while I sometimes do really stupid things to try to get his/her attention back.

Ⓣ Ⓕ   25. From a practical point of view, I must consider what a person is going to become in life before I commit myself to loving him/her.

Ⓣ Ⓕ   26. It makes good sense to plan your life carefully before you choose a lover.

Ⓣ Ⓕ   27. It is best to love someone with a similar background to yours.

Ⓣ Ⓕ   28. A main consideration in choosing a lover is how he/she reflects on my family.

Ⓣ Ⓕ   29. A main consideration in choosing a partner is whether or not he/she will be a good parent.

Ⓣ Ⓕ   30. I couldn't truly love anyone I would not be willing to marry.

Ⓣ Ⓕ   31. I wouldn't date anyone that I wouldn't want to fall in love with.

Ⓣ Ⓕ   32. A main consideration in choosing a partner is how he/she will reflect on one's career.

Ⓣ Ⓕ 33. Before getting very involved with anyone, I try to figure out how compatible his/her hereditary background is with mine in case we ever have children.

Ⓣ Ⓕ 34. It's always a good idea to keep your lover a little uncertain about how committed you are to him/her.

Ⓣ Ⓕ 35. Part of the fun of being in love is testing one's skill at keeping it going and getting what one wants from it at the same time.

Ⓣ Ⓕ 36. As far as my lover goes, what he/she doesn't know about me won't hurt him/her.

Ⓣ Ⓕ 37. I have at least once had to plan carefully to keep two of my lovers from finding out about each other.

Ⓣ Ⓕ 38. I can get over love affairs pretty easily and quickly.

Ⓣ Ⓕ 39. I enjoy flirting with attractive people.

Ⓣ Ⓕ 40. My lover would get upset if he/she knew some of the things I've done with other people.

Ⓣ Ⓕ 41. It would be fun to see whether I could get someone to go out with me, even if I didn't want to get involved with that person.

Ⓣ Ⓕ 42. I try to use my own strength to help my lover through difficult times, even when he/she is behaving foolishly.

Ⓣ Ⓕ 43. I would rather suffer myself than let my lover suffer.

Ⓣ Ⓕ 44. I cannot be happy unless I place my lover's happiness before my own.

Ⓣ Ⓕ 45. When I break up with someone, I go out of my way to see that he/she is okay.

Ⓣ Ⓕ 46. I am usually willing to sacrifice my own wishes to let my lover achieve his/hers.

Ⓣ Ⓕ 47. If my lover had a baby by someone else I would want to raise it, love it, and care for it as if it were my own.

Ⓣ Ⓕ 48. I would rather break up with my lover than stand in his/her way.

Ⓣ Ⓕ 49. Whatever I own is my lover's to use as he/she chooses.

Ⓣ Ⓕ 50. When my lover doesn't see me or call for a while, I assume he/she has a good reason.

Now score your quiz by looking at where your True answers are grouped.

LOVE STYLE	QUESTIONS	NUMBER OF TRUE RESPONSES
Romantic	1–7	
Best Friends	8–15	
Possessive	16–24	
Logical	25–33	
Playful	34–41	
Unselfish	42–50	

You likely answered True at least once in most of the categories. But look at the two or three categories where you have the highest number of True answers to get a sense of how you define love. More important, learn what values your partner uses to define love.

#4: Has Time Changed Your Sex Life?

Estimate the effect the passing years are likely to have on your sex life. Start by indicating how many times a week you had sex during your first year of marriage.

a) Once a week: 52 times a year

b) Twice a week: 104 times a year

c) Three times a week: 156 times a year

d) Four or more times a week: 208 times or more a year

What will your sex life be by your third year of marriage? Pick the letter that corresponds to your first answer to estimate how often you'll be having sex with your spouse after three years:

a) Once or twice a month

b) About once a week

c) Twice a week

d) Three times a week

What will your sex life be by your tenth year of marriage? Pick the letter that corresponds to your first answer to get a sense of your potential future sex life. In ten years, you'll be having sex with your spouse:

a) Occasionally

b) About three times a month

c) Nearly twice a week

d) Two to three times a week

Of course, these findings are averages based on a national sample. Some people sustain robust sex lives over the course of a marriage, while others experience a dramatic decline. If you're having more sex than predicted, good for you! It's a sign that sex remains an important priority in your marriage. If you're having less sex than predicted, you may want to focus on your sex life and work on restoring physical intimacy to your marriage.

#5: What Do You Want from Your Partner?

Think about five things you'd like your husband or wife to say or do during sex. Try not to focus on specific acts or positions. The goal here is to determine general behavioral changes that would give you more pleasure in bed. Perhaps you want your partner to talk more, be more loving, be more experimental or adventurous or be more specific about his or wishes. Write down your answers.

During sex, I wish my husband would:

1.
2.
3.
4.
5.

During sex, I wish my wife would:

1.
2.
3.
4.
5.

Compare your answers to those of your spouse. It may surprise you how many of your answers match. Pay attention to how your answers are different as well, and what you could be doing to make your partner happier.

Now see how your answers compare to those of other couples who were asked the same questions. Here's what research couples had to say about what they wanted from sex.

What Husbands Wish Their Wives Would Do
1. Be more seductive.
2. Initiate sex more often.

3. Be more experimental.
4. Be wilder and sexier.
5. Give more instructions.

What Wives Wish Their Husbands Would Do
1. Talk more lovingly; be more complimentary.
2. Be more seductive.
3. Be more experimental.
4. Give more instructions.
5. Be warmer and more involved.

#6: The Story of How You Met

Below are some of the questions researchers use to get couples talking about their how-we-met stories. Go through the questions and then write down your answers. You don't have to answer every question—just pick a question or two that gets you talking. The goal here is to document your recollections of the earliest days of your relationship.

It's important that you answer these questions now so you won't be influenced by the research findings, which are described after the questions.

1. Do you remember the time you first met? What were your first impressions?
2. How long did you know each other before you got married? What types of things did you do together?
3. How did you decide to get married? Was it an easy or difficult decision?
4. Of all the people in the world, what led you to decide that this was the person you wanted to marry?
5. What do you remember about your wedding? Your honeymoon?
6. When you think back to the first year you were married, what do you remember?

7. What moments stand out as really good times in your marriage?

8. What moments stand out as the really hard times? Why do you think you stayed together?

9. Why do you think some marriages work and others don't?

10. What were your parents' marriages like?

What does your how-we-met story say about your marriage? When we are happy in our relationship, we remember the early days with pretty much the same rosy-tinted optimism. But once we become dissatisfied with our partnership, at some point perceptions shift. It's not that we make up problems that never existed. It just becomes far easier to recall the negatives than the good times. And we end up recasting history to reflect our current state of discontent.

Is the story of your early courtship filled with nostalgia and optimism? Or is it tinged with negativity and regret? Do you remember getting lost in the rain together on your first date? Or do you just remember the fact that he refused to stop for directions?

Spouses who are in happy marriages often recount the early part of their relationship with laughter, smiles, and nostalgia— even when talking about difficult times like a job loss or financial struggles. Unhappy couples, however, tend to recast their past times together in a decidedly negative light.

#7: How Well Do You Know Your Partner?

In his workshops with married couples, John Gottman often suggests a quiz to take the emotional temperature of a relationship. He calls it a "love map" that helps you explore your partner's inner world.

1. I can name my partner's best friends.

Ⓐ yes   Ⓑ no

2. I know what stresses my partner is currently facing.

(A) yes   (B) no

3. I know the names of some of the people who have been irritating my partner lately.

(A) yes   (B) no

4. I can tell you some of my partner's life dreams.

(A) yes   (B) no

5. I can tell you about my partner's basic philosophy of life.

(A) yes   (B) no

6. I can list the relatives my partner likes the least.

(A) yes   (B) no

7. I feel that my partner knows me pretty well.

(A) yes   (B) no

8. When we are apart, I often think fondly of my partner.

(A) yes   (B) no

9. I often touch or kiss my partner affectionately.

(A) yes   (B) no

10. My partner really respects me.

(A) yes   (B) no

11. There is fire and passion in this relationship.

(A) yes   (B) no

12. Romance is definitely still part of our relationship.

   Ⓐ yes   Ⓑ no

13. My partner appreciates the things I do in this relationship.

   Ⓐ yes   Ⓑ no   .

14. My partner generally likes my personality.

   Ⓐ yes   Ⓑ no

15. Our sex life is mostly satisfying.

   Ⓐ yes   Ⓑ no

16. At the end of the day my partner is glad to see me.

   Ⓐ yes   Ⓑ no

17. My partner is one of my best friends.

   Ⓐ yes   Ⓑ no

18. We just love talking to each other.

   Ⓐ yes   Ⓑ no

19. There is lots of give and take (both people have influence) in our discussions.

   Ⓐ yes   Ⓑ no

20. My partner listens respectfully, even when we disagree.

   Ⓐ yes   Ⓑ no

21. My partner is usually a great help as a problem solver.

   Ⓐ yes   Ⓑ no

22. We generally mesh well on basic values and goals in life.

    Ⓐ yes   Ⓑ no

Your score: _____

> 15 or more yes answers: You have a lot of strength in your relationship. Congratulations!
>
> 8 to 14: This is a pivotal time in your relationship. There are many strengths you can build upon, but there are also some weaknesses that need your attention.
>
> 7 or fewer: Your relationship may be in serious trouble. If this concerns you, you probably still value the relationship enough to try to get help.

Source: Copyright © 2000-2007 by Dr. John M. Gottman. Distributed under license by The Gottman Institute, Inc. The Love Map quiz was written by Dr. John Gottman and reprinted from the Web site of The Gottman Institute. Dr. Gottman is a world-renowned researcher in the area of couples and family relationships. For further information on couples workshops and private therapy, training programs for therapists, and relationship books and DVDs, visit www.gottman.com.

#8: What Do You Fight About?

How are the battle lines drawn in your home? During a peaceful moment with your partner, list the top issues that are most likely to cause conflict in your relationship. Compare your answers to each other's and to the average response from couples in a national study.

	HER RANKING	HIS RANKING
Children		
Sex		

Housework
Money
Leisure
Alcohol

In the national study, this is how men and women ranked their top reasons for fighting.

	WOMEN	MEN
Children	1	4
Sex	2	1
Housework	3	6
Money	4	2
Leisure	5	3
Alcohol	6	5

#9: *Are You Complaining or Criticizing?*

Take this quiz to help you decipher the differences between conflicts, complaints, and contempt. Circle the letter that best describes the statement, and then check your score below.

1. I am upset that you didn't call to say you'd be late.

   Ⓐ Complaint   Ⓑ Criticism   Ⓒ Contempt

2. You can't be trusted.

    Ⓐ Complaint   Ⓑ Criticism   Ⓒ Contempt

3. You play too rough with the kids.

    Ⓐ Complaint   Ⓑ Criticism   Ⓒ Contempt

4. You never want to have sex.

    Ⓐ Complaint   Ⓑ Criticism   Ⓒ Contempt

5. I feel like you take me for granted.

    Ⓐ Complaint   Ⓑ Criticism   Ⓒ Contempt

6. You're just like your mother!

    Ⓐ Complaint   Ⓑ Criticism   Ⓒ Contempt

7. I wish you would initiate sex more often.

    Ⓐ Complaint   Ⓑ Criticism   Ⓒ Contempt

8. I'm upset you didn't help clean up after the party.

    Ⓐ Complaint   Ⓑ Criticism   Ⓒ Contempt

9. You're such a slob.

    Ⓐ Complaint   Ⓑ Criticism   Ⓒ Contempt

Answer Key:

1. Complaint 2. Contempt 3. Criticism 4. Criticism 5. Complaint 6. Contempt 7. Complaint 8. Complaint 9. Contempt

#10: Financial Strengths of Happy Couples

There are five simple questions that can help you determine whether money is a major issue of conflict in your relationship.

Take this quiz to see how your answers compare to the couples in the survey.

Read the following statements and note whether you agree or disagree. Don't rush, and give each question some thought. The answers will help you understand whether money and debt are positive or negative factors in your relationship.

1. We agree on how to spend money.
2. I have no concerns about how my partner handles money.
3. We are satisfied with our decisions about saving.
4. Major debts are not a problem.
5. Making financial decisions is not difficult.

What was your score? The statements are actually a litmus test for the level of happiness in your marriage. Happy couples will agree with at least four of the statements. When couples disagree with three or more of the above statements, they are also far more likely to score low on overall marital happiness tests. Here's how happy versus unhappy couples scored on the national survey.

Among couples who scored high on marital happiness tests:

89 percent agreed on how to spend money.
80 percent said they had no concerns about how their partner handles money.
73 percent were satisfied with their decisions about saving.
76 percent said major debts are not a problem.
80 percent said making financial decisions is not difficult.

Among couples who scored low on marital happiness tests, it was clear that money problems were creating problems in their marriage. Among these couples:

59 percent did not agree on how to spend money.

68 percent were concerned about how their partner handles money.

71 percent weren't satisfied with savings decisions.

65 percent said major debts were a problem.

68 percent said making financial decisions was difficult.

Source: National Survey of Marital Strengths, 2003

#11: How Money Can Hurt Your Marriage

Read the following statements and note whether you agree or disagree. Don't rush, and give each question some thought. The answers will help you understand to what extent money issues are contributing to marital conflict.

1. I wish my partner were more careful in spending money.
2. We have trouble saving money.
3. We have problems deciding what is more important to purchase.
4. Major debts are a problem for us.
5. My partner tries to control the money.

How many of these questions did you answer yes to? If you answered yes to even one, financial worries are likely taking a toll on your marriage. In the national survey, couples who scored low on marital satisfaction tests also were far more likely to be struggling with these financial stumbling blocks.

72 percent wished a partner was more careful in spending money.

72 percent said they had trouble saving money.

66 percent had problems deciding what is more important to purchase.

56 percent said major debts were a problem.

51 percent said a partner tries to control the money.

Source: National Survey of Marital Strengths, 2003

#12: Do You Have a Peer Marriage?

A peer marriage is defined by the following four goals. Mark yes or no to determine how similar your marriage is to a peer marriage.

1. Household duties and child rearing are shared equally or almost equally, with no greater than a 60-40 split.

   Ⓐ yes   Ⓑ no

2. Each partner believes the other has equal influence over important decisions.

   Ⓐ yes   Ⓑ no

3. Each partner feels he or she has equal control over family money.

   Ⓐ yes   Ⓑ no

4. Each partner's work is given equal weight when the couple makes plans.

   Ⓐ yes   Ⓑ no

#13: Assess Your Relationship Risk

To help couples get a sense of their relationship, University of Denver marriage researchers Dr. Scott Stanley and Dr. Howard Markman offer the following research-based quiz. Dr. Markman says couples should take the scores seriously but realize that there is a lot the quiz doesn't take into account about a relationship. He says high- and medium-high scoring couples should use the results to help them take a serious look at where their marriage is heading— and take steps (such as going to one of his couples retreats) to turn negative patterns around for the better.

Rate how often the following situations occur based on the scale of 1 to 3 below.

1   Never or almost never
2   Once in a while
3   Frequently

1. Little arguments escalate into ugly fights with accusations, criticisms, name calling, or bringing up past hurts.
2. My partner criticizes or belittles my opinions, feelings, or desires.
3. My partner seems to view my words or actions more negatively than I mean them to be.
4. When we have a problem to solve, it is as if we are on opposite teams.
5. I hold back from telling my partner what I really think and feel.
6. I feel lonely in this relationship.
7. When we argue, one of us withdraws, that is, doesn't want to talk about it anymore, or leaves the scene.

Calculate Your Score

Add up your points to determine your score. (Include only your scores; do not add to your partner's!) The ranges suggested are based on results from a nationwide, random phone survey of 947 people (85 percent married) in January 1996.

7 to 11 "Green Light"

If your total points are in the 7–11 range, your relationship is probably in good or even great shape at this time.

12 to 16 "Yellow Light"

If you scored in the 12–16 range, it's as if you are coming to a "yellow light." You need to be cautious. While you may be happy now in your relationship, your score reveals warning signs of patterns you don't want to let get worse. You'll want to be taking action to protect and improve what you have. Spending time to strengthen your relationship now could be the best thing you could do for your future together.

17 to 21 "Red Light"

Finally, if you scored in the 17–21 range, it's like approaching a red light. Stop and think about where the two of you are headed. Your score indicates the presence of patterns that could put your relationship at significant risk. You may be heading for trouble—or already may be there.

Source: Used by permission of PREP, Inc., and adapted from the book *Fighting for Your Marriage,* available at loveyourrelationship.com.

#14: Are You Bored?

1. In the past month, how often did you feel that your marriage was in a rut (or getting into a rut?), that you do the same thing all the time and rarely get to do exciting things together as a couple?

   Ⓐ Often   Ⓑ Sometimes   Ⓒ Rarely   Ⓓ Never

2. All in all, how satisfied are you with your marriage?

   Ⓐ Very satisfied   Ⓑ Somewhat satisfied
   Ⓒ Somewhat dissatisfied   Ⓓ Very dissatisfied

3. Select the picture that best describes your marriage.

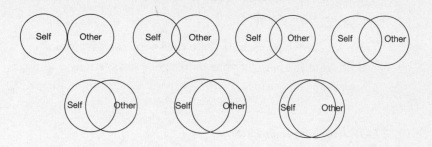

Source: A. Aron, E. N. Aron, and D. Smollan, "Inclusion of Other in the Self Scale and the Structure of Interpersonal Closeness," *Journal of Personality and Social Psychology* 63 (1992): 596–612.

Answer Key:

Question 1 measures the level of boredom you may be feeling in your marriage. Boredom is an important predictor of marital happiness. Couples in their seventh year of marriage who reported boredom were less likely to be happy or report strong feelings of closeness by the sixteenth year of marriage.

Question 2 is a simple measure of relationship satisfaction. Your answer will be self-explanatory. If you answered "A," then you are obviously happy in your relationship. But if you gave any other answer to this question, it's an indicator that you may need to work to improve your relationship.

Question 3 is a visual description of your relationship. The strongest marriages are those with a high degree of closeness in the relationship. That doesn't mean your circles have to completely overlap, but if you picked one of the overlapping circles on the bottom row, that suggests that you feel strongly connected to your partner's life. If you picked a circle on the top row—particularly one of the first three circles—that suggests you and your partner have grown apart and have larger parts of your lives away from each other than together.

How you answered each of these questions can give you some insights into the parts of your marriage that are strong and the areas where you need work.

#15: Determine Your Love Pattern

Look at the topic on each line and place an X under the High or Low column. For instance, if you rate high on Intimacy and Commitment, but low on the Passion scale, you'll place the first "X" next to Passion under the Low column. But you'll put the "X" in the High column next to Intimacy and Commitment.

Then check the answer key below to determine your love pattern.

	HIGH	LOW
Passion		
Intimacy		
Commitment		

Answer Key:

- High Passion, Low Intimacy, Low Commitment: This is *infatuated love* that lacks intimacy and commitment. Think "love at first sight."
- Low Passion, Low Intimacy, High Commitment: This is *empty love*. Married couples can be highly committed to each other, but their relationship lacks passion and intimacy. Arranged

marriages often begin as empty love, and some long-lasting marriages can begin to feel empty.

• High Passion, High Intimacy, Low Commitment: This is *romantic love*. Romantic lovers feel a strong bond and physical attraction—they are passionate and have an intimate knowledge of each other. But the relationship is typically new and hasn't reached the stage of commitment.

• High Passion, Low Intimacy, High Commitment: This is *fatuous love*. Some couples end up committing to each other after a whirlwind, passionate courtship. Their passion for each other is high and their commitment is solid, but they discover they know very little about each other, and their intimacy remains low.

• Low Passion, High Intimacy, High Commitment: This is *companionate love*. Often a lasting love is based on deep affection and commitment, but typically it's lacking in sexual desire. Commitment and intimacy are high, but the sparks of passion have died down.

• Low Passion, High Intimacy, Low Commitment: This is best described as really *liking* somebody. Some of our most intimate relationships are with friends. Some marriages become more like a long-term friendship, with intimacy at a high level, but they lack passion and commitment.

• High Passion, High Intimacy, High Commitment: This is *consummate love*. For most couples, this is the ideal. It's a complete form of love with a high level of commitment, intimacy, and passion.

#16: How Do You React to Good News?

Please take a moment to consider how your partner responds when you tell him or her about something good that has happened to you. For example, imagine that you come home and tell your partner about receiving a promotion at work, having a great conversation with a family member, getting a raise, winning a prize, or doing well on an exam at school or a project at work. Please consider to what extent your partner does the following things in response to your good fortune.

1. My partner usually reacts to my good fortune enthusiastically; he/she often asks a lot of questions and shows genuine interest about the good event.
2. My partner is usually silently supportive of the good things that happen to me; my partner says little, but I know he/she is happy for me.
3. My partner reminds me that most good things have their bad aspects as well; he/she points out the potential downsides of the event.
4. My partner seems uninterested; sometimes I get the impression he/she doesn't care that much about something good that has happened to me.

Researchers have identified four different types of personalities based on how they respond to a spouse's good news. They are:

1. Active Constructive responders are those who enthusiastically react to good news.
2. Passive Constructive responders are those who show quiet support. They don't say much, but the spouse feels loved and supported.
3. Active Destructive responders have a negative outlook, always seeing the potential downside of positive events.
4. Passive Destructive responders don't say much because they simply aren't interested.

Not surprisingly, the final two groups—the Active and Passive Destructive responders—are associated with low scores on intimacy, satisfaction, and other measures of relationship happiness.

#17: Does Your Marriage Have High Standards?

University of North Carolina psychologist Donald H. Baucom set out to determine how having high, even idealistic, standards about various aspects of a relationship can affect its quality. Couples filled out questionnaires related to their hopes and feelings about finances, affection, household tasks, relations with family and friends, religion, sex, leisure, career issues, parenting. They answered questions about how they communicate positive and negative feelings to their spouses. All told, the survey involved sixty different standards couples have for their relationships.

Here's a shortened version of the survey. Use a scale of 1 to 5 to indicate support or disagreement for the following statements:

"When my partner and I disagree on some child-rearing decision, each of us should try to get the other to agree with our point of view."

"Only one of us should have final say on decisions we make about money."

"My partner and I should take part in our leisure activities with each other."

"We should show our love for each other through physical affection."

Now answer the following questions:

"Are you satisfied with the way this standard is being met in your relationship?"

"How upsetting is it to you when this standard is not met?"

Research shows that couples on the extremes—those who expect a lot from their marriages and those who expect very little—tend to get exactly what they ask for.

#18: Measuring Social Ties

Identify your "core discussion networks," the people with whom you have close personal and social ties.

Looking back over the last six months, who are the people with whom you discussed matters that are important to you?

Take the following quiz and then compare your answers to how others responded in a national survey.

Your spouse or romantic partner _____

Your mother and/or father _____

Your siblings or other relatives _____

One or two close friends _____

Four or more close friends _____

Members of a community group/social club _____

Answer Key:

- In 2004, 80 percent of respondents said they talk *only to family members* about important matters, up from 57 percent in 1985.
- The number of people who depend totally on their spouse to talk about personal issues has jumped to 9 percent, up from 5 percent.
- In 1985, nearly one in three people said they had four to five regular confidants. By 2004, that number had dropped to just 15 percent.
- The researchers also reported a decline in the number of groups that people belong to and the amount of time they spend with clubs and other organizations.

#19: How to Reignite Romance

If you feel like your relationship is lacking a little spark lately, here's a scientifically proven prescription for reigniting the romance. Follow each step carefully.

1. Both you and your partner should start by taking the Passion-ate Love quiz (that's quiz #2 in this workbook.) Record your score on these pages. You'll want to refer back to it later

My score _____ My partner's score _____

2. Make a list of at least 10 new activities that could make fun and exciting "date night" excursions. It's essential that you choose activities that you haven't done together for the past six months. So if you regularly meet for dinner and a movie, don't put that down on your list. Ask your partner to create a similar list and compare your answers.

Here are some suggested "novel" date night activities: Go to an amusement park; take a cooking class; try an ethnic cuisine neither of you has had before; take a scenic drive to someplace new; visit a tourist attraction in your area that you've never bothered to see; attend a free lecture at the local university; attend a wine tasting; go bowling; go to a comedy club; go hiking; take a sports lesson together (golf, tennis, etc.); take a pottery or art class; race go-carts; take a long walk through your neighborhood; picnic under the stars.

My List of Date Nights	My Partner's List of Date Nights
1.	1.
2.	2.
3.	3.
4.	4.
5.	5.
6.	6.
7.	7.
8.	8.
9.	9.
10.	10.

3. Now make a data of it! Every week for the next 10 weeks, pick a new and different activity for your date night. It's important that it be an activity you both enjoy. If you love art museums but your partner doesn't, then a trip to the local modern art exhibit is not the right choice! It really doesn't matter what you do as long as it's something new and different that you both will enjoy.

4. Finally, after completing the 10-week "date night" prescription, retake the Passionate Love quiz and compare your score to your earlier score. Did you see any change your responses to this quiz? More important, have you noticed a change in your relationship? Research studies show that when couples spend time together doing new and different activities, they manage to recapture some of the novelty and excitement of the earliest days fo their courtship.

#20: Test Your Marriage IQ

How much do you really know about marriage? Take the *For Better* IQ quiz to test your knowledge.

1. In the past 40 years, divorce rates in the United States have:

   Ⓐ Stayed about the same   Ⓑ Increased dramatically

   Ⓒ Declined   Ⓓ Not followed a distinctive
                                  pattern

2. Which generation of couples has the highest divorce risk?

   Ⓐ Couples married in the 1970s

   Ⓑ Couples married in the 1980s

   Ⓒ Couples married in the 1990s

   Ⓓ Divorce risk is the same each decade

3. When it comes to being involved in the community, married people are more likely to:

   Ⓐ Socialize with neighbors   Ⓑ Become politically active
   Ⓒ Spend time with   Ⓓ None of the above
      extended family

4. Which of the following predicts a stronger marriage?

   Ⓐ Fighting rarely   Ⓑ Sharing good news
   Ⓒ Having children   Ⓓ Sharing common interests

5. Which of these activities did women say they wanted from their husbands during sex?

   Ⓐ Be more seductive   Ⓑ Give more instructions
   Ⓒ Be more experimental   Ⓓ All of the above
   Ⓔ None of the above

6. Which of these items do American couples rank highest as being important for a happy marriage?

   Ⓐ Children   Ⓑ Shared faith/religion
   Ⓒ Common interests   Ⓓ Chore sharing

7. Which of these items do American couples rank lowest in importance for a happy marriage?

   Ⓐ Children   Ⓑ Shared faith/religion
   Ⓒ Common interests   Ⓓ Adequate income

8. How does getting married change the amount of time a woman spends on housework?

   Ⓐ Marriage cuts a woman's housework time in half.
   Ⓑ Married women have about 1/3 less housework than single women.

Ⓒ Getting married increases housework for women by about 70 percent.

Ⓓ Marriage has no effect on the time women spending on housework.

9. Which of the following occurs when women shoulder a disproportionate share of housework?

Ⓐ Women get depressed   Ⓑ Men get less sex
Ⓒ Marriages are less happy Ⓓ All of the above

10. In a given year, what percentage of married people say they were unfaithful?

Ⓐ 10 percent   Ⓑ 20 percent
Ⓒ 40 percent   Ⓓ 60 percent

11. Which of the following issues is the biggest risk factor for infidelity?

Ⓐ Just had a fight with husband or wife
Ⓑ Bored in the relationship
Ⓒ Infrequent sex in the marriage
Ⓓ An opportunity presents itself

12. When a women gains financial independence, she is more likely to:

Ⓐ Get a divorce   Ⓑ Argue with her husband
                           about money
Ⓒ Have an affair   Ⓓ Stay married

Answer Key:

1. Answer: C: The divorce rate has declined, dropping to fewer than 17 divorces per 1,000 couples, down from a peak of 23 divorces per 1,000 couples in the 1970s.

2. Answer: A: Divorce risk is dropping with each generation. Couples married in the 1990s had a ten-year divorce risk of about 17 percent, compared to about 25 percent for couples married in the 1970s.

3. Answer: D: None of the above. Studies show modern marriages are far more insular than marriages of earlier generations, and couples have fewer family and community ties.

4. Answer: B: Sharing good news. Research shows that making a fuss over the small, good things that happen every day can boost the health of your marriage.

5. Answer: D: All of the above. In a national study, women were just as likely as men to ask for more communication and adventure during sex.

6. Answer: D: Chore sharing. More than 60 percent of men and women surveyed said that sharing household chores is important for a good marriage, according to a 2007 report from Pew Research Center.

7. Answer: A: Children. Only 40 percent of Americans in the Pew survey thought children were essential to a happy relationship, ranking kids lower than sex, sharing chores, money, religion, and common interests.

8. Answer: C: University of Michigan studies show that getting married increases a woman's chores by 70 percent but reduces chore time for men by 12 percent.

9. Answer: D: All of the above. How chores are divided is a key source of conflict in marriages and can even influence how often a couple has sex.

10. Answer: A: Just 10 percent of married men and women say they have had sex outside of their marriage in the past year.

11. Answer: D: Opportunity, in the form of an out-of-town trip or an interested coworker, is an important risk factor for cheating on a spouse.

12. Answer D. Stay married. Statistics show that typically, the more economic independence and education a woman gains, the more likely she is to stay married.

Score:

10-12: Great job! Your marital smarts are off the charts!

5-9: Ho-hum. Time to brush up on your marriage education.

0-4: Uh oh. You've still got a lot to learn about marriage.

NOTES

1. Barbara Dafoe Whitehead and David Popenoe, "The State of Our Unions: The Social Health of Marriage in America" (Piscataway, NJ: The National Marriage Project, 2006). Available at http://marriage .rutgers.edu.

2. Betsey Stevenson and Justin Wolfers, "Marriage and Divorce: Changes and Their Driving Forces," *Journal of Economic Perspectives* 21, no.2 (Spring 2007).

3. Stephanie Coontz, *Marriage, a History: How Love Conquered Marriage* (New York: Viking, 2005), p. 306.

4. Ibid., p. 146.

5. Barbara Dafoe Whitehead and David Popenoe. "Life Without Children: The Social Retreat from Children and How It Is Changing America" (Piscataway, NJ: The National Marriage Project, 2008). Available at http://marriage.rutgers.edu.

6. Natalie Angier, "Mating for Life? It's Not for the Birds or the Bees," *The New York Times,* Tuesday, August 21, 1990.

7. Vlad Tarko, "The Myth of Monogamous Swans: Researches Study the Sex Lives of Black Swans, *Sci-Tech News*, June 8, 2006.

8. Natalie Angier, "Mating for Life?"

9. Oliva Judson, "The Wild Side: A Commitment Pill?" *The New York Times*, September 16, 2008.

10. David O. Ribble, "The Monogamous Mating System of Peromyscus Californicus as Revealed by DNA Fingerprinting," *Behavioral Ecology and Sociobiology* 29 (1991): 161–166.

11. David J. Gubernick and J. Cully Nordby, "Mechanisms of Sexual Fidelity in the Monogamous California Mouse, Peromyscus Californicus," *Behavioral Ecology and Sociobiology* 32, no. 3 (March 1993).

12. James T. Winslow, Nick Hastings, C. Sue Carter, Carroll R. Harbaugh, and Thomas R. Insel, "A Role for Central Vasopressin in Pair Bonding in Monogamous Prairie Voles, *Nature* 365 (October 7, 1993): 545–548. doi:10.1038/365545a0.

13. H. Wallum et al., "Genetic Variation in the Vasopressin Receptor 1a Gene (AVPR1A) Associates with Pair-Bonding Behavior in Humans," *Proceedings of the National Academy of Science* 105, no. 37 (September 15, 2008): 14153–14156.

14. H. Wallum, "Link Between Gene Variant and Relationship Difficulties," Press release, Karolinska Institute, September 2, 2008. http://ki.se/ki/jsp/polopoly.jsp?l=en&d=130&a=60139&newsdep=130.

15. Claus Wedekind, Thomas Seebeck, et al., "The Intensity of Human Body Odors and the MHC: Should We Expect a Link?" *Evolutionary Psychology* 4 (2006): 85–94.

16. C. E. Garver-Apgar, S. W. Gangstead, R. Thornhill, R. D. Miller, and J. J. Olp, "MHC Alleles, Sexual Responsivity and Unfaithfulness in Romantic Couples," *Psychological Science* 17: 830–835.

17. David P. Barash, "Deflating the Myth of Monogamy," http://www .trinity.edu/rnadeau/fys/barash%20on%20monogamy.htm.

18. Tara Parker-Pope, "Love, Sex and the Changing Landscape of Infidelity," *The New York Times*, October 28, 2008, p. D1.

19. Ibid.

20. Mark A. Whisman and Douglas K. Snyder, "Sexual Infidelity in a National Survey of Women: Differences in Prevalence and Correlates as a Function of Method of Assessment," *Journal of Family Psychology* 21, no. 2 (June 27): 147–154.

21. John E. Lydon, Marta Meana, Deborah Sepinwall, Nancy Richards, and Shari Mayman, "The Commitment Calibration Hypothesis: When Do People Devalue Attractive Alternatives?" *Personality and Social Psychology Bulletin* 25, no. 2 (February 1999): 152–161.

22. John E. Lydon, Danielle Menzies-Toman, Kimberly Burton, and Chris Bell, "If-Then Contingencies and the Differential Effects of the Availability of an Attractive Alternative on Relationship Maintenance for Men and Women," *Journal of Personality and Social Psychology* 95, no. 1 (July 2008): 50–65.

23. Ibid.

24. Ibid.

25. Regina Nuzzo, "Love and Infidelity: How Our Brains Keep Us from Straying," *The Los Angeles Times*, September 15, 2008.

26. Christopher Peterson, *Positive Psychology* (Oxford: Oxford University Press, 2006), p. 251.

27. Elaine Hatfield, "The Golden Fleece Award: Love's Labours Almost Lost," *APS Observer* 19, no. 6 (June 2006).

28. David B. Givens, *Love Signals: A Practical Field Guide to the Body Language of Courtship* (New York: St. Martin's Press, 2005), p. 6.

29. M. M. Moore, "Nonverbal Courtship Patterns in Women: Context and Consequences," *Ethology and Sociobiology* 64 (1985): 237–247.

30. Daniel Coleman, "For Man and Beast, Language of Love Shares Many Traits," *The New York Times*, February 14, 1995, p. C1.

31. Marina Klimenko and Hui-Chin Hsu, "Interactional Synchrony Between Mothers and Their Toddlers During Book Reading," Paper presented at the annual meeting of the XVth Biennial International Conference on Infant Studies, Kyoto, Japan, June 19, 2006. http://www.allacademic.com/meta/p93974_index.html.

32. Edward T. Hall, *The Dance of Life: The Other Dimension of Time* (Garden City, N.Y.: Anchor Press/Doubleday, 1983), pp. 154–156.

33. Karl Gammer, Kirsten O. Kruck, and Magnus S. Magnusson, "The Courtship Dance: Patterns of Nonverbal Synchronization in Opposite Sex Encounters," *Journal of Nonverbal Behavior* 22, no. 1 (1998).

34. Helen Fisher, *Anatomy of Love: A Natural History of Mating, Marriage, and Why We Stray* (New York: Ballantine Books, 1992), p. 31.

35. Timothy Perper, "Will She or Won't She: The Dynamics of Flirtation in Western Philosophy," *Sexuality and Culture* (November 2009).

36. Claus Wedekind, Thomas Seebeck, et al., "The Intensity of Human Body Odors."

37. Linda Geddes, "DNA Dating: Can Genes Help You Pick a Mate?" *The New Scientist*, December 19, 2008.

38. S. Craig Roberts, L. Morris Gosling, Vaughan Carter, and Marion Petrie, "MHC-Correlated Odour Preferences in Humans and the Use of Oral Contraceptives," *Proceedings of the Royal Society B* 275, no. 1652 (December 7, 2008): 2715–2722.

39. G. Miller, J. M. Tybur, and B. D. Jordan, "Ovulatory Cycle Effects on Tip Earnings by Lap Dancers: Economic Evidence for Human

Estrus?" *Evolution and Human Behavior* 28, no. 6 (November 2007): 375–381.

40. K. M. Durante, N. P. Li, and M. G. Haselton, "Changes in Women's Choice of Dress Across the Ovulatory Cycle: Naturalistic and Laboratory Task-Based Evidence," *Personality and Social Psychology Bulletin* 34, no. 11 (2008): 1451-1460.

41. G. A. Bryant and M. G. Haselton, "Vocal Cues of Ovulation in Human Females," *Biology Letters* 5 (2009): 12–15.

42. M. G. Haselton and S. W. Gangestad, "Conditional Expression of Women's Desires and Men's Mate Guarding Across the Ovulatory Cycle," *Hormones and Behavior* 49 (2006): 509–518.

43. D. Marazziti, H. S. Akiskal, A. Rossi, and G. B. Cassano, "Alteration of the Platelet Serotonin Transporter in Romantic Love," *Psychological Medicine* 29, no. 3 (1999): 741–745.

44. D. Marazziti, B. Dell'Osso, S. Baroni, F. Mungai, et al., "A Relationship Between Oxytocin and Anxiety of Romantic Attachment," *Clinical Practice and Epidemiology in Mental Health* 2 (2006): 28. Published online October 11, 2006.

45. E. Hatfield, R. L. Rapson, and L. D. Martel, "Passionate Love," in S. Kitayama & D. Cohen (eds.), *Handbook of Cultural Psychology* (New York: Guilford Press, 2007).

46. N. Birbaumer, W. Lutzenberger, T. Elbert, H. Flor, and B. Rockstroh, "Imagery and Brain Processes," in Niels Birbaumer and Arne Öhman (eds.), *The Structure of Emotion* (Göttingen, Germany: Hogrefe & Huber Publishers, 1993), pp. 132–134.

47. A. Bartels and S. Zeki, "The Neural Basis of Romantic Love," *Neuroreport* 11 (November 27, 2000): 3829–3834.

48. A. Bartels and S. Zeki, "The Neural Correlates of Maternal and Romantic Love," *NeuroImage* 21 (2004): 1155–1166.

49. A. Aron, H. Fisher, D. Mashek, G. Strong, H.-F. Li, and L. L. Brown, "Early-Stage, Intense Romantic Love Activates Subcortical Reward and Motivation Regions and a Dynamic Network That Varies with Intensity of Passion, Duration of Relationship, and Gender," *Journal of Neurophysiology* 94 (2005): 327–337.

50. Tara Parker-Pope, "Is It Love or Mental Illness? They're Closer Than You Think," *The Wall Street Journal*, February 13, 2007.

51. Ibid.

52. Ahdaf Soueif, *The Map of Love: A Novel* (New York: Random House, 2000), pp. 386–387.

53. Guillermina Jasso, "Marital Coital Frequency and the Passage of Time," *American Sociological Review* 50, no. 2 (April 1985): 224–227.

54. Alexandra Brewis and Mary Meyer, "Marital Coitus Across the Life Course," *Journal of Biosocial Science* 37 (2005): 499–518.

55. Guillermina Jasso, "Marital Coital Frequency."

56. John Harlow, "True Love Is All Over in 30 Months," *The Sunday Times*, July 25, 1999.

57. Linda J. Waite and Kara Joyner, "Emotional and Physical Satisfaction with Sex in Married, Cohabiting, and Dating Sexual Unions: Do Men and Women Differ?" in E. Laumann and R. Michael (eds.), *Studies on Sex* (Chicago: University of Chicago Press, 2001), pp. 239–269.

58. Dietrich Klusmann, "Sperm Competition and Female Procurement of Male Resources," *Human Nature* 17, no. 3 (September 2006).

59. Mary Roach, *Bonk: The Curious Coupling of Science and Sex* (New York: W. W. Norton & Co., 2009).

60. Alice Buckley McCarthy, "Who's Having Sex in America?" *Third Age*, July 1, 2008, www.thirdage.com.

61. Tom W. Smith, "American Sexual Behavior: Trends, Socio-demographic Differences, and Risk Behavior," National Opinion Research Center, University of Chicago, GSS Topical Report, no. 25, updated December 1998.

62. Alice Buckley McCarthy, "Who's Having Sex."

63. Sue Shellenbarger, "Not Tonight, Honey: The Plight of Dual-Income No-Sex Couples," *The Wall Street Journal,* April 3, 2003.

64. Janey S. Hyde, "Research on Sexuality in Marriage," Congressional Briefing, March 5, 2004.

65. M. Brown and A. Auerbach, "Communication Patterns in Initiation of Marital Sex," *Medical Aspects of Human Sexuality* 15 (1981): 107–117.

66. Elaine Hatfield, Susan Sprecher, Jane Traupman Pillener, et al, "Gender Difference in What Is Desired in the Sexual Relationship," *Journal of Psychology and Human Sexuality* 1 (1988).

67. J. K. Kiecolt-Glaser, L. D. Fisher, P. Ogrocki, J. C. Stout, et al, "Marital Quality, Marital Disruption, and Immune Function," *Psychosomatic Medicine* 49, no. 1 (1987): 13–34.

68. Todd Neale, "Marriage May Protect Against Dementia," *MedPage Today,* July 30, 2008.

69. Inez M. A. Joung, Jacobus J. Glerum, Frans W. A. van Poppel, Jan W. P. F. Kardaun, and Johan P. Mackenbach, "The Contribution of Specific Causes of Death to Mortality Differences by Marital Status in the Netherlands," *The European Journal of Public Health* 6, no. 2 (1996): 142–149. doi:10.1093/eurpub/6.2.142.

70. Pam Harrison, "7 Reasons Men Should Marry," *Canadian Health Magazine,* May/June 2007. http://www.canadian-health.ca/1_4/58_e .html.

71. Robert M. Kaplan and Richard G. Kronick, "Marital Status and Longevity in the United States Population, *Journal of Epidemiology*

and Community Health 60 (2006): 760–765. doi:10.1136/jech.2005
.037606.

72. Tara Parker-Pope, "Health Matters: Is Your Wife Pushing You to See
a Doctor?" *The Wall Street Journal*, May 12, 2007.

73. James A. Coan, Hillary S. Schaefer, and Richard J. Dauzslon, "Lend-
ing a Hand: Social Regulation of the Neural Response to a Threat,"
Psychological Science 17, no. 12 (2006).

74. J. Sobal, B. Rauschenbach, and E. A. Frongillo, "Marital Status
Changes and Body Weight Changes: A U.S. Longitudinal Analysis,"
Social Science and Medicine 56, no. 7 (2003): 1543–1555.

75. M. J. Müller, J. Ruof, M. Graf-Morgenstern, M. Porst, and O. Ben-
kert, "Quality of Partnership in Patients with Erectile Dysfunction
After Sildenafil Treatment," *Pharmacopsychiatry* 34, no. 3 (May 2001):
91–95.

76. Tara Parker-Pope, "What the Viagra Experience Is Really Like," *The
Wall Street Journal*, November 11, 2002.

77. L. Dennerstein, J. Randolph, J. Taffe, et al, "Hormones, Mood, Sexuality, and the Menopausal Transition," *Fertility and Sterility* 81, no. 7
(2002): 581–587.

78. Kathleen McCann, "More Marital Happiness = Less Sleep Complaints," *American Academy of Sleep Medicine*, June 9, 2008. http://
www.aasmnet.org/Articles.aspx?id=891.

79. Brant Hasler, "Poor Sleep Is Associated with Lower Relationship Satisfaction in Both Women and Men," The Twenty-third Annual Meeting of the Associated Sleep Societies, June 10, 2009.

80. R. Cartwright, "Sleeping Together: A Pilot Study of the Effects of
Shared Sleeping on Adherence to CPAP Treatment in Obstructive Sleep Apnea," *Journal of Clinical Sleep Medicine* 4, No. 2 (2008):
123–127.

81. "Can Snoring Ruin a Marriage?" Science Blog, February 2, 2006, http://www.scienceblog.com/cms/can_snoring_ruin_a_marriage_9930.

82. W. Beninati, C. D. Harris, D. L. Herold, "The Effect of Snoring and Obstructive Sleep Apnea on the Sleep Quality of Bed Time Partners," *Mayo Clinic Proceedings* 74, no. 10 (1999): 955–958.

83. J. M. Parish, P. J. Lyng, "Quality of Life in Bed Partners of Patients with Obstructive Sleep Apnea or Hypopnea After Treatment with Continuous Positive Airway Pressure," *Chest* 124, no. 3 (September 2003): 942–947.

84. M. G. Sardesai, A. K. Tan, M. Fitzpatrick, "Noise-Induced Hearing Loss in Snorers and Their Bed Partners," *Journal of Otolaryngology* 32, no. 3 (June 2003): 141–145.

85. Tara Parker-Pope, "Dangers of Second-hand Snoring," *The Wall Street Journal,* November 18, 2003.

86. Annmarie Cano, Muzy Gillis, Wanda Heenz, et al, "Marital Functioning, Chronic Pain and Psychological Distress," *Pain* 207, no. 1–2 (January 2004): 99–106.

87. J. K. Kiecolt-Glaser, R. Glaser, J. T. Cacioppo, R. C. MacCallum, and W. B. Malarkey, "Marital Stress: Immunologic, Neuroendocrine, and Autonomic Correlates," *Annals of the New York Academy of Sciences* 840 (1998): 649–655.

88. J. Kiecolt-Glaser, T. J. Loving, J. R. Stowell, W. B. Malarkey, S. Lemeshow, S. L. Dickinson, and R. Glaswer, "Hostile Marital Interactions, Proinflammatory Cytokine Production, and Wound Healing," *Archives of General Psychiatry* 62 (2005): 1377-1384.

89. "Relationship Stress and the Heart," *Harvard Men's Health Watch* 8, no. 10 (May 2004).

90. "Divorce Undermines Health in Ways Remarriage Doesn't Heal," University of Chicago, July 27, 2009.

91. Elaine Deaker, Lisa M. Sullivan, et al., "Marital Status, Marital Strain and Risk of Coronary Heart Disease or Total Mortality," *Psychosomatic Medicine* 69 (2007): 509–513.

92. Tara Parker-Pope, "Marital Spats, Taken to Heart," *The New York Times*, October 2, 2007, page D1.

93. David M. Buss, "The Evolution of Human Mating," *Acta Psychologica Sinica* 39, no. 3 (2007): 502–512.

94. K. T. Buehlman, J. M. Gottman, and L. F. Katz, "How a Couple Views Their Past Predicts Their Future: Predicting Divorce from an Oral History Interview," *Journal of Family Psychology* 5, nos. 3 & 4 (March/June 1992): 295–318.

95. Ibid.

96. S. Carrère, K. T. Buehlman, J. M. Gottman, J. A. Coan, and L. Ruckstuhl, "Predicting Marital Stability and Divorce in Newlywed Couples," *Journal of Family Psychology* 14, no. 1 (March 2000): 42–58.

97. Suzanne Leonard, "Love Stories: How You Tell If the Story of Your Marriage Predicts the Future of Your Love," *Psychology Today*, November/December 1995.

98. Ibid.

99. Ibid.

100. Ibid.

101. S. H. Adams, "Statement Analysis: What Do Suspects' Words Really Reveal?" *FBI Law Enforcement Bulletin* 65, no. 10 (October 1996): 12–20.

102. J. W. Pennebaker, "What Our Words Can Say About Us: Toward a Broader Language Psychology," *Psychological Science Agenda* 15 (2002): 8–9.

103. M. L. Newman, J. W. Pennebaker, D. S. Berry, and J. M. Richards, "Lying Words: Predicting Deception from Linguistic Styles, *Personality and Social Pychology Bulletin* 29, no. 5 (May 2003): 665–675.

104. R. S. Campbell and J. W. Pennebaker, "The Secret Life of Pronouns: Flexibility in Writing Style and Physical Health," *Psychological Science* 14, no. 1 (January 2003): 60–65.

105. R. A. Simmons, P. C. Gordon, and D. L. Chambless, "Pronouns in Marital Interaction: What Do 'You' and 'I' Say about Marital Health?" *Psychological Science* 16, no. 12 (2006): 932–936.

106. A. Freitas-Magalhães, *The Psychology of Human Smile* (Oporto: University Fernando Pessoa Press, 2006).

107. P. Elkman, W. V. Friesen, and M. O'Sullivan, "Smiles When Lying," *Journal of Personality and Social Psychology* 54 (1998): 414–420.

108. Tara Parker-Pope, "How Eye Rolling Destroys a Marriage," *The Wall Street Journal*, August 2002, p. D1.

109. John Gottman, *Why Marriages Succeed or Fail: And How You Can Make Yours Last* (New York: Simon and Schuster, 1994), p. 66.

110. David M. Buss, "Conflict Between the Sexes: Strategic Interference and the Evocation of Anger and Upset," *Journal of Personality and Social Psychology* 56, no. 5 (1989): 735–747.

111. Daniel Goleman, "Study Defines Major Sources of Conflict Between Sexes," *The New York Times*, June 13, 1989.

112. Hilary Stout, "Family Matters: The Key to a Lasting Marriage: Combat—Even Happy Couples Aren't Really Compatible, Suggests Latest Research," *The Wall Street Journal*, November 4, 2004. p. D1.

113. Hara Estroff Marano and Carlin Flora, "The Truth About Compatibility," *Psychology Today*, September 1, 2004.

114. Dolf Zillman, "Cognition—Excitation Interdependences in Aggressive Behaviour," *Current Theoretical Perspectives on Aggressive and Antisocial Behavior* 14, no. 1: 51–64.

115. S. Carrère and J. M. Gottman, "Predicting Divorce Among Newlyweds from the First Three Minutes of a Marital Conflict Discussion," *Family Process* 38, no. 3 (Fall 1999): 293–301.

116. John Gottman, *Why Marriages Succeed or Fail*.

117. J. M. Gottman and R. W. Levenson, "Dysfunctional Marital Conflict: Women Are Being Unfairly Blamed," *Journal of Divorce and Remarriage* 31, nos. 3 & 4 (February 2000): 1–17.

118. Stephanie Coontz, "Till Children Do Us Part," *The New York Times*, February 5, 2009.

119. Barbara Dafoe Whitehead and David Popenoe, "The State of Our Unions."

120. Pew Research Center, "As Marriage and Parenthood Drift Apart, Public Is Concerned About Social Impact," Washington, D.C., July 1, 2007: Executive Summary, page i. http://pewresearch.org.

121. Barbara Dafoe Whitehead and David Popenoe, "The State of Our Unions."

122. Phillip Longman, "The Global Baby Bust," *Foreign Affairs*, May/June 2004.

123. Barbara Dafoe Whitehead and David Popenoe, "The State of Our Unions."

124. Jean M. Twenge, W. Keith Campbell, and Craig A. Foster, "Parenthood and Marital Satisfaction: A Meta-Analytic Review," *Journal of Marriage and the Family* 65 (April 2003): 574–583.

125. John M. Gottman and Julie Schwartz Gottman, *And Baby Makes Three: The Six-Step Plan for Preserving Marital Intimacy and*

Rekindling Romance After Baby Arrives (New York: Three Rivers Press, 2007).

126. Ranae J. Evenson and Robin W. Simon, "Clarifying the Relationship Between Parenthood and Depression," *Journal of Health and Social Behavior* 46 (December 2005): 341–358.

127. J. G. Grudzinskas and L. Atkinson, "Sexual Function During the Puerperium," *Archives of Sexual Behavior* 13 (1984): 85–91.

128. J. E. Byrd, J. S. Hyde, J. D. DeLamater, and E. A. Plant, "Sexuality During Pregnancy and the Year Postpartum," *Journal of Family Practice* 47 (1998): 305–308.

129. John M. Gottman and Julie Schwartz Gottman, *And Baby Makes Three*, p. 160.

130. Rachel Zimmerman, "Researchers Target Kids' Toll on Marriages," *The Wall Street Journal*, February 24, 2007.

131. Ibid.

132. Mark Lino, *Expenditures on Children by Families, 2005*, U.S. Department of Agriculture, Center for Nutritional Policy and Promotion, Misc Publications 2006, pp. 1528–2005.

133. Barbara Dafoe Whitehead and David Popenoe, "The State of Our Unions."

134. Phillip Longman, *The Empty Cradle: How Falling Birthrates Threaten World Prosperity and What to Do About It* (New York: Basic Books, 2004), p. 69.

135. Barbara Dafoe Whitehead and David Popenoe, "The State of Our Unions."

136. Jean M. Twenge et al., "Parenthood and Marital Satisfaction."

137. PBS *Frontline*, "Inside the Teenage Brain," http://www.pbs.org/wgbh/pages/frontline/shows/teenbrain/interviews/galinsky.html.

138. Richard B. Miller, "Do Children Make a Marriage Unhappy?" *Marriage and Families,* April 2001. http://marriageandfamilies.byu.edu/issues/2001/April/children.aspx.

139. "Report: Kids Take Greater Toll on Marriage Satisfaction of Affluent Couples," Press release, San Diego State University, July 22, 2003.

140. David Crary, "Key to a Good Marriage? Share Housework," Associated Press, Sunday, July 1, 2007.

141. Scott Coltrane, "Research on Household Labor: Modeling and Measuring the Social Embeddedness of Routine Family Work," *Journal of Marriage and Family* (November 2008): 1208–1233.

142. Frank Stafford, Jacquelynne Eccles, Robert Schoeni, Wei-Jun Yeung, et al, "Continuity and Change in American Economic and Social Life: The Panel Study of Income Dynamics," National Science Foundation, April 3, 2008.

143. Lisa Belkin, "When Mom and Dad Share It All," *The New York Times Magazine*, June 15, 2008.

144. Donald McNeil, "Real Men Don't Clean Bathrooms," *The New York Times,* September 19, 2004.

145. Ibid.

146. Karen Zagor, "The Chore Wars: Marriage & Kids," *The Feminist eZine,* December 5, 2006.

147. Dan Bortolotti, "The New Dad: The Changing Face of Fatherhood in Canada," *Today's Parent*, June 2009.

148. Carolyn Pape Cowan and Philpi A. Cowan, "When Partners Become Parents: The Big Life Change for Couples," *Psychology Press* (2009).

149. Lisa Belkin, "When Mom and Dad Share It All."

150. Karen Zagor, "The Chore Wars."

151. Scott Coltrane, "Research on Household Labor."

152. Sharon Jeffcoat Bartley, William Judge, and Sharon Judge, "Antecedents of Marital Happiness and Career Satisfaction: An Empirical Study of Dual-Career Managers," *Journal of Business and Public Affairs* 1, no. 1 (2007).

153. Linda Babcock and Sara Laschever, *Women Don't Ask: Negotiation and the Gender Divide* (Princeton: Princeton University Press, 2003).

154. Constance T. Gager and Scott T. Yabiku, "Who Has the Time? The Relationship Between Household Labor Time and Sexual Frequency," *Journal of Family Issues* 31, no. 135 (2010).

155. David Olson, National Survey of Marital Strengths (2003), www.prepare-enrich.com.

156. L. Sanchez and C. T. Gager, "Hard Living, Perceived Entitlement to a Great Marriage, and Marital Dissolution," *Journal of Marriage and Family* 63 (2000): 708–722.

157. Jeff Grabmeie, "Divorce Drops a Person's Wealth by 77 Percent, Study Finds," Ohio State Research Communications, http://reserachnews.osu.edu/archive/divwith.htm.

158. Council on Contemporary Families, "Are Women More Stressed Than Men by Work-life Conflict?" Unconventional Wisdom, www.contemporaryfamilies.org.

159. S. D. Friedman and J. H. Greenhaus, *Work and Family—Allies or Enemies? What Happens When Business Professionals Confront Life Choices* (New York: Oxford University Press, 2000), Bureau of Labor Statistics, www.bls.gov/opub/ted/2009/jan/wk1/art05.htm.

160. Ellen Galinsky, "Are Women More Stressed Than Men by Work-Life Conflict?" Council on Contemporary Families: Unconventional Wisdom Issue 1, www.countemporaryfamilies.org.

161. U.S. Bureau of Labor Statistics, "Wives Earning More Than Their Husbands, 1987–2006," January 9, 2009, http://www.bls.gov/opub/ted/2009/jan/wk1/art05.htm.

162. Betsey Stevenson and Justin Wolders, "Marriage and Divorce: Changes and Their Driving Forces," *Journal of Economic Perspectives* 21, no. 2 (2007): 27–52.

163. Stephanie Coontz, "Sharing the Load: Quality Marriages Today Depend on Couples Sharing Domestic Work," The Shriver Report, Center for American Progress, 2009, http://www.awomansnation.com/marriage.php.

164. Kristin W. Springer, "Breadwinner Anxiety and Husbands' Health: How Old Ideas of Masculinity Can Hurt," Columbia University Center on Family Demography and Public Policy. December 2008.

165. Lynn Prince Cooke, "Traditional Marriages Now Less Stable than Ones Where Couples Share Work and Household Chores," Council on Contemporary Families briefing document, July 5, 2008, www.contemporaryfamilies.org

166. Sanjiv Gupta, "Women's Money Matters: Earnings and Housework in Dual-Earner Families," Council on Contemporary Families Briefing Paper, September 4, 2007, contemporaryfamilies.org.

167. Scott I. Rick, Deborah A. Small, and Eli J. Finkel, "Fatal (Fiscal) Attraction: Spendthrifts and Tightwads in Marriage," September 30, 2009. Available at SSRN: http://ssrn.com/abstract=1339240.

168. Lawrence Kurdek, "Predicting Marital Dissolution: A Five-Year Prospective Longitudinal Study of Newlywed Couples," *Journal of Personality and Social Psychology* 64, no. 2 (February 1993): 221–242.

169. Jan Pahl, "His Money, Her Money: Recent Research on Financial Organisation in Marriage," *Journal of Economic Psychology* 16, no. 3 (September 1995): 361–76.

170. Carole B. Burgoyne, Janet Reibstein, Anne Edmunds, and Valda Dolman, "Money Management Systems in Early Marriage: Factors

Influencing Change and Stability," *Journal of Economic Psychology* 28, no. 2 (April 2007): 214–228.

171. Ibid.

172. David Olson, National Survery of Marital Strengths.

173. Francine M. Deutsch, *Halving It All: How Equally Shared Parenting Really Works* (Harvard University Press, 2000).

174. J. M. Gottman, R. W. Levenson, C. Swanson, K. Swanson, R. Tyson, and D. Yoshimoto, "Observing Gay, Lesbian, and Heterosexual Couples' Relationships: Mathematical Modeling of Conflict Interaction," *Journal of Homosexuality* 45 (2003): 65–91.

175. Sarah R. Holley and Robert W. Levenson, "Exploring the Basis for Sex Differences in the Demand/Withdraw Interaction Pattern," Talk presented at the Eighteenth Annual Convention of the Association for Psychological Science, New York, N.Y., May 27, 2006.

176. Joseph Harry and Willam B. Devall, *The Social Organization of Gay Males,* (New York: Praeger, 1978).

177. P. Kollok, P. Blumstein, and P. Schwartz, "Sex and Power in Interaction: Conversational Privileges and Duties." *American Sociological Review,* 1985.

178. Glenn I. Roisman, Ph.D., Eric Clausell, M.A., Ashley Holland, M.A., Keren Fortuna, M.A., and Chryle Elieff, Ph.D., University of Illinois at Urbana-Champaign, "Adult Romantic Relationships as Contexts of Human Development: A Multimethod Comparison of Same-Sex Couples with Opposite-Sex Dating, Engaged, and Married Dyads," *Developmental Psychology* 44, no. 1.

179. N. Gersteland and N. Sarkisian. "Marriage Reduces Social Ties," Discussion paper for Council on Contemporary Families: Unconventional Wisdom Issue 1, January 2, 2007, www.contemporaryfamilies.org.

180. Sharon Jayson, "More Parents Share the Workload When Moms Learn to Let Go," *USA Today,* May 4, 2009.

181. S. J. Schoppe-Sullivan, G. L. Brown, E. A. Cannon, S. C. Mangels-dorf, and M. Szewczyk Sokolowski, "Maternal Gatekeeping, Copar-enting Quality, and Fathering Behavior in Families with Infants," *Journal of Family Psychology* 22: 389–398.

182. John P. De Cecco, *Gay Relationships* (New York: Haworth Press, 1988), p. 6.

183. E. Mavis Hetherington and John Kelly, *For Better or for Worse: Divorce Reconsidered* (New York: W. W. Norton, 2002), pp. 25–33.

184. T. L. Huston, J. P. Caughlin, R. M. Houts, S. E. Smith, and L. J. George, "The Connubial Crucible: Newlywed Years as Predictors of Marital Delight, Distress, and Divorce," *Journal of Personality and Social Psychology* 80, no. 2 (2001): 237–252.

185. A. Booth, D. R. Johnson, L. K. White, and J. N. Edwards, "Predict-ing Divorce and Permanent Separation," *Journal of Family Issues* 6, no. 3 (1985): 331–345.

186. I. Olenick, "Odds of Spousal Infidelity Are Influenced by Social and Demographic Factors," *Family Planning Perspectives* 32, no. 3 (May–June 2000).

187. I. Tsapelas, A. Aron, and T. Orbuch, "Marital Boredom Now Pre-dicts Less Satisfaction 9 Years Later," *Psychological Science* (2009), in press.

188. R. J. Sternberg, "A Triangular Theory of Love," *Psychological Review* 93 (1986): 119–135.

189. Paul R. Amato, "Explaining the Intergenerational Transmission of Divorce," *Journal of Marriage and the Family* 6, no. 3 (1985): 331–346.

190. D. H. Baucom, N. Epstein, L. A. Rankin, and C. K. Burnett, "Assessing Relationship Standards: The Inventory of Specific Rela-tionship Standards," *Journal of Family Psychology* 10, no. 1 (March 1996): 72–88.

191. N. Gerstel and N. Sarkisian, "Marriage Reduces Social Ties," Discussion paper for Council on Contemporary Families, January 2, 2007.

192. Stephanie Coontz, "How to Stay Married," *The Times* (London), November 30, 2006. http://www.contemporaryfamilies.org.

193. M. McPherson, L. Smith-Lovin, and M. E. Brashears, "Social Isolation in America: Changes in Core Discussion Networks over Two Decades," *American Sociological Review* 71 (June 2006): 353–375.

194. "Americans Have Fewer Friends Outside the Family, Duke Study Shows," Press Release, Office of News and Communication, Duke University, June 23, 2006.

195. P. Brickman, D. Coates, and R. Janoff-Bulman, "Lottery Winners and Accident Victims: Is Happiness Relative?" *Journal of Personality and Social Psychology,* 36 (1978): 917–927.

196. Thomas Holmes and Richard Rahe, "Holmes-Rahe Life Changes Scale," *Journal of Psychosomatic Research* 11 (1967): 213–218.

197. Ed Diener, Carol L. Gohm, Eunkook Suh, and Shigehiro Oishi, "Similarity of the Relations Between Marital Status and Subjective Well-Being Across Cultures," *Journal of Cross-Cultural Psychology* 31 (July 2000): 419–436.

198. R. E. Lucas, A. E. Clark, Y. Georgellis, and E. Diener, "Reexamining Adaptation and the Set Point Model of Happiness: Reactions to Changes in Marital Status," *Journal of Personality and Social Psychology* 84, no. 3 (2003): 527–539.

199. Christopher J. Gearon, "Marriage and Sex," *Discovery Health,* www.discoveryhealth.com.

INDEX